Sold into Extinction

The Global Trade in Endangered Species

JACQUELINE L. SCHNEIDER

FOREWORD BY RONALD V. CLARKE

Global Crime and Justice
Graeme R. Newman, Series Editor

 PRAEGER

AN IMPRINT OF ABC-CLIO, LLC
Santa Barbara, California • Denver, Colorado • Oxford, England

Library of Congress Cataloging-in-Publication Data

Schneider, Jacqueline L.
  Sold into extinction : the global trade in endangered species / Jacqueline L. Schneider ; foreword by Ronald V. Clarke.
      p. cm. — (Global crime and justice)
  Includes bibliographical references and index.
  ISBN 978–0–313–35939–2 (hardback) — ISBN 978–0–313–35940–8 (ebook) 1. Endangered species. 2. Wild animal trade. 3. Endangered species—Law and legislation. 4. Wild animal trade—Law and legislation. 5. Endangered species—Case studies. 6. Wild animal trade—Case studies. I. Title.
QH75.S265   2012
578.68—dc23   2011051644

ISBN: 978–0–313–35939–2
EISBN: 978–0–313–35940–8

16 15 14 13   2 3 4 5

This book is also available on the World Wide Web as an eBook.
Visit www.abc-clio.com for details.

Praeger
An Imprint of ABC-CLIO, LLC

ABC-CLIO, LLC
130 Cremona Drive, P.O. Box 1911
Santa Barbara, California 93116-1911

This book is printed on acid-free paper ∞

Manufactured in the United States of America

To Bob and Audrey who represent the very best of the past
and
To Clay and Yvonne who represent the very best of the future

Some of the photographs contained in the book depict graphic images of dead animals that may disturb some readers.

Contents

Illustrations

Figures

Boxes

Series Foreword

WHATEVER THE WORD "GLOBALIZATION" means, this book surely exemplifies it. Because endangered species are found in the farthest corners of the world, the markets that Jacqueline Schneider describes and analyzes reach into those corners and tie them together into huge, global networks, connecting the poorest countries and regions to the richest. Trafficking in endangered species is the most transnational of all crimes, and because of this it challenges the justice systems of the world. Although individual countries pass laws protecting particular species, others do not. International covenants are made, but their enforcement is extremely difficult. And, as Schneider asks, even if the laws were enforced, would this result in the protection of endangered species? This book clearly demonstrates that, while laws are important in extending the idea of justice to cover animals and even plants, calling the abuse of endangered species a crime does not solve the problem, and in many cases makes it worse. While arrest and prosecution is the standard law enforcement response to those who break the law, we know that it has limited effectiveness in preventing crime. When particular species are on the brink of extinction, catching poachers or dealers who kill them for their body parts or sell them to willing collectors would seem to be too late, since the damage is already done.

This is why Schneider has adopted a marketing approach to protecting endangered species, making prevention the primary response to crime, an approach that criminologists have used successfully to reduce theft. Among other things, this approach requires an understanding of local communities that are located close to the source of endangered species and the complex networks that link those communities to the wide world of consumers. But the relationships of local communities to endangered species may be far more complex than glossy magazines of the developed world represent. Tigers are a real threat to some local communities in India; elephants may destroy valuable pastures in parts of Africa, for example. Schneider's marketing analysis uncovers such issues and many more and offers market based solutions.

But the challenges ahead are immense. Analyzing markets and designing intervention strategies requires an intimate knowledge of those markets and the collection of very detailed information. Much of this information does not exist, or if it does, is inaccessible to researchers. In this book, Schneider maps out the territory and pinpoints what needs to be done. It is a small step in search of a global justice for all the species of this planet.

Graeme R. Newman
Series Editor

Foreword

CONSERVATIONISTS HAVE WORKED TIRELESSLY for many years to protect endangered species from habitat losses. Huge tracts of forest have been designated nature reserves, especially in the developing world where so many of these species are found. In establishing these reserves, the poor countries of Africa, Asia, and South America have made many difficult choices between conserving habitats and the urgent need to feed their growing populations. Without the sacrifices these countries have made, the whole world would be impoverished through the extinction of many rare and beautiful plants and creatures. Richer countries have responded—though some would argue not quickly or generously enough— by making funds and expertise available to assist the conservation efforts.

Unfortunately, in step with the increasing number of conservation successes, a wider realization has dawned. It is that the burgeoning illegal trade in wildlife might now be as much a threat to endangered species as habitat loss. As Graeme Newman notes in his *Series Foreword*, globalization has facilitated the growth of this trade. It has fueled the demand for the products of endangered species— ivory, timber, caviar, tiger bone—and has helped to satisfy that demand through the development of worldwide communications, air transportation, international trade, and international smuggling routes. The illegal trade in wildlife is now thought to be second in volume only to the illegal trade in drugs.

In this pioneering book, the first by a criminologist, Jacqueline Schneider discusses ways to stem the illegal trade in wildlife. She resists the easy, but superficial, prescription of crackdowns on the poachers and organized criminals involved. Instead she draws on her experience of crime prevention to advocate a careful, species-by-species analysis of steps in the trading chain. This analysis helps to identify those points where opportunity-reducing measures might find their greatest effect. To achieve this effect, the interventions will need to be tailored to fit the particular nature of the species traded (or their parts), their natural habitats, the staging points in the trade, and the distribution points in destination countries. It is one thing to take a sturgeon in the Caspian Sea, remove and process the caviar, and sell it in Moscow or New York, but it is quite another to shoot a rhino in South Africa, carry the horn into Mozambique, and smuggle it to China for use in making traditional Asian medicines (TAMs). To make these forms of trade more difficult and risky, the interventions will have to be different in each case.

Dr. Schneider's approach requires an enormous investment in research. To be successful, preventive interventions must be selected on the basis of careful research into the nature of the problem. Criminologists know how to do this research, but they need to be persuaded to venture into this new field. The difficulties they face would be considerable. They will have to acquire detailed knowledge of the many different environments in which the illegal trade thrives. They will have to work hard and creatively to obtain the data for their studies, sometimes in difficult, even dangerous conditions. They will have to defend the importance of their work from skeptical colleagues—a major concern for those seeking tenure. However, crime is declining in the developed countries where most criminologists are employed and many are looking for new challenges. They will find these challenges in working on wildlife crime and other crimes of the developing world. In the long run—though perhaps not at first—the professional rewards of such work could be considerable. But the rewards of working to reduce the illegal trade in wildlife go far beyond professional advancement. Criminologists who do this work could play a vital role in preserving charismatic species for the enjoyment of future generations. They could help to make these species economically valuable to poor, rural people. They could enable endangered animals to exist alongside human populations with minimal conflict. They could reduce the profits enjoyed by organized criminals, which fuel the trade and draw others into these crimes. Finally, they could help to reduce the cruelty and suffering imposed on countless animals, birds, and other creatures. These are highly gratifying rewards and criminologists can thank Dr. Schneider's book for drawing attention to them.

Ronald V. Clarke
Rutgers University

Preface

THIS BOOK RAISES THE IMPORTANCE of including criminology in the fight against illegal trafficking in endangered species. Conservationists conduct most of the research that explores various aspects of the illegal trade, while criminology—the study of crime—has been conspicuously absent in the discourse. This book presents a crime reduction strategy that can assist current conservation efforts by examining the contributing factors that allow the illicit trade in endangered species to exist in order to design intervention strategies that reduce killing and selling of our protected species. Furthermore, it was once said "the only good criminology was useful criminology."[1] This thought provides the underpinnings of this book by offering to policy makers and practitioners a new approach in protecting threatened species.[2]

Animals and plants have been hunted since humans began living in groups. The hunt could have been for sustenance, sport, trophy, or protection. Buying and selling the spoils of the hunt on an international scale was also left to thrive without restriction or sanction. Because these practices continue, the number of extinct, functionally extinct, or critically endangered species continues to rise at alarming rates. Today, the illegal trade in endangered flora and fauna is a multi-million dollar industry that spans the globe.

The need to preserve and conserve the planet's wildlife came to light in the late 1940s with the establishment of the International Union for Conservation of Nature and Natural Resources (formerly known as The World Conservation Union). This organization was the first of its kind to focus on global environmental issues, including the protection of wild flora and fauna. Today, there are organizations around the world with missions to protect and conserve our endangered animals and plants, some of which will be highlighted in this book.

This book examines the illicit trade in endangered species from an environmental criminological perspective. The framework focuses on identifying and reducing the opportunities for carrying out crime. The traditional criminology community has ignored both opportunity-reducing approaches and the study of the unique crime of trading endangered species. This book uses opportunity-reducing techniques that can contribute to the fight against the killing of protected plants and animals, such as elephants, tigers, sharks, parrots, and the majestic mahogany. Viewing illicit goods markets as places where opportunities abound, it takes for granted that offenders, however motivated, will take advantage of those opportunities. This book looks at the main mechanisms that support and allow the trade to flourish. Recommendations are offered as a way to redress these conditions, thus reducing existing opportunities to poach, process, transport, and sell endangered and protected wild flora and fauna.

The inspiration for writing this book lay in my previous work on traditional stolen goods markets conducted with West Mercia Constabulary in England. The work centered on the implementation of the market reduction approach to stolen goods. The approach examined stolen goods markets from a different perspective— the primary focus was on the property stolen rather than on the offender responsible for the thefts. The main focus stayed firmly on the property. Once it could be determined what property was in demand, intervention strategies could be tailor-made in order to reduce the opportunities that put that property at risk in the first place. The market reduction approach had great success against stolen goods markets in England, where it was put forth as best practice. While I was working on projects there, I always wondered what impact the concept could have on the endangered species trade. Here, poaching replaces thefts and tigers and elephants replace disc players and iPads.

The book discusses the plight of some of the most endangered species on Earth, as well as those quickly becoming at serious risk of extinction by The International Union for Conservation of Nature and Natural Resources. The case studies are divided by species types: mammals, marine, plants, and avian. Each chapter provides information about the species themselves along with aspects that make them vulnerable to risk of killing or illegal harvesting. Facets of the illegal trade of the various species discussed are also described. The book concludes by presenting how the market reduction approach can assist in the preservation of natural resources.

This book is a valuable contribution to the field of criminology, criminal justice, and conservation in that it demonstrates how the two very different fields can work together in order to fight a common cause. However, my work could have gone unnoticed without the help of many people to whom I must express my sincerest thanks. Professor Graeme Newman gave me the opportunity to write this book and I am extremely grateful. Professor Ron Clarke has been instrumental in my career in so many ways. His body of work changed forever the direction of mine many years ago. For that I am indebted and very appreciative. I particularly want to thank the editors of a prestigious academic journal for rejecting my manuscript, "Reducing the Illicit Trade in Endangered Wildlife: The Market Reduction Approach." The reviewers were wholly complimentary of the paper, but it was ultimately rejected because it was not seen to be "criminological in nature."

Kaya Townsend, associate librarian at the University of South Florida St. Petersburg, worked tirelessly in order to identify suitable references and articles. Kaya made my life much easier. My thanks also go to my summer research assistant, Emily Shaw, who spent endless hours in the library rather than spending her summer on the beaches of Florida. My gratitude is also extended to my colleagues at the University of South Florida St. Petersburg for their incredible support and constant encouragement. To Dr. John Arthur, University of South Florida St. Petersburg—thank you for helping me understand indigenous communities and to Dr. Rob Rhykerd, Illinois State University—thanks for the agriculture and soils lectures. As a criminologist, I never thought I would need information about agriculture! Dr. Jason Ingram, Illinois State University, helped with my mapping. I owe thanks to Katharine Woollen, Susan Woollen, and Sheri Lerner, who worked tirelessly on notes and the bibliography. I also owe Jennifer Mailley a note of thanks for the last-minute review. I am indebted to Julie Derden, who did the editing and indexing for this book—a tornado could not even stall her work.

There are several people who helped tremendously with the photographs contained in the book: Kevin Connor, Oceana; Debbie Martyr, FREELAND Foundation (formerly WildAid Thailand); Grace Gabriel, International Fund for Animal Welfare (IFAW); Dr. Mahendra Shrestha, Save the Tiger Fund; Mook Wongchayakul, FREELAND Foundation (formerly WildAid Thailand); The Royal Thai Police; Jim Gore, University of Tampa; and Clay and Yvonne Ruffner. Dr. Ralph Weisheit is not only a distinguished professor at Illinois State University, but also a great photographer and friend. Without his help, I could not have included the photographs.

Finally, to all my family and close friends who have never doubted and who always believed—many, many thanks.

Abbreviations

AKI   **Amazon Keystone Initiative**

This initiative aims to support conservation efforts in Acre, Purús, and in the Itenez Mamore areas in the Brazilian Amazon. The financial support from this initiative will secure Amazon Region Protected Areas' long-term financial and managerial well-being.

ARPA   **Amazon Region Protected Areas**

This program aims to create and sustain a series of protected areas within the Brazilian Amazon that are managed properly so that sustainable natural resources can be nurtured.

BBC   **British Broadcasting Corporation**

The BBC is the world's largest broadcasting organization.

CCAMLR   **Convention on the Conservation of Antarctic Marine Living Resources**

This Convention came into force in 1982 in conjunction with the Antarctic Treaty System, Article IX. The aim of the Convention is to protect marine life in the Southern Ocean; however, it does not forbid fishing/harvesting so long as the activities are "rational." The Convention establishes a commission in order to manage marine living resources.

CEDEFOR **Certification and Development of the Forest Sector**

This program is part of WWF–Peru's efforts to modernize and formalize in order to make the Forest Sector more efficient. Technical assistance and financial support to the Peruvian government, local communities, and the private sector contribute to the overall conservation of forest resources.

CITES   **Convention on International Trade in Endangered Species**

This international agreement is the longest standing treaty between governments that aims to ensure that international trade of wild flora and fauna does not threaten their survival.

CMS   **Convention on the Conservation of Migratory Species of Wild Animals**

This intergovernmental treaty, also known as the Bonn Convention, aims to conserve migratory species, their habitat, and migratory routes. The Convention covers terrestrial, marine, and avian migratory species throughout their natural ranges.

CRAVED   **Concealable, Removable, Available, Valuable, Enjoyable, Disposable**

These characteristics contribute to the probability that a specific product might be at risk of being stolen. They also make products more desirable and, therefore, "hot." CRAVED is a model of products targeted by thieves.

Defra   **Department for Environment, Food, and Rural Affairs**

This is a governmental department in the United Kingdom. It is responsible for making policy and legislation related to the natural environment, biodiversity, food, farming, fisheries, animal health and welfare, environmental protection, and rural communities.

EC   **European Community**

The European Community consists of 27 member countries. These countries have transferred some of their sovereign rights to the European Union, which is a unique approach to government. Members of the European Union pool their sovereignty in order to strengthen their world influence.

E.R.A.S.O.R.   **Extra Routine And Systematic Opportunistic Research**

As part of the market reduction approach, this research adds to traditional crime analysis, thereby adding new dimensions to understanding a specific crime problem.

ESA   **Endangered Species Act**

The U.S. Congress passed the Endangered Species Preservation Act in 1966, thereby providing protection to specific native animals. Habitats of these protected species were also included in the Act. In 1969, Congress amended the Act to provide protection to nonnative species that were threatened with extinction. Finally, Congress passed the Endangered Species Act of 1973, which further expanded previous legislation to include both plants and animals, and to restrict international commerce of these specific species.

ETIS **Elephant Trade Information System**

CITES' Conference of Parties approved this comprehensive information system that tracks the illegal trade in ivory and elephant by-products. ETIS records and analyzes seizures of elephant parts from around the world.

EU **European Union**

First developed in 1945, the European Union aimed to end wars between neighboring countries. Through the decades, the European Union has worked to strengthen the political and economic well-being of European nations.

FAO **Food and Agriculture Organization of the United Nations**

The primary aim of this organization is to end hunger worldwide. It works with developed and developing nations to reach this goal. The FAO helps developing nations modernize practices in agriculture, forestry, and fisheries.

GAO **U.S. Government Accountability Office**

This government office is also known as the "investigative arm of Congress." The GAO monitors how the federal government spends taxpayers' money. Work by the GAO helps to improve federal governmental performance.

GFECP **Guianas Forests and Environmental Conservation Project**

The main aim of this project is to conserve the Guayanan Forest Ecoregion by paying particular attention to the region's native communities, species, and the sustainability of natural resources.

GFTN **Global Trade & Forest Network**

The aims of this worldwide initiative are to eliminate illegal logging and to make the international marketplace of forestry products more conscious of the need for sustainability.

HIV **Human Immunodeficiency Virus**

HIV is the virus that can lead to the acquired immune deficiency syndrome (AIDS).

ICCAT **International Commission for the Conservation of Atlantic Tunas**

The ICCAT is an intergovernmental organization that is responsible for conserving tuna and tuna-like fish species in the Atlantic Ocean. This organization is responsible for compiling and maintaining statistical information on these species, as well as acting as a source of information for the fishing industry.

INTERPOL **International Criminal Police Organization**

This organization is the world's largest international police agency. It facilitates interagency cooperation in order to prevent and disrupt international crime. INTERPOL agents do not have arrest power, nor do they conduct investigations. Rather, they help police forces around the world to conduct their investigations when they cross national boundaries.

IPOA   **International Plan of Action**

These plans are voluntary initiatives that call for countries to take action on a specific topic.

IPOA–IUU   **International Plan of Action to Prevent, Deter, and Eliminate Illegal, Unreported, and Unregulated Fishing**

This plan assists in the participation and coordination of fishing regulation. Individual nations are to develop and implement these plans of action in order to prevent, deter, and eliminate illegal, unreported, and unregulated fishing. The plans must be comprehensive and integrated in order to maximize international efforts to combat these illegal activities.

IPOA–Sharks   **International Plan of Action for the Conservation and Management of Sharks**

The purpose of this action plan is to conserve and manage shark stocks in order to promote their long-term, sustainable use.

IUCN   **International Union for Conservation of Nature and Natural Resources (formerly known as World Conservation Union)**

The IUCN is the world's oldest and largest conservation network that aims to develop realistic solutions to the world's most pressing environmental problems. The agency supports governments, nongovernmental agencies, UN agencies, companies, and local communities to develop strategies and policies that aim to protect natural resources.

IUU   **Illegal, unreported, and unregulated fishing**

These activities are criminal. Illegal fishing practices negatively affect the sustainability of many species. These illicit practices also impinge on the economic well-being of many local fishing communities.

MIKE   **Monitoring Illegal Killing of Elephants**

The goal of MIKE is to provide information about illegal hunting trends, changes in trends, and to determine causal factors associated with any changes. Once the data are analyzed, range states can make adjustments to policy and practice.

NFRC   **Neotropical Fund Raptor Conservation Program**

Funded by The Peregrine Fund, this program focuses on the conservation of birds-of-prey living within the Caribbean, Central and South America. The aim of the program is to conserve the raptors, their habitats, and their biodiversity through research and education.

NGO   **Nongovernmental Organization**

These organizations are not affiliated with any given government, but they are structured to advocate for a specific cause and, therefore, the creation of specific policies aimed at supporting their cause.

NPOA **National Plan of Action**

Much like international plans of action, these plans call for individual countries to develop initiatives at the domestic level.

PROFEPA **Procuraduría Federal de Protección al Ambiente (Federal Attorney for Environmental Protection)**

This Mexican governmental agency is tasked with protecting the environment.

REIO **Regional Economic Integration Organization**

These organizations are collectives of foreign nations, whereby each country has conferred sovereign authority in order to make binding decisions.

RFMO **Regional Fisheries Management Organization**

Established by various treaties, these organizations exist in order to co-operatively conduct research and to set sustainability rules for fisheries.

RSPB **United Kingdom Royal Society for the Protection of Birds**

The RSPB is a registered UK charity that works to provide conservation and protection to native bird species in the United Kingdom.

SIFORZAL/ SIFORCO **Société Industrielle et Forestière Congo Allemand**

The Danzer Group subsidiary, SIFORCO (formerly SIFORZAL) owns various forest concessions and is responsible for much of the logging in African and South American countries.

SIV **Simian Immunodeficiency Virus**

This disease, also known as African green monkey virus and also as Monkey AIDS, is a retrovirus that infects several species of African primates.

TAMs **Traditional Asian Medicines**

Traditional Asian medicines are remedies for physical and/or mental aliments that have been used for centuries. Modern scientific analysis does not support their claims.

UK **United Kingdom**

The United Kingdom consists of England, Wales, Scotland, and Northern Ireland.

UN **United Nations**

The United Nations is an international organization founded in 1945. The aim of the United Nations is to promote international peace and security. Additionally, the United Nations assists the development of countries to improve their standard of living.

UNCLOS **UN Convention of the Law of the Sea**

This Convention is also known as the "constitution of the oceans" and has 154 signatory states. The Convention has 320 articles organized into parts and 9 annexes. It covers all the different maritime zones, straits that are used for navigation, archipelagic waters, the continental shelf, and the high seas, among other areas. The basic premise of the Convention aims to seek the protection of the environment, marine scientific research, and the development of marine technology.

UNESCO   **UN Educational, Scientific, and Cultural Organization**

UNESCO seeks to improve the human condition through intercultural dialogue using education, science, culture, and sharing of information.

WCS   **World Conservation Strategy**

The IUCN, the UN Environmental Programme, the WWF, the FAO, and UNESCO worked together to develop this worldwide strategy. The Strategy aims to preserve genetic diversity of species and to ensure the sustainable use of species and ecosystems.

WWF   **Formerly known as World Wildlife Fund**

The WWF has offices in 40 countries around the globe. The mission of WWF is to conserve the world's biological diversity, to ensure the sustainability of natural resources, and to stop the destruction of the Earth's natural environment. Each country that hosts a WWF office develops various projects and implements various programs aimed at the country's specific ecosystems. WWF has been at the forefront of the protection of wild flora and fauna since 1961, its first year of operation.

List of Species

Common Name	Scientific Name
African forest elephant	*Loxodonta africana cyclotis*
African savanna elephant	*Loxodonta africana africana*
Amur (Siberian) tiger	*Panthera tigris altaica*
Asian elephant (also Indian elephant)	*Elephas maximus indicus*
Bali tiger	*Panthera tigris balica*
Basking shark	*Cetorhinus maximus*
Beluga sturgeon (also European sturgeon, Giant sturgeon, Great sturgeon)	*Huso huso*
Bengal tiger	*Panthera tigris tigris*
Big leaf mahogany (also Large-leaved mahogany)	*Swientenia macrophylla*
Black mantled tamarins	*Saguinus nigricollis*
Black spider monkey (also Guiana spider monkey and Red-faced black spider monkey)	*Ateles paniscus*
Blue shark	*Prionace glauca*
Borneo elephant	*Elephas maximus borneensis* or *Elephas maximus*
California tiger salamander	*Ambystoma californiese*
Caribbean mahogany	*Swietenia mahogoni*
Carpet sharks (39 species)	*Order: Orectolobiformes*
Caspian tiger	*Panthera tigris virgata*

Clouded leopard	*Neofelis nebulosa*
Cross River gorilla	*Gorilla gorilla diehli*
Eastern lowland gorilla	*Gorilla beringei graueri*
Giant otter (also Giant Brazilian otter)	*Pteronura brasiliensis*
Goeldi's monkey	*Callimico goeldii*
Great white shark	*Carcharodon carcharias*
Grey nurse shark (also Sand Tiger, Spotted Ragged-tooth)	*Carcharias taurus*
Gulper shark	*Centrophorus granulosus*
Himalayan black bear (also Asiatic black bear)	*Ursus thibetanus*
Honduras mahogany (also Mexican mahogany, Pacific Coast mahogany)	*Swietenia humilis*
Indian elephant	*Elephas maximus indicus*
Indo-Chinese (Corbett) tiger	*Panthera tigris corbetti*
Jaguar	*Panthera onca*
Javan tiger	*Panthera tigris sondaica*
Killer whale	*Orcinus orca*
Leopard	*Panthera pardus*
Leopard shark	*Stegostoma fasciatum* or *Triakis semifasciata*
Malayan tiger	*Panthera tigris jacksoni*
Mountain gorilla	*Gorilla beringei beringei*
Nile crocodile	*Crocodylus niloticus*
Oceanic whitetip shark	*Carcharhinus longimanus*
Olive Ridley turtle (also Pacific Ridley)	*Lepidochelys olivacea*
Patagonian toothfish (also known as Chilean seabass)	*Dissostichus eleginoides*
Porbeagle (shark)	*Lamna nasus*
Pygmy marmoset	*Cebuella pygmaea*
Savanna/bush elephant (African bush elephant)	*Loxodonta africana africana*
Scalloped hammerhead	*Sphyrna lewini*
Scarce blue tiger	*Tirumala gautama*
Scarlet macaw	*Ara macao*
School shark (also Whithound, Liver-oil shark, Miller's Dog, Oil shark, Penny dog, Rig, Snapper shark, Soupfin, Soupie, Southern tope, Sweet William, Tiburon, Tope, Toper, Tope shark, Vitamin shark)	*Galeorhinus galeus*

Silky shark	*Carcharhinus falciformis*
Silvertip whaler shark	*Carcharhinus albimarginatus*
Snow leopard	*Panthera uncia*
South China tiger	*Panthera tigris amoyensis*
Spiny dogfish shark (also known as Piked Dogfish)	*Squalus acanthias*
Squat-headed Hammerhead Shark (also Great hammerhead shark, Hammerhead shark)	*Sphyrna mokarran*
Sri Lankan elephant	*Elephas maximus maximus*
Sumatran elephant	*Elephas maximus sumatrensis*
Sumatran tiger	*Panthera tigris sumatrae*
Sunda pangolins	*Manis javanica*
Tibetan antelope	*Pantholops hodgsonii*
Tiger	*Panthera tigris*
West Indian mahogany (also American mahogany, Cuban mahogany, Caribbean mahogany, Small-leaved mahogany)	*Swietenia mahagoni*
Western lowland gorilla	*Gorilla gorilla gorilla*
Whale shark	*Rhincodon typus*

PART I

Framework of the Problem

1 ──

Introduction to the Opportunity Structure for the Illicit Endangered Species[1] Trade

EACH YEAR ABOUT 50,000 species of plants and animals disappear from the planet as a result of human activity.[2] Conservationists and environmental activists have been trying to elevate the priority given to the protection of the environment and its inhabitants for many years, but the public, politicians, and criminologists have largely ignored their efforts. Various media outlets report stories of people tying themselves to trees in order to save spotted owls, or of large-scale construction projects that are halted because an endangered frog's habitat might be in jeopardy. When the public hears stories like these, reactions are varied. Some see these actions as moral victories while others see them as simply absurd. As more prominent public figures become active in the fight against crimes involving nature, the problem of illegally trading endangered species will gain prominence in society. As an example, the awarding of the 2007 Noble Peace Prize to former U.S. Vice President Al Gore and the UN Intergovernmental Panel on Climate Change reminded people that environmental causes are noteworthy. CNN reporter Anderson Cooper highlighted the plight of various species in his special series, *Planet in Peril*. Other celebrities have lent their names to various campaigns, for example, actress Minnie Driver was the spokesperson for Scotland Yard's wildlife unit, actor Martin Sheen supports the Sea Shepherd Conservation Society, and actor Harrison Ford works on tiger conservation. Regardless of how the message is spread, the important fact is that the environment and efforts to safeguard it are emerging and gaining the public's attention.

Conservation agencies have taken the lead on studying how and why species are threatened with extinction. Fault for the demise of many species is planted firmly on human activities, both legal and illegal. Although poaching and illegal destruction of habitat lie at the core of the problem, a criminological approach is conspicuously absent from the discussion. This omission is not surprising because the extirpation of various species of wild flora and fauna is seen as the domain of conservationists as opposed to criminologists. Many traditional criminological scholars question the appropriateness of inclusion of this subject matter in the realm of a science that has historically focused on crimes that include murder, rape, robbery, and burglary. Additionally, criminologists have histori-cally studied the motivations of offenders—why they commit crimes and how society should punish or rehabilitate them. Further, crime prevention efforts have traditionally focused on social or dispositional factors, such as drug addiction or a history of abuse that may contribute to an offender's desire or motivation to commit crime. Social scientists, social workers, and psychologists have all tended to the needs and motivations of offenders. Situational-based criminology, a small but growing discipline, aims to reduce crime by focusing on environmen-tal cues that facilitate the commission of crime. Situational crime prevention offers the most effective framework that can positively impact environmental crimes, especially the illegal trafficking of endangered species.

It was Cesare Beccaria in the eighteenth century,[3] who first suggested that it is far better to prevent crime rather than to react to it. From Beccaria's time until the 1970s, criminologists have reacted to crime by focusing on offender behavior rather than focusing on understanding how and under what conditions actual crime events occur. During the 1970s, it was hypothesized that to truly reduce crime, researchers should change their perspective to one that advocated the manipulation of the envi-ronment or situation so that opportunities to engage in particular criminal activities could be reduced or eliminated. More simply stated, that hypothesis caused a shift in criminological sciences to the crime rather than behavior of the offender.

Unfortunately, the perspective and the utility of research based on situational or environmental constructs continue to be dismissed or marginalized among mainstream criminologists. They believe that efforts are only useful if geared toward furthering our understanding about offenders, victims, and crime control mechanisms like police, courts, and corrections. This book veers from tradition in two ways. First, the topic of the illegal trade in endangered species is explored. Second, it does so from an opportunity-reducing approach that does not center on motivations of offenders. The book also presents alternatives to traditional crime control mechanisms in crime prevention by suggesting that the involvement of noncriminal justice partners may actually be more effective in reducing crime than if the criminal justice system acted in isolation.

THE ILLICIT TRADE IN ENDANGERED SPECIES

Research on endangered species is primarily the product of the scientific commu-nity, comprised of conservationists, biologists, zoologists, botanists, and ecolo-gists. Additionally, anthropologists also study species and their relationship with humans, as well as how societies adapt when species become extinct. All told, their combined work identifies species at risk of imminent danger and the contributing factors that threaten the species. Information about the geographic locations and habitat of species, as well as how the species are catalogued regard-ing the level of threat and protection needed, are all provided by these scientific fields.

Conservation agency reports published by agencies like WWF and TRAF-FIC provide the vast majority of what is known about the trafficking in endangered flora and fauna. While these reports offer valuable information about the illicit trade, established trade routes, and the extent of the problem, they are devoid of detailed discussions or descriptions of the manner in which their data are collected and analyzed. This opens the reports of their findings to criticism and raises questions about the validity and reliability of their methodology and conclusions, thus making them vulnerable to independent scrutiny. Sometimes conflicting information is published in different reports sponsored by the same organization! These reports are merely snapshots in time about local activities, which rarely provides a holistic viewpoint or a deeper understanding of the crime. It is important to note that conservation agencies are extremely under-funded and, therefore, inordinately strained in their ability to conduct compli-cated, international research.

The Extent and Nature

In general terms, the majority of the trade in wildlife is legal and provides a great deal of income to impoverished countries and regions. However, the illegal trade—hunting, processing, and trafficking—in endangered flora and fauna is among the fastest growing of international crimes. This illicit trade has a devas-tating effect on species survival, which in turn has negative, long-term effects on humans. Moreover, it is said that the illicit trade in endangered flora and fauna is second only to that of drug trafficking from a profitability standpoint.[4] It is well known that profits from the illegal wildlife trade are immense; however, they are difficult, if not impossible, to accurately calculate. For example, one annual figure of US$159 billion is based on declared values of items imported; yet the Metropolitan Police in the United Kingdom offer a much more modest figure of US$25 billion, of which only a quarter is attributed to illegal trading.[5] Further, an even more modest amount of US$8 billion is provided and is based on a com-bined illegal trade of ozone depleting substances and wildlife.[6]

Globally, the number of declared (legal or possibly illegal) wildlife ship-ments increased 61 percent from 111,296 (FY 2000) to 179,323 (FY 2007).[7] What is not clear from these figures is just how many individual pieces of wild-life goods, legal or illegal, were contained in each shipment. The estimated value for the illegal and legal contents contained in the shipments was US$1.2 billion and US$2.88 billion for each year, respectively.[8]

The United States is not a large supplier of wildlife products—legal or ille-gal. However, it is considered to be an active consumer nation for both legal and illegal products derived from endangered species. The United States accounts for approximately 20 percent of all global purchases of illegal wildlife goods.[9] Table 1.1 explores data about the number of refused shipments versus counts of individual items refused.

Table 1.1 The Top 10 Countries from Which Wildlife Imports Were Refused, 2000–2004*

Country	Shipments Refused
Mexico	3,772
Canada	1,560
People's Republic of China	1,138
Philippines	728
Hong Kong	591
Russia	562
No Shipping Label	524
Thailand	473
Italy	406
South Africa	341

*Liana Sun Wyler and Pervaze A. Sheikh, "CRS Report for Congress: International Illegal Trade in Wildlife: Threats and U.S. Policy," *Congressional Research Service* (August): 6.

No one may be able to agree on amounts of actual profits generated by illicitly trading endangered wildlife or on how those profits are calculated, but all agree that scarcity and rarity affect costs. The basic principles of economics stipulate that limited supply increases demand. This holds true in the illegal trade of species: the more rare and scarce the plant or animal, the more valuable it is on the black market. Scarcity increases demand, which in turn inflates prices. Plants and animals listed on the International Union for Conservation of Nature and Natural Resources[10] (IUCN) Red List of Threatened Species[11] will be extremely valuable, expensive, and profitable because of the high bounty placed on them. Efforts to acquire the desired item, coupled with the level of official protection attached to it, will determine the final price of the demanded commodity.[12]

The potential for profit is extraordinary, but perhaps more important is the incalculable costs of losing species and of the destruction of habitat caused by the illicit trade in endangered species.[13] While there are some international control mechanisms in place such as customs/border patrol and international trade treaties, the crime remains practically invisible to authorities, making law enforcement efforts extremely difficult, if not impossible. A large proportion of these crimes occur in regions and countries where scarce resources are diverted to other priorities, such as civil war or terrorism. Nations where these crimes thrive generally have weak legislative and enforcement controls coupled with very porous borders, providing conditions for the illegal conditions for practices to continue unabated, confounding the problem even further.

The Markets

Research from Wolverhampton University in the United Kingdom identified five types of illegal activities associated with the trade in endangered species.[14] These include the illegal trade in (1) timber; (2) caviar; (3) skins, furs, and traditional Asian medicine (TAM); (4) specialist collections; and (5) activities pertaining to drugs and narcotics. The five types of activities all have their own unique characteristics, including methods of acquisition, processing, transshipping, trading, and trafficking.[15] These researchers also claim that trade routes for illegal drugs are being used for the purposes of importing and exporting endangered species. What is difficult to ascertain, however, is the accuracy of the researchers' claims. No other academic or scientific research can be found that substantiates their claim of the link between trafficking in drugs and that of trafficking endangered flora and fauna.

The natural habitat or the country of origin of a particular species is known as a range state. Species are usually taken from their range state and moved through a series of intermediary/transshipment points. Transshipment points are locations where the animals or plants are processed into smaller parts in order to facilitate shipping. These points play an important role in that it is far simpler to move a butchered tiger or elephant, for example, compared to that of the entire carcass. By organizing their shipments, traffickers can consolidate their goods so that the number of destinations can be managed in a way that reduces suspicion. Once processed, the parts of the demanded wild flora and fauna are moved through a series of handlers until they reach their final destinations—the consumers.

Consumers want products for different reasons—all of which keep the trade in endangered species vibrant. Luxurious goods or trophies made from ivory or mahogany are status symbols, as are exotic fashions made of animal pelts. Bushmeat serves as a source of nutrition. TAMs provide remedies for physical or psychological ailments. These are only a sampling of reasons that compel consumers to participate in the illegal species trade.

Innumerable global ports of call exist where the illegal goods are delivered. For example, tiger bones are used in TAMs and therefore may be shipped to a factory in China that manufactures the remedies; whereas the skins may be demanded by tourists in Thailand or by residents in Tibet. Intervention is exceptionally difficult due to the vast distances and areas that the species must travel from capture, slaughter, to consumption. Officials must develop a systematic understanding of the entire process in order to design interventions at various points of opportunity.

THE ROLE OF CRIMINOLOGY

The illegal killing of wild endangered flora and fauna violates a number of international treaties and national laws. The illegality does not stop with the killing. Once harvested, the goods move through a series of steps from the point of kill or harvest through to the end-consumer. This process includes the buying and selling of protected species, which is also a violation of international treaties and national laws. These criminal activities are clearly the domain of criminologists.

Engagement of the criminological community to undertake situational or environmental studies that address the dynamics of illicit market activities rather than those focusing on offender behavior is a possible way forward. Situational, environmental, and/or conservation criminologists do indeed have a role to play in conservation by examining what factors contribute to the loss of species. With the knowledge gained from systematic research, effective crime reduction interventions can be designed in order to negatively impact opportunities that facilitate the criminal activities that reduce the survivability of endangered animals and plants.

There is an unusual and exciting union to be formed here. Crime reduction is best done in partnerships with police and other relevant agencies. Criminologists, working in conjunction with conservationists, can provide multidimensional intervention strategies that are limited only by imagination.

Applying Criminology: The Market Reduction Approach

The market reduction approach is a crime reduction strategy initially designed to reduce traditional forms of theft-related crimes by targeting stolen goods markets rather than thieves. The approach is offered here as a tool for enforcement and conservation officials to use for reducing the occurrence of trafficking in endangered flora and fauna by making it more risky for the trade to continue. The market reduction approach is a multifaceted strategy built upon the foundations of situational crime prevention and routine activity theory, in addition to several proactive policing strategies. It is situational in that the strategy aims to understand *how* the crime event occurs rather than *why* it happens. By developing this understanding, practitioners are able to design holistic intervention strategies that are monitored for success, thus allowing for changes in the intervention to be made, if necessary.

Situational crime prevention was constructed with routine activity theory in mind. Routine activity theory states simply that in order for crime to occur, a motivated offender (poachers, handlers, consumers) and a target (endangered species) must converge in time and place in the absence of a capable guardian (local villagers, conservationists, law enforcement, other interested parties). These three elements often meet through a person's daily routine, offering opportunities for victimization to occur. A change in just one of the three elements (target, offender, or absent guardian) will prevent the crime event from occurring. Furthermore, reducing criminal opportunities decreases the probability that crime will occur.

Correlated to routine activity theory is research conducted on travel-to-crime. Historically, law enforcement officials have long believed that criminals travel great distances to commit their crimes. However, research conducted in England has dispelled that notion.[16] The research demonstrated that, instead, criminals travel very short distances in order to offend. Additionally, it confirmed that offenders commit crimes near to where their routine activities occur, such as where they live, where they work, or where they engage in recreational activities. The exception to this tenet is the greater distances some very specialized offenders, like rapists, are willing to travel in order to commit their crime.

When first introduced, situational crime prevention provided an entirely new approach to reducing crime. This theory requires a thorough analysis of the physical setting and circumstance where specific crimes occur. Once contributing factors are identified, the physical setting can be modified or changed in order to reduce existing criminal opportunities. Hot spots of activities are explored in addition to the distances that offenders are willing to travel in order to commit crime.

For crime reduction strategies like the market reduction approach to be successful, they must be designed with particular forms and types of crime events in mind. Effective efforts, therefore, must be targeted and evidence-based. In order to reduce the illegal trade in endangered species, it would not be helpful to create a generic intervention for illegal trade in all types of threatened flora and fauna. It would also be unhelpful to apply strategies that were designed to reduce illegal markets that involved iPads or flat screen televisions. To illustrate the meaning, successful initiatives that reduce the trafficking in elephant ivory may not be helpful in reducing the trade in shark fins; therefore, detailed analyses of both situations/crimes must be conducted before practitioners can figure out how to make each crime more risky and less rewarding.

A modified model of the market reduction approach as it pertains to the illegal trade in endangered species is outlined in Figure 1.1.[17] As applied to the illicit endangered species trade, the market reduction approach specifically aims to make hunting, harvesting, processing, shipping, and trafficking in protected species more risky for all those involved in the process by designing specific intervention strategies in partnership with relevant agencies. In order to do this, the routine activities of humans, as well as animals, must be documented so that "pinch points" can be identified. Where appropriate, market reduction approach interventions can then be implemented. The approach states specifically that while this is a crime reduction approach, police cannot be the sole participants in trying to reduce its occurrence. The market reduction approach relies on the involvement of relevant partner agencies that can help provide data and other resources in order to help develop a thorough understanding of the problem and solutions to it. Conservation agencies have a critical role to play in conjunction with various local, national, and international police officials.

Analytical tools are necessary in order to determine the nature and extent of the illegal hunting, processing, and trading of particular species. There are two possible sets of useful official data to analyze. The first are police/customs

Figure 1.1 The Market Reduction Approach Interagency Model

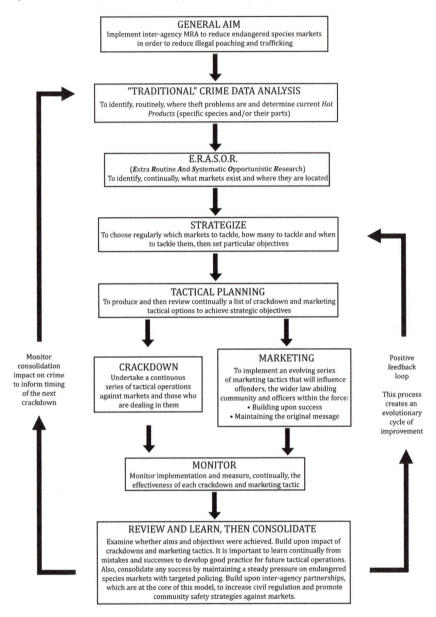

seizure data, which helps to determine what types of animals/parts are being targeted. Seizure data are constructive proxy measures that help identify animals and/or their by-products demanded by consumers, thus fulfilling a market niche. Additionally, these data, when available, will hopefully reveal detailed information about how the offender operates and with whom the offender trades. Oftentimes, however, seizure data are either missing or incomplete. The second potentially useful data are those included in the Red List. It is important to note that this dataset is compiled for conservation purposes—not crime reduction, but there is scope for its use by criminologists. This dataset is searchable and therefore can be arranged by specific species, which will then yield a case study of the endangered status of the animal or plant, along with descriptions of its location, habitat, and threats.

Official crime data tell only a partial story about crime events, whereas "Extra Routine And Systematic Opportunistic Research" (E.R.A.S.O.R.) data draw upon sources of information not normally used for crime-related purposes. Interviews with known offenders (past or current), known traffickers (past or current), local nonpolice authorities, conservationists, and members of the local community are all considered to be sources for E.R.A.S.O.R. data. Migration, mating, nesting, and other behaviors will add a dimension when designing interventions and would be considered E.R.A.S.O.R. data.

It is ideal to explore all facets of the illicit trade in flora and fauna in practice, which include people who hunt, kill, dissect, transport, and arrange for the sale of the various products, to the final consumer. Interviews should also be conducted with conservationists who monitor the routine movements of animals, local farmers whose crops may be at risk of animal stampedes, and shopkeepers, among others.

When all the data are synthesized and analyzed, strategic decisions are made as to which illegal market to disrupt. This is a decision that is dependent on available resources and skill sets. Once the intervention team has decided a course of action, tactical planning takes place with the aim of identifying approaches or operational plans that may yield the most positive and sustained results. Alongside the operational crackdowns, marketing campaigns are implemented, which have a number of purposes: to inform the public about the intervention activities underway; to educate the public about the negative consequences of partaking in the illegal trade of endangered species; and to reiterate the need to conserve natural resources. Finally, the market reduction approach requires constant monitoring. Operations must be evaluated in terms of process and outcome in order to determine their effectiveness. It is at this point where adjustments can be made if data show that tactics had no discernable effect.

The market reduction approach addresses concerns expressed by the International Criminal Police Organization (INTERPOL) Wildlife Working Group. As early as 1994, the working group expressed the need to collect reliable and valid data on wildlife crime. Additionally, this group suggested that a global wildlife database, including illicit trading in protected species, would greatly aid an individual nation's efforts in their fight against the growing problem. Currently, efforts are left to individual nation-states to devise data capturing systems. This confounds not only conservation efforts, but also makes crime reduction nearly impossible. The implementation of the market reduction approach would enable INTERPOL and police from various countries to design an appropriate data collection process, which will inform policy responses.

In order to become truly systematic in our understanding of the illegal trafficking in endangered species, specific data must be uniformly collected by affected nation-states. Because of the international aspect of this crime, it is unhelpful for one country to collect data in one way and another country to use completely different methods. Data capturing mechanisms like those set forth by the market reduction approach could be designed and disseminated to parties of the Convention on International Trade in Endangered Species (CITES). However, access to resources becomes a potential stumbling block. Problems will, no doubt, arise given that countries are stratified by income and financial resources. Not all countries will have the money, technology, knowledge, or the training needed to carry out the data collection that will enable the implementation of the market reduction approach. CITES does have problems with getting party members to fill out annual reports, so it might take considerable effort to persuade nations to submit market reduction approach information.

Typology: Stolen Goods Markets

In 1995, a typology of traditional stolen goods markets was developed as a result of an analysis of British Crime Survey data and a small-scale study in southeastern England.[18] Markets include thieves and someone to purchase the goods from thieves in order to sell them on to consumers. This intermediary is known as a fence or handler of stolen goods. These markets are commercial fence supplies, residential fence supplies, network sales, commercial sales, and hawking. Each market type operates differently, thus requiring different intervention types. Descriptions of the various markets are:

- Commercial fence supplies: thieves sell their goods directly to fences operating out of commercial establishments;
- Commercial sales: commercial fences sell illicit goods directly to the public, who may or may not know their provenance;
- Hawking: thieves sell illicitly obtained goods directly to the public via various methods;
- Network sales: the buyer obtains the illicit goods via a network of friends or acquaintances; and
- Residential fence supplies: thieves sell stolen goods to fences at their homes.[19]

Identification of these typologies and their practices will enable researchers and practitioners to determine the extent to which these market types relate to endangered flora and fauna.

These typologies were instrumental in the development, implementation, and evaluation of the market reduction approach in three constabularies in

England. The evaluations concluded that the market reduction approach was indeed a useful tool to combat traditional illegal stolen goods markets. As a result, this concept was put forth as best practice in the United Kingdom. However, there has been confusion over the title of the concept—market reduction approach. At first glance, practitioners assume that "market" means the local or village market stall where all types of goods are sold. Within the context of the market reduction approach, a market is defined as the exchange relationship between various participants in the illicit trade. In other words, it is the manner in which the hunter provides the plant or animal to the person who harvests the essential parts and how this person then sells the goods to the next person in the chain until ultimately, the goods wind up in the hands of the final consumer. As part of the problem solving research, it is imperative to discover the process by which the animals or their by-products are bought and sold.

The illegality of trafficking in endangered species is rooted in international and national law. The foundations of these laws are introduced next, along with the main organizations that have championed the fight against this crime. Because the market reduction approach requires partnerships, the following agencies can provide valuable and necessary assistance.

RELEVANT AGENCIES AND INTERNATIONAL LEGISLATION

There are many conservation and quasi-legal agencies that play important roles in the fight against illegal trafficking. They do not necessarily offer intervention strategies, but they aid in helping to frame the problem of illegal endangered species markets. The following set forth these agencies' current role in providing a foundation for investigation.

The United Nations (UN) provides the legal-political foundation for the fight against the illicit, international trade of protected species and plays a dual role in the protection of endangered flora and fauna. First, the UN Convention on Transnational and Organized Crime and its protocols is one of the most relevant legal foundations for the protection of endangered species. This Convention deals with illegal trafficking in firearms, endangered species, cultural property, human organs, migrants, and humans, especially women and children. Second, the UN Environment Programme serves as the Convention on International Trade in Endangered Species of Wild Fauna and Flora (CITES) Secretariat.

CITES is one of the longest standing international treaties in existence. The treaty sets forth a system and process by which endangered species are provided protection from trade and overexploitation. The Secretariat of the United Nations has an advisory role for the CITES by monitoring the treaty's implementation among signatories. The Secretariat also organizes the Conference of Parties, which is the "supreme decision-making body"[20] of the Convention and is comprised of all member parties. During the Conference of Parties, signatory parties are able to submit proposals to amend the precepts of the Convention. Proposals are then discussed and are eventually put to a vote. Depending on that vote, CITES is either amended or not.

CITES encourages each signatory country to develop and enforce national legislation that offers protection to species under the auspice by the Convention. Since CITES is not designed to punish offenders of the Convention, it relies on individual countries to self-monitor. Each country has various sociolegal and economic factors that influence the degree to which these national laws are written and enforced.

A number of nongovernmental organizations (NGOs) are involved actively in the conservation and protection of endangered flora and fauna. The International Union for Conservation of Nature's (IUCN) network is uniquely structured to represent more than 1,000 organizations in 140 countries. IUCN sponsors research and assists governments in the implementation of laws, policy, and best practices.[21]

One of the most significant contributions by the IUCN is the joint effort by the IUCN Species Programme and the IUCN Species Survival Commission. Their work, for over 40 years, has assessed the status of species in order to identify those at risk of extinction with the aim of drawing attention to the need for conservation activities. Based on scientific data, the IUCN produces the Red List. The IUCN Species Programme holds the data contained in the Red List as part of IUCN's Species Information Service. These data are searchable and available to the general public via their Web site.[22]

The WWF (formerly the World Wildlife Fund for Nature) is perhaps the most notable and recognizable agency that has provided information about endangered animals around the world for decades. WWF also sponsors research and partners with other conservation agencies worldwide to further their protective and educational work.

TRAFFIC is an international agency that monitors illegal trafficking in endangered species and works to determine if this activity threatens species' survival. TRAFFIC is considered the worldwide leader in providing information about the illegal trade in endangered species. TRAFFIC has initiated research on the illegal hunting and trafficking of animal by-products. The organization is monitored by the TRAFFIC Committee, which consists of members from IUCN and WWF.

INTERPOL is the world's largest police force with 187 countries contributing to its efforts. INTERPOL's primary function is the facilitation of cross-border police operations and investigations. Agents of INTERPOL do not have enforcement powers; rather they assist and support police agencies worldwide in their efforts against crime. INTERPOL has a variety of areas of work, including wildlife crimes. In 1992, INTERPOL began working on wildlife crimes, and despite the appointment of only one full-time officer, work pertaining to wildlife crime has "grown significantly."[23] Their wildlife crimes program has appointed a Wildlife Working Group in order to assist CITES Parties in their mission to protect flora and fauna. The Group works to exchange information about wildlife crimes between nations, coordinate activities between countries when wildlife crime crosses borders, train wildlife officers, and assist CITES countries with their domestic conservation and enforcement efforts.[24]

BOOK OUTLINE

Chapter 2 of the book describes the global patterns of illegal hunting and trafficking of endangered animals. It also reviews CITES data pertaining to the traded species as a way to show how the legislation works in order to protect endangered flora and fauna. Seizure data, where available, is presented to illustrate the types of species confiscated, thus serving as a proxy measure of demanded goods.

Chapter 3 explains the legal framework within which global agencies must work. The UN Convention on Transnational and Organized Crime has specific provisions that address the illegal trafficking in endangered flora and fauna. The details of this Convention are discussed along with the provisions of CITES. Individual examples of national legislation are explored in order to show how international agreements are operationalized at the nation-state level.

Claims are being made that the endangered species trade is affiliated with organized crime and the trade in other illicit goods, such as drugs and weapons. These claims will be explored in Chapter 4 along with the influence that market forces have on the development and sustainability of legal markets. Of particular importance to this chapter is the exploration of the market reduction approach that has been used to impact traditional forms of stolen goods. The chapter describes in detail how this concept can be applied to the illicit trade in flora and fauna.

Chapters 5 through 8 present case studies on a variety of species contained in the Red List. Each plant or animal has varying IUCN levels of protection. The chapters are organized by animal type: terrestrial, marine, plants, and birds.

The final chapter, Chapter 9, summarizes conservation and preservation efforts, as well as ways the market reduction approach can be applied. The chapter concludes with the market reduction approach, thus providing readers, policy makers, and researchers a new paradigm with which to work.

Data and Patterns

DATA PERTAINING to the endangered species trade are sparse. Some police data exist about poaching crimes, but police data about buying and selling endangered species are severely limited. The quality of data varies tremendously from country to country.[1] This variability is due to the skills sets of those working in the various agencies, the availability of technology and equipment, and the level of governmental resources allocated to the enforcement of crimes involving endangered species. Wealthier countries are better able to ensure that the appropriate tools and personnel are available to combat this crime problem, but even in these countries, there is no guarantee that data are complete or accurate. Developing nations and those in economic transition are less likely than wealthier countries to have the requisite resources at their disposal to combat transnational crimes. Therefore, data availability and quality become a serious issue when trying to combat trafficking crimes.

Only a few types of data are available that describe the nature of the endangered species problem. Where available, official police data yield important information about offenses, locations, and active participants in crimes related to the illicit market in endangered species. CITES organizes three databases that will inform crime reduction strategies: (1) species, (2) trade, and (3) trade data dashboards. Finally, the Red List is the primary vehicle through which data about threatened species are catalogued. The combination of police data, CITES data, and the Red List will illustrate the nature of threats that various species face.

POLICE DATA

Police data are not openly available to the public and therefore are difficult to critique here. Largely, these data remain a mystery to the public. Whatever data are collected by agencies like INTERPOL's wildlife unit, United States Fish and Wildlife Service (USFWS), the UK Border Agency, or the Metropolitan Police in London remain closed and unavailable for public use or scrutiny. What is known is that agencies worldwide do not collect the same data, nor do they collect data in a uniform or unified manner. This lack of uniformity makes it extremely difficult to use the information with any level of confidence, especially when trying to make comparisons. It literally becomes a task of comparing apples to oranges or in this case, tigers to trees. Because trafficking in endangered species is an international/transnational crime, efforts must be made to systematize data and data collection.

Intelligence also plays an important role in determining the nature and extent of the crime problem. Local villagers, businesses, and agency workers most probably have critical information that is absent from police reports or datasets. Interviews with these types of groups would be an additional source of data and knowledge. As a way forward, partnerships must be forged between relevant law enforcement agencies, conservation agencies, and researchers in order to strategize a way to reduce the illicit trade. The first step is to determine what police data are available and how that data can best be utilized. The next step is to identify what different types of data can be collected in the future in order to provide the most accurate and thorough understanding as to the nature of the *specific* problem.

Historically, police have focused their efforts on thieves when trying to tackle stolen goods markets. Consequently, police data are rich in details about the various activities and motivations of thieves, but void of details of information pertaining to stolen goods markets. Research has begun to deconstruct the process of stealing, buying, and selling stolen goods,[2] and while thieves are part of illicit markets, the entire process must be understood or else theft will continue to rise.

In the case of the endangered species trade, the emphasis has largely been focused on catching poachers, who are akin to thieves in traditional stolen goods markets. A more thorough approach would be to monitor how the poachers decide what species to hunt, how they deliver the flora and/or fauna to the handler who, in turn, prepares it for processing and transshipment to the final customers. If this process were understood, police data could assist in the creation of more effective crime reduction strategies.

CITES DATA

CITES also has several databases that can be freely accessed via the World Wide Web. Three are relevant here: (1) the species database, (2) the trade database, and (3) the trade data dashboard, which offers views on a global scale and on individual nations.

The species database allows the user to search individual countries by taxonomic categories or by common names. Taxonomic categories include phylum, class, order, family, and genus. These may not be the most useful to use for crime reduction purposes because within each category there can be hundreds of species. This database yields very similar information to that of the Red List, but CITES search results are less detailed. The species database is not extremely user-friendly, as there is no mechanism that enables the user to search all countries. Therefore, researchers must know a species' range state (place of natural existence) in order to proceed with searches.

The CITES trade database currently holds ten million records of trade in protected wild flora and fauna.[3] The database contains nearly 50,000 scientific species names listed by CITES. Furthermore, there are roughly 700,000 records about CITES-listed species. The data are based on information provided by signatory parties to CITES. Hence, data are not complete because some countries do not file their annual report to CITES as dictated in the treaty. Even if filed, confusion exists about the content of the report. Most nations do not discern if the number reported is the number of permits issued or if the data reflect the actual number of species that were traded.[4] Other problems include missing or inaccurate information about seized items, and absence of standardized units of measures, making it difficult to accurately count the volume of trade. Annual reports submitted by nation-states frequently do not explain if the species is wild, farmed, or for personal use or commercial use.

In theory, the CITES trade database should assess whether or not party members are adhering to CITES regulations. The analyses of party members' compliance should help determine if they are in violation of the treaty's tenets. The measure of the trade volume should be evident through this database. It could also show the type of trade occurring between parties. Again, in theory, the data provide an excellent way to monitor the trade in protected species. It is, however, prudent to approach the CITES trade database with caution, especially when trying to make or assess policy. Reporting errors and deficiencies affect the success of policies that are implemented.

The novice user is offered a step-by-step process in order to effectively search the databases. The aim is to explore where trade of a particular endangered species is occurring at the nation-state level. The first task is to set date parameters from 1975 through to the current year. Next, the researcher can choose the scope of his/her search. All party members are included to determine the trade occurring between importing and exporting countries. The database allows for granular searching such as choosing specific parts (for example legs, teeth, claws, skin) or the finished product (chess sets made from ivory). A menu of options is offered for trade investigation, ranging from captive-bred to illegal. Finally, the database lists a number of purposes for the items, including breeding, use in circuses, educational, and as hunting trophy. The end result is a comparison table generated from the various options selected. Additionally, tables can be generated based on gross/net imports and/or exports.

The comparative reports are the most frequently used of the tables. They are not easy to decipher, and CITES explains that records often do not match because of the inconsistent manner in which items are counted or reported. One example offered by CITES shows a discrepancy in the numbers because the respective importer and exporter did not use the same purpose code.[5] Another example offered by CITES was that of an exporter reporting that 500 belly skins from the Nile crocodile left Botswana, but the importing country, Japan, only listed the cargo as skins.[6] According to CITES, both are technically correct, but the individual records of items exported will not correlate with records of items imported. Therefore, final statistics will vary depending on how items are recorded by CITES party members and categorized from a database perspective.

To complicate matters further, products can be re-exported and re-imported. For instance, Uganda may export 10 Nile crocodile (*Crocodylus niloticus*) belly skins to the United States and then, the skins may be re-exported to France. Those 10 skins must be accounted for at all steps in transportation. Furthermore, it is necessary to verify that only the original 10 skins are counted and entered into the CITES database. The correct number of exported skins to record, in this case, is 10. Oftentimes, the number recorded includes the re-exports are included in the final count, which is incorrect.

The CITES dashboard database offers a cursory look at data on mammals, birds, reptiles, amphibians, fish, invertebrates (noncorals), corals, orchids, cacti, and other plants.[7] Any party nation can be selected in order to examine the volume of trade over time in that specific country. The primary problem with this database is that specific species in the categories cannot be examined. Data are only provided for *all* mammals traded in that country, therefore, a researcher cannot tell if tigers are among the mammals traded and, if so, how many were traded in a given period of time. This database is useful for an extremely broad overview, but it is imprecise for studying specific types of illicitly traded mammals or for crime reduction strategies for said trade.

IUCN RED LIST OF THREATENED SPECIES

The compilation of this dataset is the result of partnerships between the IUCN Species Programme, the IUCN Species Survival Commission, the IUCN network of scientists, and other relevant agencies.[8] The purpose of the Red List is to determine which species are at risk of extinction and therefore, most in need of conservation and protection. The Red List is the primary database used by conservationists and other scientists worldwide. Data held in the Red List provide a baseline for monitoring and assessing populations, habitat, and conservation needs.[9]

Red List data are available publicly and are relatively easy to manipulate. The Red List aims to provide a transparent process of assessing species and to allow for external review. It does not have an in-house team of scientists who are responsible for updating every single species in the database. Instead, teams of scientists from around the world contribute to the Red List. These scientists welcome external scrutiny, challenges, and/or corrections to their assessments in order that the most accurate case study can be put forward. In the late 1990s, weaknesses were uncovered about the documented assessments. At that time, the existing assessments could not be verified; therefore, changes had to be made for the data to be taken seriously and to be viewed as the primary authority on threats of extinction.

For all species already included in the Red List and for those eventually added, there is a "minimum documentation protocol." A justification must be made to Red List partners as to why a new species should be included. In addition to the justification, the following must be provided: taxon's name, status, criteria, and distribution, a map of where the species is located, population trends, conservation efforts in existence and future conservation needs, and information on the utilization of the species.[10] The breadth and quality of information provided has increased over time and has become much more substantial in recent years, thus providing conservationists a richer understanding of the current state of threatened and protected flora and fauna.

For consistency, five standard categories of information can be viewed when searching the Red List. A **summary** of most of the categories is provided as a general overview, but the summary does not contain information on the list of habitats, major threats, conservation actions, external links, nor the bibliography. The **classification schemes** include lists of habitats, major threats, and conservation actions. **Images and external links** provide photographs when available and other external links that take the researcher to other relevant sources. A **bibliography** is provided so the researcher can go to original sources of material included in the category or to other relevant readings. The **full account** includes all of the information contained in all categories.[11]

Scientists in the various sciences and conservationists use appropriate scientific names and details of species. Therefore, the higher taxonomy details are shown for kingdom, phylum, class, order, and family. Common names, like tiger and elephant, can be used to search the Red List database. However, problems can arise when using common names. For example, if a researcher searches "tiger," three pages of results will follow, with a total of 108 different species that have the word "tiger" included in their common name, which ranges from the California Tiger Salamander (*Ambystoma californiese*) through to the Scarce Blue Tiger (*Tirumala gautama*), a butterfly.

Placement in one of the IUCN categories is dependent on the assessment data compiled[12] (see Figure 2.1). The categories are cumulative; if a species is listed as critically endangered, it is also considered vulnerable and endangered. Red List data are built upon the best estimations of population, threat, and projections. The Red List categories are extinct, extinct in the wild, critically endangered, endangered, vulnerable, near threatened, least concern, data deficient, and not evaluated.

Ambiguity does exist when determining the appropriate threat category. The IUCN explains that natural variation, vagueness of terms and definitions, and measurement error all contribute to assessing species.[13] This does not mean that the Red List should be discounted as a valid measure of species' status; rather, these data are the best science can offer at this point in time. The categorization of species does not dictate conservation priorities, which are influenced by financial resources, logistics, and chances of success.

Figure 2.1 IUCN Red List of Threatened Species Categories

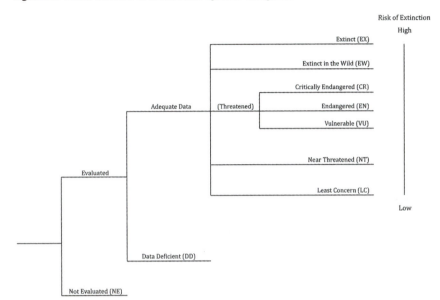

The placement of a plant or animal in any category may shift over time. The IUCN has specific rules on how that transfer can take place. First, moving from a higher threat level to a lower one can be made if the criteria for the higher level are not met for five or more years. Second, movement between categories can take place if the original assessment data are deemed flawed. Finally, the Red List suggests that moving from a lower level to a higher one take place as soon as feasibly possible.

The Red List categories have very lengthy and specific criteria used to help determine appropriate listings.[14] A cursory overview of those criteria is presented here. Variables that are assessed include reductions of population size over time, geographic region size and structure, actual counts of individual animals/plants, and the probability of extinction.

To qualify for **extinct**, there is no reasonable doubt that the last living taxon has died. Studies must be conducted at various times throughout the year over the species' historic range for the species' typical lifespan. If none of the taxon is seen, it is considered extinct. Flora or fauna are **extinct in the wild** if the remaining plants or animals only live in captivity, or in cultivation. As with the extinct label, exhaustive surveys are done in order to assess the species properly.

To warrant being listed as **critically endangered**, populations must be reduced by 90 percent or more over the last 10 years or for a course of a generation and that the cause of the reduction is reversible, understood, and stopped. There are additional clauses that stipulate a lower percentage drop (80% or more), but the causes are unknown or uncontrolled. The geographic range is extremely fragmented and continues to decline. Also, the area of occupancy shrinks to such levels that it cannot sustain the flora or fauna. The geographic range is less than about 39 mi^2 (100 km^2), and the area of occupancy is less than four mi^2 (10 km) and is extremely fragmented or only exists in a single locale. The estimated count of individuals is less than 250 mature members and continues to decrease or is estimated to decline at lease 25 percent over a three-year period or a generational span, whichever is longer. To be critically endangered, an actual count can be as low as 50 mature individuals. The probability of extinction in the wild is at least 50 percent within 10 years or three generations, whichever is longer.

For **endangered** species, the reduction in population size has a slightly higher threshold of 70 percent or more with causes being reversible and stopped within 10 years or three generations, whichever is longer. Furthermore, if the population size decreases by 50 percent or more and the causes have not been rectified or reversed, the species is considered endangered. The geographic range is estimated to be less than 1,031 mi^2 (5,000 km^2). The range is extremely fragmented, exists in no more than five locations, and continues to decline. The area of occupancy is less than 193 mi^2 (500 km^2), severely fragmented, and in constant decline. For endangered status, there are less than 2,500 mature individuals alive. Additionally, it requires further declines by at least 20 percent within five years or two generations, whichever is longer. The probability of extinction in the wild within 20 years or five generations, whichever is less, is at least 20 percent.

To qualify as **vulnerable**, a species' decline in population is 30 percent or greater over the past 10 years or three generations, whichever is longer. Causes for the decline are known, reversible, understood, and stopped. The categorization can also be based on population reductions of more than 30 percent, but causes have not stopped or reversed and the reasons for the decline have not yet been understood. The geographic range is less than 7,722 mi^2 (20,000 km^2) and severely fragmented or known to be in less than 10 areas. Areas of occupancy are less than 772 mi^2 (2,000 km^2). The number is less than 1,000 mature individuals. The risk of extinction within 100 years is at least 10 percent.

Near threatened species have been assessed, but their survivability levels are not as critical as those in the other categories. A species will be placed in this category if the flora or fauna do not quite meet the other criteria and it is thought that the species might warrant reclassification to a higher status in the future. Species classsed as **least concern** have been evaluated and do not meet the thresholds of the higher categories. The species are in abundance in the wild. When there is a lack of material and information on the species, it will be classified as **data deficient**. This is not a category that denotes threat; rather it is one that simply acknowledges there is more research to be done. **Not evaluated** is very clear—the species has not yet undergone rigorous analyses.

ARRANGING IUCN RED LIST DATA

Red List data are meant for use by scientists. It presents an interesting challenge for those who do not have a biology or zoology background! Red List data are presented as summary statistics in table form. Summaries are presented by taxonomic groups, by country, and list of past and present Red List threatened species.[15] Before beginning, nonbiologists/zoologists may find it useful to decipher scientific classifications. All flora and fauna have scientific classifications. The classifications are broken down by several categories: (1) Kingdom, (2) Phylum, (3) Class, (4) Order, (5) Family, (6) Genus, and (7) Species. For example, the tiger's scientific classification is:

Kingdom:	Animalia	
Phylum:	Chordata	
Class:	Mammalia	
Order:	Carnivora	
Family:	Felidae	
Genus:	*Panthera*	
Species:	*tigris*	
Subspecies (subsp.):	*P. t. altacia* (Siberian)	*P. t. amoyensis* (South China)
	P. t. balica (Bali)	*P. t. corbetti* (Indochinese)
	P. t. jacksoni (Malayan)	*P. t. sondaica* (Javan)
	P. t. sumatrae (Sumatran)	*P. t. tigris* (Bengal or Indian)
	P. t. virgata (Capsian)	

Knowing the taxonomic information of the targeted species is useful when analyzing Red List data. The Red List summary table includes 26 classes with varying numbers of orders within each of the class categories (see Table 2.1). Within each class there are a number of orders, which have a number of families, which further have a number of genus, and then finally a number of species and subspecies that fall within a specific genus. It is impossible to tell, from the way the data are presented and organized, exactly what specific animals are extinct, critically endangered, endangered, vulnerable, threatened, or data deficient. The data can tell researchers which of the mammalia orders have the most threatened species, but without knowing microlevel data, the information is nothing more than rankings of the different classes. Surely, it would be far better to have more detailed accounts of which species and subspecies are in need of protection. In order to drill down to that level, researchers would have to simply search the Red List species by species.

Similar summary data are also available for plants. There are 18 classes that have a total of 364 families of plants that are considered threatened. In those families, there are a total of 8,724 plants that are considered threatened: 113 are either extinct or extinct in the wild; 1,619 are critically endangered; 2,397 are

Table 2.1 All Animal Classes and Orders that Are Threatened, Red List, 2010

Animal Class	No. of Orders	EX	EW	CR	EN	VU	NT	Lr/cd	DD	LC	Total
Mammalia	27	76	2	188	450	493	324	0	836	3,122	5,491
Aves	25	132	4	190	372	678	838	0	62	7,751	10,027
Reptilia	4	20	1	106	200	288	189	3	526	1,473	2,806
Amphibia	3	37	2	486	658	654	387	0	1,596	2,376	6,296
Cephalaspidomorphi	1	1	0	2	0	1	2	0	3	10	19
Myxini	1	0	0	0	0	0	0	0	2	1	3
Chondrichthyes	10	0	0	25	42	114	134	0	488	241	1,044
Actinopterygil	40	57	9	348	358	959	278	10	1,459	4,299	7,777
Sarcopterygii	2	0	0	1	0	1	0	0	0	3	5
Echinoidea	1	0	0	0	0	0	1	0	0	0	1
Arachnida	3	0	0	3	5	11	2	0	9	3	33
Chilopoda	1	0	0	0	0	1	0	0	0	0	1
Diplopoda	1	0	0	1	6	7	0	0	7	10	31
Crustacea	18	11	1	116	145	335	53	9	781	701	2,152
Insecta	15	60	1	89	166	478	192	3	798	1,482	3,269
Merostomata	1	0	0	0	0	0	1	0	3	0	4
Onychophora	0	0	0	3	2	4	1	0	1	0	11
Hirudinoidea	1	0	0	0	0	0	1	0	0	0	1
Oligochaeta	1	1	0	1	0	4	1	0	0	0	7

Olychaeta	2	0	0	1	0	0	0	1	0	2
Bivalvia	4	32	0	59	35	21	63	59	112	384
Gastropoda	13	279	14	314	293	556	222	749	312	2,763
Enopla	1	0	0	0	0	2	1	3	0	6
Turbellaria	1	1	0	0	0	0	0	0	0	1
Anthozoa	5	0	0	6	23	202	175	147	289	842
Hydrozoa	1	0	0	1	2	2	1	2	8	16
Total Fauna	187	707	34	1,940	2,857	4,821	2,866	7,530	22,192	42,989

endangered and 4,708 are vulnerable. There are 1,147 near threatened, 817 data deficient, and 225 considered lower risk. The class of plants that has the largest number of threatened species is the *magnoliopsida* class, which contains over 250,000 specimens of flowering plants. It is the largest phylum of land plants worldwide. The same Red List problematic issues that were present in the animal kingdom are present in the plant kingdom. As the data are currently arranged, there is no way to clearly know which plant within a given class and family is at risk.

Data can also be arranged by country. The number and types of species will, of course, vary because of natural habitat and climate amenable to particular types of species. Again, these data are organized in such a way that they may present challenges to crime reduction experts. The Red List categorizes and sub-categorizes animals as vertebrates (mammals, birds, reptiles, amphibians, fishes) or invertebrates (insects, mollusks, crustaceans, others) while plants are catego-rized and subcategorized as mosses, ferns, allies, gymnosperms, dicotyledons, and nonocotyledons. These categories are extremely broad and serve as the basis for all other Red List tables. For instance, in 2010, Cameroon reported the fol-lowing taxonomic data: 39 mammals, 16 birds, 4 reptiles, 53 amphibians, 110 fishes, 11 mollusks or crustaceans, 13 other type of invertebrates, and 378 plants, for a total of 624 threatened species. The same problem exists with these data. There is no way to discern exactly which mammals, birds, reptiles, amphibians, fishes, mollusks, or plants are threatened.[16] For effective crime reduction inter-ventions, police and conservationists must know exactly what species within these very broad categories is in danger, as well as which are being illegally traded.

These tables can reveal interesting differences that raise questions. Nigeria is a border country that has similar wildlife as Cameroon, but Nigeria has far fewer endangered species with 27 mammals, 13 birds, 4 reptiles, 13 amphibians, 56 fishes, 1 mollusk or crustacean, 11 other type of invertebrates, 172 plants, for a total of 397 endangered species. Both Nigeria and Cameroon have similar geog-raphies and climates, and yet Cameroon has 64 percent more endangered species than its neighbor. What are the contributing factors that can account for that large of a difference? Are there policy differences or more strict law enforcement? Is there a larger presence of conservation agencies? More extensive details about individual species are needed before addressing these larger questions.

MARKET REDUCTION APPROACH DATA

Without having access to data from INTERPOL and other relevant police agen-cies, it is difficult to assess their usefulness when implementing this crime reduc-tion strategy. Developing partnerships with local, regional, national, and international police officials is vital. Without access to official police data, it would be much more difficult to implement the market reduction approach.

However, nontraditional police information is also an important part of the strategy. Existing data, thus far, lies in the hands of conservation agencies. It is fair to say, however, that existing data collected and arranged by various conservation agencies fall somewhat short in terms of crime reduction.

Traditional crime data encompasses information such as locations of crime, types of crime committed, and spatial distribution of these crimes. It also includes information on "hot products." Evidence regarding stolen goods markets should also be examined.

E.R.A.S.O.R. data fall outside the scope of regular crime analyses. Law enforcement agencies typically do not collect these atypical forms of data. Largely, E.R.A.S.O.R. data are those derived from qualitative interviews with a variety of individuals and groups. Offenders are a rich source of information that can be used to help construct interventions. However, law enforcement officials interview offenders for evidence used to convict criminals. E.R.A.S.O.R. interviews would not be used for prosecution; rather, the interviews help to frame the problem. They reveal patterns of buying or selling illicit goods, reasons why the items are stolen, and locations where poaching, processing, and sales take place. It might be helpful to think of E.R.A.S.O.R. data as the "who," "what," "where," "when," and "how" that typically frame a journalist's story (see Table 2.2).

Because the market reduction approach is built with partnerships in mind, interviews with various law enforcement officers, other nonlaw enforcement officials, conservation agency workers, and local community members should also be conducted. Results from these structured interviews can be invaluable to the development of an understanding about the nature of the crime, which informs effective intervention strategies. Oftentimes, these groups are outside the scope

Table 2.2 Differences Between Traditional and MRA Data

Focus	Traditional	MRA
Who	Individual offender	Thief, handler, consumer
What	Individual crime; e.g., burglary, theft from motor vehicle, shoplifting	Specific types of property
Location	Individual address	Type of location; e.g., shop, shed, house, school, business
Date	Date of victimization	Seasonality
How	Individual MO of offender	How things are bought and sold: i.e., the type of stolen goods market
Why	Drugs, poverty, greed, childhood abuse	Demand

of traditional law enforcement investigations. The change in the underlying purpose of the interviews moves away from prosecution toward that of collaboration is often a challenge. Community members may be reluctant to be interviewed by policing officials, whereas they may be very candid with researchers trying to uncover patterns of crime. Therefore, it is crucial that nonpolice participants conduct the interviews with relevant constituents.

PATTERNS

Patterning the hunting, poaching, production, transportation, and purchasing of endangered flora and fauna is nearly impossible to do on a global scale. These actions are dependent on the demand of individual species, sociolegal jurisdictions, and quality of mapping data. Generalities can give some indication of how goods are moved from the species' natural range, but generalities are hardly useful in trying to develop an in-depth understanding of the intricacies and patterns of the illicit trade. Further, trafficking routes most likely vary by species type, which complicates matters even more.

For example, elephant ivory can originate in only a few places worldwide—select countries on the African continent and select countries on the Asian continent. Once the illegal ivory is removed from the elephant carcass and then readied for shipment as either unworked or worked ivory, it can literally be transported to any destination worldwide. Shipment is largely dependent on who is transporting the illicit goods, how they are transported, and where in the world the goods are wanted/consumed. Continuing with the elephant ivory example, unworked ivory is highly demanded in Japan, where there are no naturally occurring elephants, but where expert craftsmen can transform the ivory into tourist souvenirs or other treasures. Since Japan is an island nation, there are only two ways to enter the country: via airports or seaports. There are approximately 47 public airports in Japan and 1,020 seaports. Of these, 106 are main ports, and 892 local ports, and 22 are for special purposes.[17] This total does not include any private docks or airstrips. At the majority of ports worldwide, officials respond reactively when illicit goods are discovered, often by chance. This approach is not only too time-consuming, but it is infeasible given the number of police available to search every cargo shipment or every traveler's suitcase.

To complicate matters, ivory (worked or unworked) is not only demanded in Japan; individuals in other parts of the world also want to possess works of ivory. This trade is a perfect example of the economic laws of supply and demand. Products will make it through to whoever demands it, no matter where the person is located. The riskier the process is, the higher the price of the goods demanded.

The point to be taken here is that no specific city is the entry point for illegal ivory in *any* country. Additionally, countries can merely be used as a pass-through for other destinations. Seizure data suggest that ivory is removed from either Africa or Asia and moved to Japan via the Middle East, Singapore, among many other countries. Moreover, there is no specific city within a country that is the throughway. This scenario is true of any other endangered species by-product. Literally anything can be smuggled into any city in any country. This makes it incredibly difficult or impossible to map specific routes at this point in time, with any degree of certainty.

Legislation and Enforcement Efforts

THE DANCE OF LEGISLATION that aims to protect wild species is a complicated one. This chapter outlines the more relevant historic legal mechanisms that protect flora and fauna that are at risk of extinction and discusses current international accords, as well as a small number of national laws enacted as part of international efforts.

Individual nations alone cannot effectively reduce the illegal practices of trading endangered species. Regardless of whether the nation has the best intent to protect its natural animal and plant resources, nature itself inhibits efforts. Animals and plants are obviously not aware of geopolitical boundaries as their natural migratory patterns cross borders. This, coupled with the fact that criminals use destinations worldwide to process and market protected wild species, makes legal intervention and conservation extremely complicated and difficult. In order for efforts to be successful, nations must work in unison in order to combat the illicit trade in endangered wild fauna and flora.

The role of international agreements and treaties pertaining to the protection of endangered species cannot be dismissed. Despite the difficulties involved in developing and enforcing these agreements, the international conservation efforts serve as a vital mechanism through which real protection can be afforded to the threatened and at risk species. International legislation that protects endangered species is a global conservation tool[1] that plays a central coordinating role for conservation and protection issues, but these international efforts are dependent on nation-states having strong domestic laws that restrict and penalize illegal hunting, killing, and trading protected species.

HISTORIC PERSPECTIVES

There is a rich history of attempts to protect endangered wild species through international agreements and legislations. Sustainability of natural resources, including wild flora and fauna, has been the subject of many national and international agreements for several years. Historically, international legislation and subsequent programs based on that legislation focused on species that exist across many national borders or those which migrate across nation-states. In large part, work was focused on ensuring sufficient breeding populations remained so that wild harvesting practices could still take place. Today, conservation and protective legislation is more complex. Treaties categorize flora and fauna based on the varying levels of needed protection. From that list of wild species, transnational trade can be restricted, and proof of the species' sustainability documented as the treaty enforcement process.

Conservation agencies have started to implement a step-change in the manner in which conservation and protection is approached. Rather than simply trying to save wild species, humans are being told that their relationships with nature and their environs must change in order for the survival of all humans and wild species. Conservationists have witnessed the shift from traditional and historical approaches, such as simply focusing on one ecosystem at a time and in isolation of others. In 1971, the Convention on Wetlands of International Importance especially as Waterfowl Habitat first highlighted the symbiotic relationship between species and habitats, thus negating the approach of focusing on only one species at a time in isolation of the habitat. These early conservation agreements were largely negotiated between small numbers of countries and truly only focused on one species at a time.

Countries have entered into wildlife agreements with foreign governments for centuries. For example, in 1893, the Convention for Preservation and Protection of Fur Seals (in force, 1911) was agreed between Russia, the United States, the United Kingdom, and Japan. This Convention provided the foundation for the League of Nations negotiating the Geneva Convention for the Regulation of Whaling (1934), which limited high seas whaling of depleted species in addition to the prohibition of calf whaling. However, Japan, Germany, and the former Soviet Union were not party to the agreement. In 1937, the International Agreement for the Regulation of Whaling, while not considered terribly helpful, did designate a whaling season for hunters, but no other limits were imposed such as animal size or allowable numbers of catches. After World War II, the main whaling states passed the International Convention for Regulation of Whaling (1946), which remains the governing agreement today.

General agreements on wildlife protection, albeit unsuccessful, began in the early 1900s. The first was the London Convention Designed to Ensure the Conservation of Various Species of Wild Animals in Africa Which Are Useful to Man or Inoffensive (1900). Although this convention was relevant among colonial states of Africa, it never went into force. The second was the London Convention Relative to the Preservation of Fauna and Flora in their Natural State (1933). Both of these conventions limited hunting on certain protected or threatened species in addition to requiring licenses to export wildlife products derived from these protected species. The 1933 Convention was activated in 1936, but with the fall of colonialism and the lack of oversight, it failed in every way. In 1940, the Washington Convention on Nature Protection and Wildlife Preservation in the Western Hemisphere was created. Perhaps somewhat ahead of its time, what it sought to accomplish is mirrored in current CITES practices. The Convention aimed to control the trade in protected species by creating a permit system for exporting and importing these animals and plants. It also required the creation of national parks and other wildlife conservation areas that prohibited hunting; however, this Convention was never fully implemented and eventually collapsed, as there were no mechanisms to govern the treaty.

THE ROLE OF THE UNITED NATIONS

The United Nations provides the legal-political foundation upon which to focus on the illicit trade of protected species. This organization provides several avenues through which endangered species are afforded protection. The first is through the work of the Economic and Social Council (ECOSOC). The ECOSOC must convene a Crime Congress every five years as stipulated by Article 62 of the UN Charter and General Assembly Resolution 415(V) of 1950. Commissions are functional bodies of the ECOSOC in which member states can discuss issues and work to adopt resolutions, which serve as the basis for developing international policies on crime prevention or matters pertaining to the administration of justice. The work conducted at and during congresses help the UN Crime Commission determine a focus of future work.[2] Within ECOSOC, the UN Office of Drugs and Crime is responsible for implementing the mission of the Crime Commissions, which identified transnational and organized crime as an area of focus. The UN Convention on Transnational and Organized Crime identified several items that are trafficked: humans, specifically women and children; weapons, including those of mass destruction; cultural items; endangered species of wild fauna and flora, among others. These items become national and international crimes to combat.

A second role of the United Nations lies firmly with its Environment Programme. The UN Environment Programme plays a major role in monitoring and promoting scientific research related to environmental causes. One of its most significant roles is to help develop and implement international agreements pertaining to the sustainability of wildlife and communities.

The UN Environment Programme is run by a General Council, which consists of 58 members that serve four-year terms. There is regional representation from Africa, Oceania, Europe, North and Latin Americas, and Asia. The Council meets every two years in addition to holding special sessions when special issues arise. The founding resolution calls for the UN Environment Programme "to keep under review the world environmental situation in order to ensure that emerging environmental problems of wide international significance should receive appropriate and adequate considerations by governments."[3]

The UN Environment Programme coordinates all UN-based environment programs and provides and administers the secretariat role for two major conventions: CITES and the Convention on Migratory Species (CMS). In addition to these, the UN Environment Programme sponsors several related programs, such as World Conservation Strategy (WCS), which began in 1980 when 35 nations, international NGOs, and UN agencies came together through the joint efforts of the UN Environment Programme, IUCN,[4] and WWF.

The goal of WCS was to combine development efforts with those of conservationists. The fundamental aim of the program was to work with communities at the local and national levels to see the value in conservation. Furthermore, the program aimed to combine sustainable development and use. In other words, it was the first time that conservation was married to economic development. From the work of that organization, the IUCN drafted the World Charter for Nature,[5] which was adopted by the UN General Assembly in 1982. This reinforced the ideal that countries had a legal obligation to protect their own natural resources, especially endangered species. Additionally, nations had an added protection from the exploitation of natural resources by other nations. Therefore, the aim was to implement a project that would encompass protections at the nation-state level, as well as those between nation-states.

CITES

The most laborious and enduring work on protecting endangered wild species began in the 1960s when a dramatic increase in species trade was noticed by the IUCN. IUCN continues to be one of the world's most important conservancy agencies that strives to safeguard endangered fauna and flora. In 1963, IUCN's General Assembly called for the creation of a treaty whose purpose was to regulate trade in rare or threatened wildlife. Disputes between import and export countries thwarted efforts until the 1972 Stockholm Convention, where an action plan was agreed upon that included a working conference to negotiate terms of agreement between the sparring countries.

In 1973, a new draft that focused on protecting endangered species through trade regulation was agreed to and CITES was enacted and in force by 1975. CITES has been called the "magna carta" for wild fauna and flora.[6] It is considered one of the most successful international treaties in general, as well as worldwide, and it is the definitive tool by which endangered species are provided protection globally. Today, CITES is a global conservation agreement that has 175 signatory parties.

Initially, CITES' sole concern was the preservation of species. Increases in the trade of a few species such as spotted cats, chimpanzees, and crocodiles, contributed to the increased concern among scientists and policy makers. Activities centered on mechanisms that protected those animals and plants that were most at risk of extinction. These activities were designed to merely protect these animals; no attention was paid to the larger issue of ecosystem conservation or community development. It was not until later that CITES realized that, in order for endangered species to recover, work was needed at a macrolevel to ensure that local communities were provided alternatives to relying on fauna and flora for sustenance or on the illegal trade for economic gain.[7]

CITES aims to protect endangered species by prohibiting trade of those wild fauna and flora that are most threatened with extinction. The fundamental idea behind CITES is that if trade is regulated strictly, animals and plants faced with extinction will have time to regenerate and therefore, increase their survivability in the wild. Without doubt, regulation is the key factor CITES uses to enforce the tenets of the treaty. A signatory party of CITES agrees to design domestic legislation aimed at protecting endangered species along with the creation and designation of a management authority and a scientific authority. In each country, the management authority seeks to monitor the implementation of CITES policy at the nation-state level. This scientific authority guides principles in the identification of species in need of protection and monitors the status of those species already listed by CITES.

Three appendices lie at the heart of CITES. Wild fauna and flora are listed in one of the appendices based on their standing in the wild. Trade is restricted based on the status. For example, animals and plants listed in Appendix I are those species most severely threatened with extinction and, therefore, trade is extremely restricted. Commercial trade is prohibited entirely, and other forms of trade are considered only if parties can show that the trade will not further threaten or harm the overall species. In theory, species listed in Appendix I can only cross over national borders if the requisite CITES permits accompany the animals or plants.

Animals and plants listed in Appendix II require intervention and regulation in order that their tenuous status is not further threatened with extinction, so trade is tightly regulated. Species or their by-products can only be traded if parties can show that the trade is not harmful to the overall health and survival of the species. Additionally, those wishing to trade must demonstrate that the species or their parts were not obtained illegally under respective domestic laws. Finally, those who wish to trade must show the required trade permits, along with evidence that the trade will not harm the species.

Appendix III provides signatory parties some degree of latitude when listing species within their borders that are in need of protection domestically. In essence, a nation-state that believes a species within its jurisdiction is in need of protection seeks support from CITES and other signatories. The requested species is therefore added to Appendix III, which then requires proof that no harm will come to the listed species and that export permits were granted through management authorities for trade in that species. Under these conditions, CITES provide international recognition to locally protected wild species. Because CITES-listed species are limited in their trade, import and export documents must be shown to legal authorities. If the documents are found to be forged or missing, the items are confiscated and a criminal investigation may take place.

Aside from the Appendices and authorities, CITES creates a Conference of Parties, which meets every two years with the purpose of doing treaty-related business. It is at the Conference of Parties where signatories can ask for amendments to the Appendices listings. Species can only be added to Appendix I or II with approval of two-thirds of the Conference of Parties. There are processes that allow for nations to register reservations to decisions and for disputes to be resolved. Generally, the Conference of Parties provides general policy guidance for signatory parties and prepares reports about the transfer of species, compliance, and infractions by nation-states.

Each signatory party to CITES voluntarily submits an annual report that accounts for all imports and exports of CITES-governed species. Parties also submit biennial reports that detail their nation's efforts to protect endangered species. The reporting rate is not encouraging with only 8 to 30 percent of countries submitting annual reports.[8] The high of 80 percent took place in 1987 and because of the subsequent decline, CITES sent letters out to the parties explaining that a failure to report was a "major implementation problem."[9] In theory, export and import data should correspond perfectly; however, because of inaccurate or incomplete data or due to law enforcement problems, the data do not match.

The Secretariat also publishes a report of infractions, which lists those parties who have violated trade rules. Training is provided to a nation's officials when infractions do occur, but it must be said that there are very few penalties for noncompliance. The CITES Standing Committee can recommend action against an offending nation. Restriction of trade with and outright banning of a member state are examples of penalties.

Overall, CITES has had mixed results. Without doubt, thousands of wild species have been given protected status; however, in practice, several problems have been identified. Perhaps the most glaring issue is that there is no consensus on how to measure CITES success. For example, the U.S. Government Accountability Office (GAO) reports that the Minister of Agriculture in Chilé measured the effectiveness of CITES by saying that no wild species became extinct during its implementation in that country. Because of data quality issues, measurement of success or impact on species is difficult.

Perhaps the major issue of concern with CITES is the enforcement of the treaty's policies. Article VIII authorizes member nations to penalize those who violate the tenets of the Convention. However, the Convention fails to explain to countries how punishment works. While some training is provided to countries that implement CITES, enforcement remains one of the biggest problems with the Convention. Nations are left to implement and enforce local laws that they may not have either the expertise or the resources to do. CITES does not specify penalties, which has resulted in inconsistent sentences and financial repercussions being identified. While the Secretariat is a central figure of CITES, the position holds no authority to enforce penalties. It is important to note that since CITES is a voluntary treaty, there are no remedies for nonparty nations who violate the spirit and tenets of the treaty.

CITES is an international treaty that is imposed on sovereign nations, albeit on a voluntarily basis. Individual nations create laws that protect that nation's best interests, economically, socially or politically. When tensions arise between sovereign nations and international treaties such as CITES, the tension can quickly become a barrier to success. The U.S. GAO expresses concern when economically deprived signatory countries are faced with the dilemma of ignoring the lucrative practice of trading in endangered wild species or enforcing CITES.[10]

CITES in Action

The United States

The United States is reported to be the largest importer of wildlife and wildlife products—making up approximately 20 percent of the legal trade.[11] No figures rank the United States in terms of illegal consumption of protected wildlife and wildlife products. In the United States, the primary vehicles through which CITES is implemented and enforced are the Endangered Species Act (ESA) of 1973 and the Marine Mammal Protection Act.[12] The U.S. Fish and Wildlife Service is the U.S.-designate to act as the CITES management and scientific authority. However, the U.S. Fish and Wild Service and the U.S. Commerce Department's National Marine Fisheries Service are responsible for the administration of these laws. The U.S. Fish and Wildlife Service is primarily responsible for terrestrial species, such as protected bats, rats, large cats, and bear, whereas the U.S. National Marine Fisheries Service is responsible for oversight of marine wildlife. Although CITES, the ESA, and the Marine Mammal Protection Act all are dedicated to preserving wild species, they approach the problem from different angles. CITES aims to prevent the threats posed by illegal trading, whereas the ESA extends CITES by adding the conservation of ecosystems to its mission. The Marine Mammal Protection Act only allows the use of marine mammals for public display and scientific research. The only exceptions are afforded to Native Alaskans who are permitted to continue their ancient hunting rights and to some commercial fishing activities. The majority of species protected by the ESA are mammals, birds, and reptiles, which fall under the auspice of the U.S. Fish and Wildlife Service. However, marine mammals are governed by the Marine Mammal Protection Act and monitored by the U.S. National Marine Fisheries Service.

The ESA prohibits the take[13] of listed species as well as the interstate or international trade of wildlife that is protected by the ESA. The ESA provides both civil and criminal sanctions. While the ESA supports the mission of CITES, its scope is far more broad as it aims to protect, not only by prohibiting illegal trade, but also by preserving habitat. Therefore, the aim of the ESA is to provide the mechanisms to conserve the ecosystems of endangered and threatened species, as well as to ensure that treaties and conventions are adhered to by relevant parties. For example, the ESA requires the creation of a "critical habitat" for listed species when "prudent and determinable." Critical habitats may not actually house the listed species, but these geographical areas host environments that are essential to the conservation and survival of the protected species.

Without doubt, protections afforded by the ESA are far stricter than those provided by CITES. There are instances where trade is allowed by CITES, but restricted by the ESA; the cheetah is one example where contradictory policies are in place. Botswana, Namibia, and Zimbabwe have instituted a quota for exporting hunted wild cheetah. Under the ESA, the U.S. Fish and Wildlife Service does not allow the importation of hunting trophies pertaining to the cheetah because U.S. officials do not believe that current hunting and animal management programs in these countries are allowing for sustainable populations of the animals.[14] An American can legally hunt cheetahs in the three African nations, but it would be illegal for any of its parts to be brought into the United States.

The ESA categorizes species as either threatened or endangered.[15] Threatened species are those likely to become endangered within a foreseeable future throughout all or a significant portion of its habitat range, whereas endangered species are those at risk of becoming extinct throughout all or a significant portion of its range.[16] Five designating factors are used by the United States when determining if a species is threatened or endangered. These include (1) alteration of habitat; (2) overuse for commercial, recreational, scientific or education reasons; (3) disease or predation; (4) inadequacy of legislation; and (5) other factors, manmade or natural, that affect survival. Species are evaluated for listing on a five-year basis. In order to qualify for protection under the ESA, a species must meet at least one of the five designating criteria.

The Marine Mammal Protection Act[17] aims to ensure that populations of marine mammals are maintained at optimal levels of sustainability—regardless of the threat. The Marine Mammal Protection Act prohibits the take of marine mammals in U.S. waters and by U.S. citizens on the high seas. Additionally, it prohibits the importation of marine mammals and their products into the United States. It should be noted that the U.S. Fish and Wildlife Service is responsible for protecting walruses, manatees, otters, and polar bears, whereas the U.S. National Marine Fisheries Service protects whales, dolphins, porpoises, seals, and sea lions.

By 1972, various marine mammals were inching toward extinction. As a result, the U.S. Congress passed the Marine Mammal Protection Act in order to help these species recover to sustainable levels. The intent of Congress was aimed at species stock replenishment, in addition to learning about the animals' total ecology. In 1994, the Marine Mammal Protection Act was amended to add the aforementioned exceptions for native communities, commercial fishing operations, and studies of various mammal stocks.[18]

The Pelly Amendment to the Fishermen's Protective Act of 1967[19] allows the president to block the importation of wildlife from any country that fails to protect threatened species. Additionally, action can be taken against countries that fail to observe international treaties that aim to protect endangered wild species. The Pelly Amendment requires the Secretary of the Interior to provide information to the president as to which countries are actively engaging in the illegal trade of endangered wild species. The president authorizes embargos on all fish or wildlife products for a specific period of time. Congress is notified of the intent to embargo the violators. In 1994, trade sanctions were levied against Taiwan for CITES violations of trading in rhinoceros and tiger products. China was also cited under the Pelly Amendment; however President Clinton did not pursue action.

The European Union

The European Union's (EU) role in regulating trade in wild endangered species rests within the European Community (EC). The European Community is not a signatory party to CITES. However, through common regulation, which is applicable to all EU Member States, provisions of CITES have been enforced throughout the European Community since 1982. The European Union is a Regional Economic Integration Organization (REIO), which permits sovereign nations to transfer all or some of its capabilities to the REIO. The Gaborone Amendment to CITES in 1983 authorizes the accession of REIOs, which enabled the European Union to become a party to the treaty.

Council Regulation (EC) No. 338/97,[20] enforced in 1997, is the legal framework under which the European Community regulates the trade of endangered wild species. The latest Commission Regulation (EC) No. 865/2006 stipulates detailed rules pertaining to the implementation of Council Regulation (EC) 338/97. Combined, these two pieces of legislation instruct the European Union on the internal trade, import, export, and re-export of endangered wild fauna and flora listed in the legislation's four Annexes. Annex A corresponds with CITES Appendix I (if no EU member lodges a reservation) with the addition of some CITES II and III species for which the European Union has enacted stricter laws. Annex B contains all other CITES Appendix II species save those upon which an EU member has registered a reservation, along with some Appendix III and some non-CITES species. Annex C corresponds to CITES Appendix III—again, unless an EU member has registered a reservation. Finally, Annex D contains some CITES Appendix III species and some that are not protected by CITES. These laws cover live and dead animals, as well as their by-products.

The United Kingdom

Being obliged to adhere to the EC regulations and CITES provisions, the United Kingdom has implemented comprehensive domestic legislation that allows CITES to be enforced within the United Kingdom. The Control of Trade in Endangered Species (Enforcement) Regulations 1997 is the national legislation that covers endangered species trade offenses once the protected wild fauna and flora species enters UK borders. Control of Trade in Endangered Species (Enforcement) Regulations 1997 was amended to allow prosecution of offenses related to the commercial trade in those wild species safeguarded by CITES. Some species, subspecies, or populations are divided between the Annexes. The Amendment allows for the presumption of a species belonging to Annex A, if there is doubt as to which annex a split-listed specimens belongs.

The UK Management Authority is the Department for Environment, Food, and Rural Affairs (Defra)—specifically Animal Health. This agency assures that CITES permit requirements are monitored and followed. The United Kingdom has two scientific authorities: the Joint Nature Conservation Committee and the Royal Botanic Gardens, Kew. The Joint Nature Conservation Committee monitors and advises on animal-related activities, whereas the Royal Botanic Gardens is responsible for plant species. Enforcement activities and responsibilities lie with the UK Border Agency (formerly Her Majesty's Revenue and Customs) and UK Police agencies.

The primary legislation that protects indigenous endangered or conserved species in the United Kingdom is the Wildlife and Countryside Act 1981 (WCA).[21] The WCA has provisions that qualify some activities as arrestable[22] offenses. Similar to the U.S. approach, the United Kingdom has taken a holistic approach to protecting endangered species. Legislation is in place that addresses conservation: the Conservation (Natural Habitats, &c.) Regulations 1994, the Natural Environment and Rural Communities Act 2006, the Nature Conservation (Scotland) Act 2004, and the Wildlife (Northern Ireland) Order 1995.

Crimes against protected species include killing, taking from the wild, collecting eggs or skins for personal collection and/or trading items, and using them in taxidermy practices. Destruction of nests, breeding sites, and other habitats described in the legislation are also illegal. In addition to these activities, the United Kingdom has passed legislation that criminalizes cruelty and persecution of some wildlife species, such as badgers.

China

China is the fourth largest country in the world geographically and the largest in terms of population. China ranks eighth in terms of biodiversity worldwide and is the first in the Northern Hemisphere.[23] About 10 percent of the world's plant species exist in China, as do about 10 percent of all terrestrial species. China is home to 100 animal species unique only to China. Its natural resources are among the highest in the world, but due to population pressure, they are relatively scarce. Endangered species are particularly at risk within China's borders. Native species are among the 10 most endangered in the world: the panda, Siberian tiger, Asiatic black bear, black rhinoceros, and Indo-Chinese tiger. Two of the four Chinese tiger species are already extinct. The main reason for their demise is the loss of habitat because of expansion, growth, and development. The illicit trade in endangered species in China is second only to that of the illegal drug trade.[24]

As early as the twenty sixth century B.C.E., China had restrictions relating to the consumption of natural resources. During 359–206 B.C.E., China's rulers banned logging in forests, as well as burning of grasslands. There were established penalties for taking fish and timber, which included the possibility of criminal punishment from 619–1730 C.E. These laws demonstrated how important natural resources were to the rulers and people of China.[25]

After the Stockholm Convention's Declaration of 1972, China's commitment to land use and resource consumption paved the way for new laws adopted in the 1980s. Since then a series of statutes, local laws, and regulations have been designed for the protection of wildlife and the environment. Currently, the following legal mechanisms are in force: the Environmental Protection Law, the Marine Environment Protection Law, the Grasslands Law, the Forestry Law, and the Administrative Measures for Forest and Wild Animal Nature Reserves. Due to the political structure of the People's Republic of China, nature reserves are created to serve the interests of the state. Within their borders, no fishing, hunting, cultivation, collection, or exploitation of wild plants or animals is allowed. Chinese national parks were created as a form of conservation.

Wild animal protection laws are in place to achieve three objectives. The first is to restore the populations of endangered species. The second is aimed at recovery efforts for those species that have become extinct in China, but live elsewhere. Finally, as with other countries, China aims to expand the idea of saving endangered species to include conservation of habitat.[26]

Primarily, these laws fall under the premise that all wild flora and fauna are the property of the state; therefore, it is the responsibility of the state to manage and conserve it. There are also, however, local responsibilities. The main agencies involved are the Forestry Administration and the Fishery Department of the State Council. Their top priority is the plight of endangered species. Class 1 species, which are primarily the endangered ones, are managed by the national government, while provincial governments govern Class 2 species. Hunting and killing Class 1 animals is strictly prohibited. Buying and selling Class 1 species is illegal; only in exceptional cases will the State Council approve these activities. Provincial officials must approve activities surrounding Class 2 species.[27]

African Nations

CITES has been relatively futile in Africa. The main reasons for the failure are primarily due to noncompliance and the lack of enforcement. Furthermore, noncompliance is due to social, economic, and political unrest throughout the continent. Specific reasons include corruption, wars, lack of human resources, limited financial resources, lack of political commitment and stability, and internal conflict.

In 2006, a study of compliance with CITES among African nations reported that 49 of 52 countries were signatories of CITES—accounting for 32 percent of total CITES membership.[28] The study, entitled the National Legislation Project, examined and evaluated domestic wildlife protection laws aimed at implementing and complying with CITES. In order to determine the level of compliance, four questions were asked:

1. Has there been legislative designation of authorities responsible for implementing CITES?
2. Has legislation addressed all species listed in the Convention?
3. Does domestic legislation expressly prohibit illegal trade and designate specific departments or agents responsible for the Convention?
4. Does domestic legislation facilitate the confiscation or return of species that are legally traded?

From the responses to these questions, countries are categorized three ways. Category I countries adequately implement CITES in order to ensure compliance. Category II countries have implemented some provisions of CITES, but are in need of more activity in order to meet legislation requirements. Category III countries meet no requirements of CITES.[29]

Study results indicated that only four African countries were classified as Category I. Only 20 countries were classified as Category II and 24 as Category III. The African continent is home to some of the most endangered species on Earth. Moreover, some of the species located on the continent are not found anywhere else on Earth. Without strong domestic legislation, enforcement, and strict compliance, these African-specific endangered wild fauna and flora are at extreme risk of extinction.

Canada

Canada has been trying to secure legislation that protects endangered species for many years with little success.[30] Finally, in 2002, the Species At Risk Act received Royal Assent and was signed into law and implemented in 2003. As a signatory party to CITES, Canada is required to enact domestic legislation that aims to protect endangered species. The Species At Risk Act has three aspects. First, official recognition of a species can only be offered protection if it is listed. Second, it offers habitat protection so that listed species have a greater probability of survival. Finally, the Species At Risk Act stipulates clearly that the federal government can act if a province fails to offer protection to listed species.[31]

Similar to CITES, Canada has a scientific management board, which is an independent advisory board[32] that makes listing recommendations to the government. Unfortunately, government does not oftentimes accept the recommendation of the board, which results in flora and fauna being excluded from the list and hence, protection. Politics and economics play an important role in whether a species is listed. Five years after the Species At Risk Act was enacted, about 80 percent of recommended species were actually listed.[33]

The Species At Risk Act requires all governments in Canada (federal and provincial) to work together to conserve wildlife. The Canadian Endangered Species Conservation Council works with the National Aboriginal Council on Species at Risk and with the scientific committee in order to develop sound policy pertaining to listed species. However, the Species At Risk Act applies only to federal land, leaving the provinces to develop their own specifications. Because the Species At Risk Act only protects species on federal land, the scope of the legislation has limited impact. Several organizations, including Environment Canada, Fisheries and Oceans Canada and Parks Canada Agency, are actively helping to educate the citizens of Canada about the tenets of the Species At Risk Act.

The Debate

Many countries have stricter domestic laws than what CITES provides. For example, Australia bans the exports of live native wildlife even if CITES approves the movement of those species. Ecuador and Nigeria have banned all commercial export of wild fauna and flora. Costa Rica and Paraguay both prohibit all international trade in wildlife. When domestic laws are more stringent than international conventions, heated debates quickly take place. There are a number of arguments that support harsher laws. Provisions for protection can be put in place without applying for approval through the Conference of Parties, thus, providing greater protection to wild species facing survival problems. Attention is given to animals and plants under threat, which perhaps allows for prevention programs to be put in place far in advance of a species reaching endangered status. These countries, by adopting harsh laws, are announcing to the international community that they take the protection of species and their ecosystems very seriously.

The negative side of more severe legislation is as compelling as the positive. It is thought that when nations develop strict domestic laws that developing countries are discouraged from establishing their own conservation programs. Additionally, harm from the lack of trade of species not banned by CITES can negatively affect economic strategies and development. When economic development is suppressed or depressed, conservation programs are at greatest threat of losing funding. This obviously is not a desired outcome, especially when many of the countries with economies in transition are those with the highest population of endangered wild species. Finally, countries with more severe domestic conservation laws are thought to be contravening the philosophy of CITES, which is an international agreement based on consensus. To openly impose stricter legislation beyond the constraints of the international treaty can be seen as a message that "our way is better." The appearance of arrogance is never helpful when working to build consensus.

CONVENTION ON THE CONSERVATION OF MIGRATORY SPECIES OF WILD ANIMALS

The CMS[34] is an intergovernmental treaty reached under the auspice of the UN Environment Programme. The purpose of the treaty is to conserve terrestrial, marine, and avian migratory species throughout the range of their habitat. As of August 1, 2009, there were 112 signatory parties from countries in Africa, Central and South America, Asia, Europe, and Oceania. Conspicuously absent from the list of signatories is the United States, who only signed a Memorandum of Understanding on the Conservation and Management of Marine Turtles and their Habitats of the Indian Ocean and South East Asia.

The CMS classifies wild species in two appendices. Those included in Appendix I are threatened with extinction, thus requiring the greatest international attention. Signatory parties must protect not only the animals, but they must also conserve or restore the habitat and ranges where these animals live and breed. They must also identify migration obstacles and identify solutions to problematic migration barriers in order to remove those obstacles so that migration can proceed. Animals listed in Appendix II would benefit from conservation efforts. No direct protection efforts are required for these species; however, if regional action is not taken to fortify and preserve migration areas, the species could be in further jeopardy.[35]

In addition to the efforts of the Convention, agreements that range from legally binding to memoranda of understanding outline plans for conservation and management of the species in question. Memoranda of understanding allow regional problems to be rectified through conservation and preservation efforts.

The UN Environment Programme provides support for the Convention and serves as the Secretariat. A Conference of Parties is the decision-making body for the Convention and meets every three years. Like CITES, a Scientific Council gives technical and scientific support and helps to set priorities. The Standing Committee provides policy and administrative support for member parties.

Enforcement—CITES and CMS

Enforcement capabilities are only as strong as their legal foundations and the resources available to perform various activities. CITES and CMS are among several international laws that aim to protect endangered species. They are the primary mechanisms that provide the international foundations for police activity. At the international level, INTERPOL, the world's largest law enforcement agency, has a specific Wildlife Working Group as part of its operating structure. INTERPOL coordinates investigative activities for their membership, which currently has 188 member states. If a member country is investigating transnational criminal activities, police representatives can request assistance via INTERPOL to help with the investigation in those countries related to the offenses.

INTERPOL's structure has several component parts.[36] The General Assembly is the overarching governing body that makes decisions related to policies, resources, modes of operation, and also has financial decision-making capabilities. The Executive Committee consists of a president, three vice presidents, and nine delegates covering four worldwide regions. It is an elected body of 13 members, chosen from the general nation membership. The General Secretariat, located in Lyon, France, operates year-round, 24 hours a day, and serves as the operational nexus of INTERPOL. The General Secretariat has seven regional offices that help with operations, with offices located in Argentina, Cameroon, Côte d'Ivoire, El Salvador, Kenya, Thailand, and Zimbabwe. It also has a presence at the United Nations in New York City, and for the European Union in Brussels.[37] National Central Bureaus are located in each member country and are staffed by members of that country's national law enforcement personnel. These bureaus serve as points of contact for the General Secretariat. The Commission for the Control of INTERPOL's Files is the final component of INTERPOL. The commission is an independent body that has control over how INTERPOL's data are used and stored.

The Wildlife Crime Working Group, a subunit of the Environmental Crime Unit of INTERPOL organizes cooperative arrangements in order to investigate transnational wildlife criminal activities.[38] Environmental, and subsequently wildlife crimes, are not part of INTERPOL's primary purpose or focus. However, the General Assembly acknowledges that these types of crime are a growing international menace and, as a result of the UN's various conventions, INTERPOL must begin to acknowledge their role in today's emerging policing issues.

In 2006, INTERPOL appointed a full-time officer to manage wildlife activities within the Environmental Crime unit. The Wildlife Working Group defines wildlife crime as, "the taking, trading, exploiting or possessing of the world's wild flora and fauna in contravention of national and international laws."[39] The appointment of only one full-time person to help coordinate worldwide wildlife policing activities is perhaps a perfect example of where, in terms of priority, these types of crime fall.

Because CITES requires each member party to devise its own domestic endangered species laws, each country must develop its own enforcement capabilities and structures to correspond with the legal mechanisms. The ability for each country to successfully enforce its endangered species laws is dependent upon a number of variables. First and foremost, laws must be written in such a way to sustain enforcement actions. Second, resources are necessary to properly protect endangered wild flora and fauna. Third, for enforcement to be successful, corruption must be uncovered at every possible opportunity or, preferably, eliminated altogether. Fourth, the general populace must be willing to develop an understanding of how the elimination of protected species affects the entire ecosystem and eventually their own survival. Finally, effective policing strategies must be developed so that these crimes, which are committed around the world in areas that literally span hundreds of thousands of miles, can be effectively and successfully enforced.

Policing efforts are largely reactive—hoping to find illegal goods at ports— or they are in the form of antipoaching patrols. While antipoaching patrols are proactive, they can only be successful on extremely small scales. Most endangered species have range states that literally cover hundreds of thousands of miles. Due to the vastness of their patrol space, antipoaching patrols can only have limited success, if at all. Antipoaching patrols can be likened to street crime directed police patrols in high crime areas. Directed patrols are used to tackle specific crime problems and have been met with less than favorable results. In the case of antipoaching patrols, various reports state that they are successful. However, what these reports fail to take into account is that, while there may be arrests of poachers taking place, the patrols are extremely limited in area and scope. While arrests are being made in one location, there is no practical way to detect and detain poachers in other areas, which may be thousands of miles away. There are multiple antipoaching teams, but the small numbers pale in comparison with the distance to be covered.

The Phoenix Fund supports antipoaching patrols in Russian Far East.[40] Antipoaching patrols are considered their number one force to combat poaching of the Amur tiger and leopards. "Operation Tiger" enabled the purchase of equipment, including vehicles, communication, and video capabilities to enforce conservation laws in the region. Continual administrative changes have made it difficult for efforts to remain consistent; however, the project has claimed thousands of arrests, confiscated weapons, animal skins, and various hunting tools.

A major obstacle to effective policing against any crime is corruption. Corruption involves bribery of public officials, forgery of official documents, among other crimes that affect the ability of public officials to execute assigned responsibilities entrusted to them by the public. Corruption has been an issue throughout much of the African continent. The Global Corruption Report, 2009 ranks most of African nations at the higher end of the corruption scale.[41] Countries charged with CITES violations are among the most corrupt. Until corruption is addressed, the chances of reducing the illicit trade in endangered flora and fauna remains extremely low. Cameroon's President Paul Biya admitted that corruption affects economic advancement, social development, and governmental controls.[42] Cameroon is both a party to CITES and to the UN Convention Against Corruption and as such, President Biya promised to tackle corruption by creating the Anti Corruption Commission and the National Financial Investigation Agency. His seriousness was evidenced by his firing of a government magistrate for failing to properly apply the nation's Wildlife Law of 1994 in the case of a trafficker. The country's Minister of Forestry and Wildlife, Professor Elvis Ngolle Ngolle, admitted that wildlife trafficking is rooted in corruption and that more needed to be accomplished in the country's fight against these crimes.[43] Furthermore, the Minister stated that "these animals demand the sympathy and care of humanity."[44]

The United States

The ESA provides the foundation for law enforcement efforts in the United States. At the federal level, the U.S. Fish and Wildlife Service is the agency responsible for enacting CITES. If the U.S. Fish and Wildlife Service claims a CITES' violation, penalty proceedings take place at the Department of the Interior's Office of Hearings and Appeals, which is administrative rather than criminal law. However, the ESA also criminalizes certain actions, such as the taking of listed species. Federal wildlife officers are charged with protecting U.S. borders from the illegal importation and exportation of listed species. This is a daunting task, considering that the United States is a large nation-state with thousands of miles of borders and 327 official ports in the country.[45]

Furthermore, there are roughly 11 million cargo containers that reach U.S. soil each year. The U.S. Customs and Border Patrol is responsible for ensuring that these containers are safe for importation and that the goods being shipped are legal. Obviously, it is impossible to search each and every container; therefore, a threat assessment is undertaken. The Container Security Initiative is a multinational partnership that helps to minimize the risk of terrorist attacks. Combining the use of intelligence and risk-based analysis, the U.S. Customs and Border Patrol examines 100 percent of all containers deemed to be "suspicious."[46] At the point of origination, those wishing to ship a container must provide a manifest of items contained therein. These data help in deciding if the cargo container is at high risk and, therefore, necessary to be screened. It remains unclear how containers are assessed in terms of suspicion of containing illegal wild flora and fauna. However, according to the U.S. Customs and Border Patrol, on any given day 4,291 prohibited plants, meat, and animal by-products are seized.[47]

Without a doubt, terrorism is the primary, if not sole, focus of the U.S. Customs and Border Patrol searches. Since the terrorist attacks of September 11, 2001, terrorism is at the forefront of governmental protective services. While the illegal trade in endangered wild flora and fauna is legislatively grounded, it is a low enforcement priority when compared to crimes like terrorism and trafficking in humans.

The United Kingdom

Several agencies have a stake in enforcing CITES and the EU laws against trafficking in endangered wild flora and fauna. The UK Border Agency is responsible for uncovering smuggling operations at the various ports of entry. UK Customs and Excise helps to enforce CITES. At Heathrow International Airport, the fourth largest airport in the world and the largest that handles international passengers, a dedicated team of special officers exists. The Customs Wildlife and Endangered Species officers are on constant alert for illegal import and export of CITES-protected species.

The Metropolitan Police[48] launched Operation Charm in 1995 with the aim of reducing the illegal trade of endangered species in London. In 2006, the Metropolitan Police partnered with WWF, the Metropolitan Police Wildlife Crime Unit, the Greater London Authority, the International Fund for Animal Welfare, and the David Shepherd Wildlife Foundation.

Operation Charm used public education alongside traditional policing techniques to achieve their goal. Since its inception, the Metropolitan Police have seized tens of thousands of items of endangered species, with the majority related to TAM[49] generated from bear bile, tigers, and rhinos. Operation Charm also was part of one of the largest, if not the largest, seizure of shahtoosh shawls, which are made from the wool of the critically endangered Tibetan antelope (*Pantholops hodgsonii*). Operation Charm accepts donations from the general public in order to ensure the Metropolitan Police maintains its function in this endeavor. This is another example of how low the priority of these types of crimes actually is—taking private dollars to ensure a public service from being cut from budgets.

Canada

Under the Species At Risk Act, law enforcement activities in Canada include inspections and investigations of suspected illegal wildlife activity. Law enforcement officials have the authority to compel compliance in lieu of court action or through court action.[50] Canada has, at last count, 21 wildlife enforcement officers under the Species At Risk Act. By 2007, Fisheries and Oceans Canada had over 600 officers, who had been trained and designated as Species At Risk Act officers. Furthermore, Parks Canada Agency no longer had enforcement capabilities due to *Canada Labour Code II*, but to ensure that maximum efforts continued, a partnership between the Parks Agency and Environment Canada was made. This partnership allowed for the continued protection of Canada's valuable natural resources.

As with those of the United States, the Canadian borders are large and vast; the two countries share over 5,000 miles of border. Canada is partner to the Container Security Initiative program that allows for searching at risk or suspicious cargo containers. However, the primary purpose of the searches is to uncover potential terrorist activities and threats. Canada Border Services Agency is responsible for undertaking searches and for the security of Canada's border.[51]

INVESTIGATIVE SUCCESSES

The United Kingdom, France, and the United States are host to national forensic laboratories tasked with the analyses of evidence pertaining to wildlife crime. These laboratories help investigators in a number of ways. The identification of the species from which the suspected illicit product is derived is a key part of the investigation. For example, in Thailand a seller of shahtoosh shawls was arrested; however, he claimed that he was only guilty of deceiving the buyer, as the shawls were not made from the endangered Tibetan antelope, but from a common goat. Samples were sent to the U.S. Fish and Wildlife Service's Wildlife Crime Laboratory. Analysis confirmed that the shawls were indeed shahtoosh and the seller had no other alibi. Thai officials prosecuted him for the sale of endangered species' by-products.[52]

As with other traditional crime laboratories, evidence links victims (in this case, protected wildlife) to suspects and offenders. Also, these specialized laboratories have the ability to determine the cause of death for the endangered species, such as poisonings. French laboratories have been instrumental in discerning bird deaths as killings rather than accidental, which aids in the prosecution of offenders. UK's Defra published a guide for wildlife investigators on the benefits and uses that the wildlife crime laboratory can provide to them.[53] As officers become more educated about what these facilities can do, no doubt they will assist in successful investigations and, subsequently, convictions of the offenders.

Arrests and Confiscations

The following are brief synopses of law enforcement successes from around the globe. The majority of the stories were taken from TRAFFIC, the wildlife trade monitoring network's Web site. This organization is the leader in the field for publishing stories of arrests and confiscations.

Police in Viet Nam Uncover Wildlife Bone Trade Network, September 20, 2010[54]

The Hanoi Environment Police, along with other agencies, uncovered a wildlife bone trade network that a couple operated from their home. From four locations, police seized approximately 2,000 pounds (900 kilograms), including six whole tiger skeletons, six tiger skulls, a compilation of other tiger bones, two elephant tusks, three clouded leopard (*Neofelis nebulosa*) skulls and one complete skeleton, and one bear head. Additional seizures included 1,609 pounds (730 kg) of other animal species bone and by-products. The case remains open, but six people have been arrested.

Seized Notebooks Give Unique Insight into Scale of Illicit Pangolin Trade, October 28, 2010[55]

Logbooks confiscated from traffickers in Kota Kinabalu, the capital of Sabah, a state in Malaysia, showed that more than 22,000 Sunda Pangolins (*Manis javanica*) were illegally traded by a single crime organization over a 21-month period. During that time period, about 1,840 pounds (834.4 kg) of Pangolin scales were supplied to the crime group. The logbooks contained detailed descriptions and details of the illicit activities, which tremendously helped enforcement agencies.

Chinese Citizens Risk Imprisonment for Ivory Smuggling, September 13, 2010[56]

Congolese police arrested three Chinese men at Lumumbashi's airport while attempting to depart for Nairobi, Kenya. They were charged with transporting a suitcase full of elephant ivory. Kenyan officials sentenced another Chinese man to eighteen months for the illegal possession of worked elephant ivory in the form of multiple chopsticks and bracelets. Furthermore, Chinese officials seized ivory from their fellow countrymen on 710 different occasions. In September 2010, 384 African elephant tusks that originated from Tanzania were seized in Hong Kong. Many of the Chinese travelers are believed to be aware of the laws about transporting endangered species, but continued to knowingly take the risk.

Beluga Caviar Seized in Transit, December 3, 2010[57]

An Italian CITES officer stopped a passenger who was traveling from Istanbul, Turkey. In the passenger's luggage was over 33 pounds (15 kg) of caviar thought to originate from Iran. Tests revealed that the caviar was beluga, the most expensive roe of the species. The shipment did not contain requisite CITES documentation, and therefore the caviar was confiscated.

Man Arrested Over Tiger Poisoning Incident, June 22, 2010[58]

In the Jambi province of Indonesia, a man was arrested for allegedly poisoning and skinning a Sumatran tiger, one of the most endangered of all tiger species, in a state-run zoo. After hours, the offender was alleged to have placed poisoned bait in the animal's enclosure. The man was the second person arrested for the horrific crime. Police authorities are still pursuing those who planned the killing. Indonesia has consistently been one of the global hot spots for illegally trading endangered species, including the critically endangered Sumatran tiger.

Monkey Smuggler Arrested in Mexico, July 20, 2010[59]

Mexican authorities arrested a man for attempting to smuggle 18 monkeys from Peru into the country. The monkeys were wrapped in socks and smuggled in luggage. Two died in transit. The seizure included pygmy marmosets (*Cebuella pygmaea*), black-mantle tamarins (*Saguinus nigricollis*), and Goeldi's monkey (*Callimico goeldii*). Each of these species is included in the IUCN Red List of Threatened Species. Their populations are decreasing and their status ranges from least concern to vulnerable. Mexico is considered an endangered species gateway from South America to other global destinations.

Thai Customs Seize Four Suitcases Filled with Ivory, September 27, 2010[60]

Thai Customs officers apprehended a man who illegally transported cut ivory into the country from a flight out of Addis Ababa, Ethiopia. Officers seized nearly 200 pounds (90 kg) of ivory along with 16 worked pieces. This is only one of a string of other ivory seizures that ranged from two tons to 1,763 pounds (800 kg) during 2010. The Elephant Trade Information System (ETIS) data show that Nigeria, Thailand, and the Democratic Republic of Congo are the three hottest spots in the world for the illegal ivory trade.

The Serpent King, December 28, 2010[61]

A five-year prison term was given to Anson Wong Keng Liang, the "world's most notorious wildlife trafficker,"[62] for transporting 100 baby boa constrictors, two vipers, and a South American turtle. This is considered an extremely harsh sentence, which was handed down in a Malaysian court. Wong was known as the man who could get literally anything. He has trafficked anything from lizards to elephants, including some of the most endangered species on the planet. This was not Wong's first arrest for trafficking in endangered species. International law enforcement began to notice Wong in the late 1990s. The elite undercover squad of the U.S. Fish and Wildlife Service targeted Wong in Operation Chameleon. They conducted a sting operation by setting up a storefront that dealt in reptiles and began trading with Wong. A deal lured Wong out of Malaysia and into Mexico, where U.S. officials (in partnership with Mexican authorities) took him into custody.

In June 2001, Wong was sentenced to nearly six years in prison, fined US $60,000, and banned from exporting goods to the United States for three years post-release. None of this deterred him. Wong returned to Malaysia with plans to open a tiger zoo. He received government-backed funding and land in order to open his "zoo." A high-ranking official in the Department of Wildlife and Natural Parks considered him to be a legitimate businessman and vouched for his character and credibility. A *National Geographic* article uncovered his illegal operations and illustrated his plans for the new tiger zoo. Eventually, the Malaysian Anti-Corruption Commission investigated his colleague at the Department of Wildlife and Natural Parks. Upon his most recent arrest, the Malaysian government revoked Wong's business licenses, shut down his zoo, and seized his entire collection of animals.

FINAL COMMENTS

It is difficult to garner support for international treaties, and even more difficult to implement them successfully. CITES is touted as the most successful international treaty of its kind. The majority of countries around the globe have become signatory parties to it, thus agreeing to devise domestic laws to protect the world's endangered species. The weak link in reducing these illicit crimes is enforcement. Size is a component factor for the weakness. Range size is simply too large for traditional types of enforcement activities to be of use. Priority is another contributing factor. Other crimes claim the attention of the international and national law enforcement community. Crimes of human trafficking and terrorism take precedence over law enforcement activities trying to reduce the illegal trade in protected wild flora and fauna. However, the international community and individual nations must acknowledge that our ecosystem is at risk and that these illegal activities are generating billions of dollars in profit.

One way forward is the exploration as to how the market reduction approach might reduce and disrupt this type of illegal market. The market reduction approach is part of a larger body of research that offers alternative techniques of addressing crime problems. As with some of the antipoaching patrols, the market reduction approach seeks to include educational components so that consumers of illicit goods come to realize how their desire for the illicit goods are damaging ecosystems and causing the extinction of species.

Organized and Transnational Crime

THE TERM "ORGANIZED CRIME" brings to mind images of Al Capone, Don Vito Genovese, John "Dapper Don" Gotti, and the Costa Nostra or Mafia. Organized crime has been sensationalized by Hollywood in movies like the *Godfather* collection, *Goodfellas*, and *Casino*. The face of organized crime has been largely depicted as those from Italian descent, and the activities of organized crime have been highlighted to include drug trafficking, racketeering, prostitution, and gambling. These stereotypes are now challenged with good reason.

There are innumerable definitions of organized crime that vary by country. The UK Home Office[1] acknowledges that there are various definitions, but the majority states that organized crime involves (a) more than two people who commit various crimes over time, and (b) have the capacity to operate outside their country's boundaries.[2] Australia relies on the UN's Convention on Transnational and Organized Crime, Article 2,[3] which agrees with the British component of having multiple people involved to commit serious crimes over time, but it adds a financial element to the definition. The UN Convention on Transnational and Organized Crime states clearly that organized crime operates in order to seek financial benefit. The Federal Bureau of Investigation (FBI) in the United States distinguishes between organized crime and criminal enterprise. The former includes a group that has some degree of formal organization or structure and works to gain financial benefit through crime. The latter criminal enterprises are groups of six or more people, where leader-subordinate relations exist in order to generate considerable income through continued criminal activities.[4]

Whatever definition is used, the common and underlying characteristic of all organized crime activity is that of large profit. There exists some cursory evidence that organized crime has expanded into the realm of trafficking in endangered species. This should not come as a surprise as the profits from this specialized international illicit market are said to generate profits second only to those produced by illicit drug trade.

Transnational crime is the illegal procurement, transportation, and distribution of goods across international borders.[5] Transnational crime is committed by criminal enterprises, whose activities include, but are not limited to, drug trafficking, terrorism, human trafficking, trading in weapons of mass destruction and arms, trafficking in arts and antiquities, and trafficking in endangered species.

Organized crime is an element of transnational criminal activities. Because of the complicated nature of moving illegal goods across national boundaries and extremely long distances, organized criminal enterprises seem a natural avenue for moving illegal goods across geographic boundaries, given their lengthy experience in narcotics trafficking. The two concepts, organized crime and transnational crime, have been used interchangeably in common literature and in the social science research academy. It is important to note here that they are different, but extremely dependent.

ORGANIZED CRIME AND ENDANGERED SPECIES

The relationship between organized crime and the endangered species trade, at this point in time, is largely speculative but understandable. So little research has been done on the relationship that it is difficult to say with any degree of certainty what the relationship is and to what degree organized crime is involved in the illicit trade. Several UN reports on the trafficking of endangered wildlife claim that organized crime groups in China, Japan, Italy, and Russia play an instrumental part in the endangered species trade.[6] These various crime groups are not thought to be actively involved in the trafficking of all endangered wildlife, but it has been found they are "strongly present"[7] in some of the more lucrative ones such as caviar, TAM, ivory, and reptile skins. Again, it should be noted that much of the evidence is largely anecdotal.

Traffickers are thought to be connected, on an international scale, to an endless number of suppliers willing to provide exotic plants and animals. This is particularly evident in developing countries and those with economies in transition. Government is often fragile in these countries, and as a vulnerable nation-state, organized criminals make their presence known through corruption, bribery, and violence. Without a doubt, organized crime groups disrupt political and social functions.[8] It is also believed that even if traditional organized crime is not present, much of the trafficking activities require significant organization. Even if the sophistication does not warrant the label of organized crime at the present time, it may very well in the near future.

Organized crime has an astute ability to adapt. It is able to change operations, targets, and form in order to keep in tune with public demand, prosecutorial redress, and, of course, opportunities.[9] In the illegal wildlife trade, as with all transnational crime, adaptability is important, if not critical. When changes occur in the demand of various endangered species, organized crime syndicates or groups seem more than willing and able to do that which is necessary to ensure supply.

East Asian Triad societies have historically been known for their roles in drug trafficking. However, recent reports say the Triads, particularly the Wo Shing Wo and the Japanese Yakuza have been involved in the trafficking of elephant ivory, rhino horn, tigers, shark fins, abalone, and whale meat.[10] The

Yakuza is one of the most powerful, structured, and criminally versatile syndicates in the world. In Japan, there are 3,000 Yakuza groups with 60 percent of the 90,000 members concentrated in three main groups: Yamaguchi-Gumi, Sumiyoshi-Kai, and Inagawa-Kai. The Russian syndicate is known for their propensity for extreme violence. They are more decentralized than their Japanese counterparts, but nonetheless successful in their illegal activities. The Russian Mafia have been in control of the illicit trade in sturgeon, caviar, bear, and tigers.[11] The Italian Mafia and the former Medellin drug cartel in Columbia, along with groups in central Asia and Brazil, were instrumental in trafficking of rare parrots and falcons.[12]

Lines between the illicit trade in narcotics and the illicit trade in endangered species are beginning to blur. Anecdotal evidence indicates that illicit wildlife traffickers use drug trafficking routes in order to smuggle their products. Cali drug cartel in Columbia and the Mexican drug gangs have allegedly begun mixing shipments of both illegal goods in order to maximize their smuggling potential.[13] The Brazilian National Network Against the Trafficking of Wild Animals (RENCTAS) estimates that roughly 40 percent of an estimated 400 criminal rings that smuggle animals were involved in other criminal activity, especially drugs.[14]

In the late 1990s, the U.S. Customs and U.S. Fish and Wildlife Service ran a three-year operation entitled, Operation Jungle Trade, which involved more than 40 individual investigations into the illicit trade in protected flora and fauna.[15] Sophisticated smuggling rings sold birds and other illegally obtained animals in several states and in 10 different countries: Australia, South Africa, New Zealand, Brazil, Ghana, Egypt, Panama, Honduras, Belize, and Costa Rica. The birds traded were worth an estimated US$600,000 and 662 valuable endangered species were seized. Forty traffickers were arrested as a result of the operation.[16] The profits to be made from trafficking in endangered species are second only to that from drugs—pound for pound, exotic, endangered birds are worth more to smugglers than cocaine.[17]

Reporters for the United Kingdom's newspaper, *The Guardian*, uncovered a link between terrorism and the illegal trade in endangered species.[18] Poachers and traffickers are being recruited by affiliates of Al Qaeda to hunt, kill, and sell protected species in the UN Educational, Scientific, and Cultural Organization (UNESCO) World Heritage site, Kaziranga, which is located in the northeastern part of India on the Bangladeshi border. As with other militant and terrorist movements, the realization of large profit and extremely low detection probabilities and the practice of trafficking in endangered species is an attractive alternative for raising money. While newspaper reporters may have access to stories such as these, researchers have much more limited entry to explore and verify these types of claims. However, there are some truths beginning to surface. Rebel warriors and insurgent groups in various African and Asian countries have retreated to protected national parks for their own cover, but also for the immediate access to valued resources that can help fund their activities.[19] The U.S. Congressional Research Service reports that INTERPOL has intelligence reports indicating that Somali poachers have links to warlords who had offered protection to the al-Qaeda operations in the Kenyan and Tanzanian bombings of U.S. embassies in 1998.[20]

In Africa, law enforcement officials cite organized crime enterprises as being active in the ivory trade. Large-scale operations occur in the African source countries and trade routes through Tanzania, Djibouti, UAE, Hong Kong, Macao, Philippines, and Singapore. Within Africa, poachers from Sudan and Somalia cross into Kenya and Chad to slaughter elephants in order to harvest the coveted ivory. In 2006, Taiwanese officials confiscated a major consignment of elephant ivory—more than five metric tons over a three-day period. The ivory was concealed in cargo shipments. The ship's documents, if accurate, state that the origination point was in Tanzania with a final destination in the Philippines, but it did travel through Malaysia to Singapore where the ship docked for several days before it left for Taiwan and then, the Philippines. Cargo was not offloaded in Taiwan, and prior to debarkation in the Philippines, it was found that the original documents had been altered to show a different importer than first noted. At this point, Taiwanese authorities seized all the ivory onboard the ship. Later, five tons of ivory that were housed in a storage facility contracted by Philippine customs authorities disappeared. An investigation began immediately.[21]

The route from source-to-consumer is a complicated one that requires various networks. The markets that are sophisticated and extremely profitable are most likely influenced by organized crime. The criminal enterprises involved with larger-scale operations can include terrorists, drug traffickers, and rebel soldiers—all of whom are able to elude detection at every stage in the trafficking process. The local hunters who supply the various species, those who help transport the plant and animals or their by-products, the legitimate companies that serve as a laundering mechanism, and the corrupt officials all work in concert in order to get the goods to the end point—the consumers. In other words, a complicated, global conspiracy takes place every time an endangered species is brought to market.

There are several techniques for smuggling endangered species. The first includes hiding products/animals/plants in luggage, shipping containers, or on the smuggler's body. Recently, there have been accounts of customs officers in airports stopping smugglers with birds literally strapped to their legs,[22] with reptiles in underpants,[23] and with turtles in luggage.[24] A second method of smuggling involves false declarations and falsified trade permits at points of entry. This includes fraudulently identifying look-alike, nonprotected species in place of the protected ones, changing customs forms to indicate a different number of items shipped, changing declared values of items, declaring a wild species as a captive-bred one, and using forged or stolen trade permits to make the transportation seem legal.[25] Various customs officials around the world seized 86 pounds (39 kg) of cocaine stuffed in condoms, which were found in 225 boa constrictors; elephant tusks filled with hashish, and exotic birds shipped with methamphetamine tablets.[26]

Finally, ecologists at the University of Canberra[27] in Australia found that the Internet has become instrumental as an important element in the trafficking of protected species. Specifically, online auction sites have become the tool of choice among organized criminals in Australia. The researchers claim that Australia's weak criminal penalties are to blame for the blatant use of the Internet for illicit transactions of wildlife stashes. The researchers discovered 197 listings of elephant ivory for sale on an Australian online auction site; however, only two were in CITES compliance!

It is important to note that the structure and nature of trafficking in protected wildlife is species-dependent. In other words, there is no single model that can encompass the trade in general.[28] For instance, in some southern African countries the presence of organized crime is said to be limited to abalone;[29] however, other accounts indicate organized crime is responsible for ivory trade. One study found that developing a profile of poachers was an arduous undertaking.[30] There was considerable variation in those who poached and the species they hunted. Most of the poachers were individuals rather than organized crime operators. Both blacks and whites engaged in illegal hunting in South Africa, Namibia. Foreigners also operated in the various southern African nations. Poachers are farmers, fishermen, pet shop owners, tourists, private game/zoo owners, collectors, and those who live near protected state-run game reserves. This research showed that poachers were not professional hunters. The level of organization among the poachers ranged from nonexistent to loosely defined networks of friends and collectors.[31]

The same study paints traffickers in a picture slightly short of organized criminals. As with poachers, the type of trafficker was dependent on the type of species being traded. It was found that traffickers were prominently individuals, but there was evidence of loosely organized groups forming to move the products through to their destinations.

A U.S. interagency working group[32] assessed the threat of international crime, which is believed to also be a threat to national security.[33] These crimes include drug trafficking, trafficking of women and children, international smuggling, smuggling of diamonds and gems, smuggling of weapons of mass destruction and other arms, foreign economic espionage, money laundering, high-tech crime, and piracy. Environmental crimes are taken into account when they relate directly to safety, health, stability, values, and other related interests. They are among the most rapidly growing types of international crimes. Environmental crimes are hazards that harm health and the environment, exploit scarce natural resources, and affect protected flora and fauna. The U.S. government estimates that local and international crime syndicates earn an annual estimated US$22–US$31 million from hazard waste dumping, smuggling regulated/banned hazardous material, and endangered flora and fauna.[34]

International transportation has assisted the commission of transnational crimes. The volume of commercial cargo being shipped globally is at an all-time high. In 1999, U.S. seaports have accepted over 4.4 million shipping containers, holding over 400 million tons of cargo. There were 395 containers that entered U.S. soil on roadways from Canada and Mexico and an additional 76 million arrived via commercial and private flights. There are 135 million vehicles annually that cross into the United States from Canada and Mexico. There are innumerable statistics such as these, but the most discouraging fact is that the U.S. Customs officials are only able to search 3 percent of all the containers that enter the United States. That 3 percent is expected to decline to less than 1 percent in the coming years. Globalization has facilitated the growth and expansion of organized crime and transnational criminality. Table 4.1 lists the global criminal groups involved in various illegal activities pertaining to environmental crime.

Caviar

Caviar has been a delicacy for centuries. Various species of sturgeon produce the roe (eggs), but the most coveted is that of the beluga sturgeon found in the Caspian Sea and Vogla rivers in Russia. Beluga sturgeon (*Huso huso*) roe is undoubtedly the most prized and sought after of the various species, but it is also one of the most overfished and endangered species of sturgeon. Known as black gold, Beluga caviar can be found in duty free shops throughout Europe and can fetch up to US$1,500/250 grams (about nine ounces).

In the nineteenth century, the United States was the prominent producer of caviar, which was taken from the Atlantic sturgeon. In the late 1800s, Russia

Table 4.1 Crime Groups Involved in Illegal Environmental Crime*

Environmental Abuse	Criminal Syndicates
Illegal Trade in Endangered Species	
Birds	Asian, European, Latin America
Ivory and Rhino Horn	Asian, African
Reptiles and Insects	Asian, European
Tigers	Asian, Chinese Triads
Wild Game	Asian, Chinese Triads, African
Illegal Fishing	
Abalone	Asian, Chinese Triads
Caviar	Russian
Shark Fin	Vietnamese, Chinese
Sturgeon	Russian, Japanese
Illegal Logging	
Asian, Latin American, Chinese, Italian, Turkish, Afghan, Pakistani, Bosnian, Herzegovian	

*Adapted from International Crime Threat Assessment (n.d.)

displaced the United States as the top-trading caviar nation in the world. At its peak, harvests by the Russians were seven times higher than the previous peak of the U.S.'s Atlantic sturgeon.[35] During the 1900s, stocks were depleted due to the high demand of the product. CITES regulated legal trading of caviar in 2001, so all of the sturgeon caviar traded today must be accompanied by documents. The main exporters of caviar are Iran, Russia, Azerbaijan, Kazakhstan, and Turkmenistan, which all border the Caspian Sea and make up the range states for the species. There are no formal agreements between the countries on the use or preservation of the fish stocks,[36] which would greatly enhance the survivability of this great fish.

Legal Trade

According to CITES import data, more than 1,300 tons of caviar were legally traded between 1998–2006 worldwide. Iran has been the largest exporter allowing over 480 tons to leave its borders. Russia follows with 138 tons of exported caviar; Kazakhstan ranked as a distant third with 95 tons of exported caviar (see Table 4.2 for details). Of those 1,300 tons, 45 percent (491 tons)

Table 4.2 Importers, Exporters, and Seizures of Black Gold Caviar (Legal), 1998–2000

Largest Importers		Largest Exporters	
Countries	**Tons (US)**	**Countries**	**Tons (US)**
All EU Member States	237	Iran	445
France	234	Russian Federation	140
USA	297	Kazakhstan	97
Switzerland	151	Azerbaijan	36
Japan	134	China	29
		Romania	26

Caviar Seized* in the European Union, 2000–2007			
Year	**Lbs/Kg**	**Year**	**Lbs/Kg**
2000	9,535/4,325	2004	223/101
2001	2,163/981	2005	520/236
2002	672/305	2006	174/79
2003	3,031/1,375	2007	106/48
		Total Seizures	16,424/7,450

*Official seizure data underestimates the size of the illegal market.
Source: TRAFFIC, "Fact Sheet: Black Gold: The Caviar Trade in Western Europe," accessed March 13, 2010, http://www.traffic.org, 2009.

was imported by the European Union, 24 percent (313 tons) by the United States, and 13 percent (175 tons) by Switzerland.[37] These numbers actually reflect a decline in the legal harvest and export of sturgeon caviar. In 1998, legal harvest from wild and aquaculture peaked with 314 tons, but dropped to 100 tons in 2004.

In 2000, CITES parties agreed to significantly review the practices and trade pertaining to sturgeon and paddlefish. The main reason for this review was to investigate compliance with the CITES treaty. The investigation revealed that trade has affected the status and survivability of all sturgeon fished in the Amur, Danube, and Siberian rivers. Sturgeon from the Azov, Black, and Caspian Seas have also been compromised. Parties agreed that range states had to file annual export reports in addition to adopting a standardized labeling system for all caviar exports. Therefore, all caviar containers, whether imported, exported, re-exported, or within a domestic market, must have a label that contains specific information about the country of origin and the year of harvest. CITES parties agreed to only accept shipments that contain cargo with this label.

Illegal Trade

The caviar black market is thriving. It has strong links to organized crime, specifically Russian. Many think that Russian organized crime rose with the fall of the Soviet system of government. However, the Russian syndicate helped the Soviet system run by providing state-run industry with necessary supplies. They exploited the privatization movement after the fall of the Soviet Union, which facilitated the increase in the illegal and fraudulent trade in a variety of types of caviar, especially the beluga. Today, the U.S. government estimates that 200 sophisticated organized crime groups operate in Russia and worldwide. U.S. officials report that the Russian Ministry of Interior claims that there are 89 criminal communities operating in Russia.[38] However, these 89 are comprised of 1,000 smaller criminal groups, 11 of which are made of 243 groups with 50,000 members, who operate in Russia and approximately six other countries in Europe, the Americas, Caribbean, Asia, and Africa. Russian organized crime is notorious for their ruthlessness. For example, Russian border guards intervened in the illegal caviar trade and in retaliation, poachers blew up the guard's house.[39]

Caviar is the perfect CRAVED[40] product; it is Concealable, Removable, Available, Enjoyable, and Disposable. This makes the illegal trafficking in caviar—of any variety—much easier than other end products of endangered species, such as tiger skins, or elephant ivory. Russian organized crime recognizes this and has taken advantage of the product's size and its consumption in relation to its high demand.

Despite the CITES ban, the international market continues to demand caviar, and therefore, it is flooded with low quality and inexpensive caviar. Prior to the CITES ban on the trade, the estimated annual value of the legal Russian caviar trade was US$40–US$100 million, whereas the illegal Russian exports were worth US$250–US$400 million. The price of black caviar can cost up to US $10,000/kg.[41] Virtually all of the black caviar traded is illegal.[42] Unfortunately, the demand for black and other types of caviar has not diminished. The products of illegal harvests are filtered through legal commercial channels.

Countries worldwide are getting more serious about policing the illegal caviar trade. Officials in Germany began intensive policing actions against caviar smuggling, which resulted in the culmination of several successful operations in 2008. In a six-week period, authorities confiscated about 132 pounds (60 kg) of illegal caviar originating from the Caspian Sea. Dealers that were targeted nationwide included hotels, luxury restaurants, and caviar dealers.[43] Additionally, a Frankfurt businessman was arrested in France for caviar smuggling. He smuggled 88 pounds (40 kg) of beluga caviar and also smuggled 1.1 tons of caviar into Germany. German officials believe that the large-scale operations emanated from Russian crime groups.

In the United Kingdom, British customs officials, along with the National Criminal Intelligence Service, raided a number of luxury shops in the exclusive Kensington neighborhood in London. Operation Ribbon revealed that the illegal caviar trade was linked to murder, extortion, and corruption by criminal gangs on three continents.[44] In Operation Ribbon, the National Wildlife Crime Unit seized 200 tins of caviar that were labeled Iranian Sevruga, Osietra, and Beluga. However, analysis showed that the caviar was smuggled illegally from Russia. No shopkeepers were prosecuted simply because they were ignorant of the caviar's origin and illegality. In the five years prior to Operation Ribbon, UK Customs made 67 seizures of illegal caviar, amounting to 1.5 UK tons with an estimated value of £3 million (US$4.6 million).[45]

Russian authorities are also committed to reducing the illegal markets in illegal caviar. In 2009, police in Askrakhan, a major city in southern Russia, destroyed 661 pounds (300 kg) of illegal black caviar.[46] Two thousand tins of caviar deemed to be unsafe were crushed and buried at the city dump. In July 2009, 551 pounds (250 kg) of contraband, black caviar worth 30 million rubles (US$960,000) were burned due to its infestation with staphylococcus.

While there is no specific measure for the volume and values of illegal caviar, large seizures and anecdotal evidence indicates that it is far larger than the legal trade. The large seizures are also indicative of a large, well-organized smuggling system. The illegal caviar trade is believed to have strong ties to organized crime groups.[47] The CITES Secretariat's antismuggling and fraud unit also identifies Middle Eastern ports as conduits for laundering illegally obtained caviar into international markets.[48]

In a report of the Russian Federation at the International Sturgeon Enforcement Workshop to Combat Illegal Trade in Caviar, then-President Vladimir Putin called for legislation that required the destruction of all illegal sturgeon products when seized in order to keep them from entering international black markets.[49] The conclusion is that the link to organized crime and illicit trade in caviar cannot be understated.[50]

In a report to the U.S. Congress, the global trade in endangered wildlife is considered to be a national security threat due to the link with drug trafficking and organized crime. The report continues to warn that some terrorist groups may be entering the realm of endangered species trafficking due to the profits that can be generated for the support of their terrorism-related activities.[51]

Shark Finning

Much less is known about the shark fin trade than the caviar trade. "The lucrative and unregulated nature of the trade [of shark fins] attracts involvement by criminal elements, with fierce competition for shark fins leading to widespread corruption, gangland wars, and contract killings."[52] Furthermore, WildAid research in 2005[53] showed that in Columbia, drug dealers were becoming involved in the shark fin business, simply as a way to launder money.

Rob Stewart wrote and directed *Sharkwater*,[54] a film about the sharks and the threats they currently face. Stewart is an award-winning underwater photographer and also a marine biologist. He traveled with Captain Paul Watson to the shark-infested waters of the Galapagos Islands, Ecuador and Cocos Islands, Costa Rica. During their travels, they uncover corruption, organized crime, as well as, efforts to save the shark.

Captain Paul Watson,[55] founder of Sea Shepherd Conservation Society (1977), is known as the "renegade of the conservation movement" and was personally responsible for sinking Norwegian whaling vessels, effectively ending pirate whaling in the north Atlantic. The president of Costa Rica hired the ship *Sea Shepherd* (recently renamed the *Steve Irwin*) to help protect its waters against illegal and unregulated fishing. The ship, with Rob Stewart's film crew aboard, intercepted a long-line fishing vessel, the *Varadero*, which was illegally catching shark in the waters off Cocos Island, which is located about 360 miles from Costa Rica. This area is host to one of the largest and last remaining shark populations in the world. The *Sea Shepherd* gave the order to the *Varadero* to stop in the name of Costa Rican authorities. The crew of the *Varadero* continued. Captain Watson took aggressive action and began ramming the vessel until such time the *Varadero* stopped their shark killing.

While the crew of the *Sea Shepherd* prepared to board the vessel, a critical turn of events took shape. The Costa Rican Coast Guard approached the *Sea Shepherd* and demanded that her crew surrender. The crew had contacts within official channels, which no doubt helped to protect the profits generated by its illegal finning industry. As the *Varadero* escaped, officials boarded the *Sea Shepherd* with the intent of arresting Captain Paul Watson and Rob Stewart and to confiscate all of Stewart's film. The charges were extremely serious—attempted murder. The men were allowed to remain on the ship, but were expected to present themselves to authorities for criminal processing.

They heard that the Taiwanese Mafia was running the shark finning industry so Stewart and his crew went into Costa Rica looking for evidence. Costa Rican shark fins were finding their way to various Asian markets. Shark fishing is illegal in Costa Rican waters, but Stewart's pictures show another reality. Regardless of the illegality, shark fins line the roofs of multiple buildings—so many it almost appears as if they are the roof tiles themselves. Private docks in affluent neighborhoods are the actual processing plants for the shark finning industry in Costa Rica. Here, fins from dozens of species are processed, packed, and distributed to Asian markets. The fins bring millions of dollars to Costa Rica. Again, the practice is illegal, but extremely valuable to local economies. For example, the Taiwanese donated millions of dollars to Costa Rica for infrastructure improvements. Corruption ensures that fishermen are provided protection when illegally fishing for sharks, and fin processors are provided protection when preparing fins for shipment. It is interesting that the president of the country called for help to protect against the illegal fishing, but neglected to ensure that the criminal justice system was free from corruption.

CONCLUSION

Organized crime as it pertains to the trade in endangered flora and fauna is still somewhat an unknown. There appears to be a growing body of literature related to the nature of the caviar trade, but a far more sparse volume about other protected species. While anecdotal evidence points in the direction of organized crime having a substantial role in the illegal trade in a number of species, there is the need for more definitive "proof" of this idea.

PART II

Examples of the Problem

5

Terrestrial Species

TERRESTRIAL MAMMALS are perhaps the most visible victims of illegal hunting and trafficking. These animals are most recognizable and familiar to the public. Many of us grew up watching films that glorified the African safari and the kills yielded from them. Products from these safaris included tiger skin rugs or intact whole elephant tusks. For decades, these trophies brought the exotic into living rooms around the world. At the time, no one thought about these practices having such severe consequences.

The Red List includes approximately 5,488 mammals, representing 412 subspecies. The IUCN estimates that the majority (63%) of mammals are not threatened, but approximately 22 percent of mammals are globally threatened with extinction, and inadequate data exists for the remaining 15 percent of mammalian species.[1] In some parts of the world, mammals are at more risk of threat than others. For example, Indonesia is home to the largest number of threatened species, but it is also home to the most diverse mammal population with about 670 different mammalian species found throughout this island nation.[2] Mexico is second to Indonesia in terms of the numbers of threatened species within the mammal genus. Research also shows that half of the top twenty countries hosting the largest number of endangered mammalia are located in Asia.[3]

This information is the starting point for crime reduction experts to explore what animals are most at risk and which range states produce the greatest opportunities for animals to be illegally hunted and eventually trafficked. The animals presented in this chapter—tiger (*Panthera tigris* subsp.), gorilla (*Gorilla gorilla* subsp.), African elephant (*Loxodonta africana* subsp.), and Asian elephant (*Elephas maximus* subsp.)—are among the most endangered in the world. A case study that describes each of these animals, its habitat, and the threats it faces is followed by a discussion of conservation efforts both in terms of enforcement and conservation.

TIGER (*Panthera tigris* subsp.)

Panthera tigris, commonly known as the tiger, is the largest and most majestic of the big cats and represents the most powerful in nature. The tiger is also one of the most endangered of all species on the planet. Of the nine subspecies, three are extinct; one is functionally extinct; and the remaining subspecies are critically endangered or endangered (see Table 5.1). No one knows exactly how many tigers are living in the wild; however, estimates of all combined subspecies total fewer than 4,000. At the turn of the 20th century, estimated populations were at 10,000, but by the beginning of the new millennium, that number was roughly halved.

Table 5.1 *Panthera tigris*, Tiger Subspecies

Panthera tigris tigris Bengal Tiger	Habitat	Dry and wet deciduous forests, grassland, sal forests and temperate forests, mangrove forests
	Range State	Bangladesh, Bhutan, China, India, Myanmar, Nepal
	Wild Population	1841–2463 (approximately 333 in captivity, mainly in zoos in India)
	Status	Endangered
Panthera tigris altaica Amur (Siberian) Tiger	Habitat	Boreal Forest
	Range States	China, North Korea, Russia
	Wild Population	431–529 (approximately 490 in captivity)
	Status	Endangered
Panthera tigris corbetti Indo-Chinese Tiger	Habitat	Tropical, subtropical, moist broadleaf forests
	Range States	Cambodia, China, Lao PDR, Eastern Myanmar, Thailand, Vietnam
	Wild Population	736–1225 (approximately 60 in zoos in Asia and the U.S.)
	Status	Endangered
Panthera tigris jacksoni Malayan Tiger	Habitat	Southern Part of the Malay Peninsula
	Range States	Southeast Asia
	Wild Population	491–510
	Status	Endangered
Panthera tigris sumatrae Sumatran Tiger	Habitat	Peat moss forest, lowland forest to sub-mountainous and mountainous forest
	Range States	Indonesian Island of Sumatra
	Population	400–500 (approximately 210 in captivity worldwide
	Status	Critically Endangered

Table 5.1 (Continued)

Panthera tigris amoyensis South China Tiger	Habitat	Mountainous subtropical evergreen forest close to provincial borders; habitat is highly fragmented, with most blocks smaller than 500 km^2
	Range States	Central & Eastern China
	Population	47 (18 in China)
	Status	Critically Endangered/Functionally Extinct in Wild
Panthera tigris balica Bali Tiger	Status	Extinct
Panthera tigris sondaica Javan Tiger	Status	Extinct
Panthera tigris virgata Caspian Tiger	Status	Extinct

Characteristics[4]

The structure and appearance of the remaining tiger subspecies appear to be exhibiting a cline, which occurs when a single species begins to take on slight variations due to adaptation to climate and habitat. Therefore, tigers in Sumatra, Indonesia may have slightly different physical attributes than their Amur cousins in far eastern Russia. Tigers in the north are larger than those in the southern locations. The Amur tiger is the largest of the subspecies with the adult male weighing up to 800 pounds (363 kg) and 10 feet (3 m) in length. Females can weigh between 200 to 370 pounds (136 kg) with a length of roughly 8 feet (2.5 m). Male Bengal tigers can weigh up to 480 pounds (217 kg) with a length up to 9.5 feet (2.9 m). Females are smaller with an average weight of 300 pounds (136 kg) and are about 7.5 feet long (2.3 m). The South China male tigers weigh about 330 pounds (150 kg) and are 8 feet (2.4 m) in length. The females weigh nearly 100 pounds (45 kg) less then the males and only reach 7.5 feet (2.3 m) in length. Adult male Indo-Chinese tigers can weigh 400 pounds (181 kg) and grow to 9 feet (2.7 m). Their mates weigh roughly 250 pounds (113 kg) and are a foot shorter. The Malayan tiger was only recognized as a separate subspecies of tiger in 2004. They are physically similar to the Indo-Chinese tigers in size. Males can weigh up to 265 pounds (120 kg) while the females reach 220 pounds (100 kg). The male Sumatran tigers only weigh about 265 pounds (120 kg) and measure approximately 8 feet (2.5 m) from nose to tip of tail. The females are smaller weighing less than 200 pounds (100 kg) and measuring about 7 feet long (2.1 m).

The color of the various tiger subspecies ranges in shades of orange with stripes ranging from light brown to black. There is a recessive gene that produces white fur and skin, but these cats are not considered to be albino as they do not have red-colored eyes, and they also have stripes. Tigers are the only big cats to have stripes both on their fur and skin. Stripes are located on their faces, sides, legs, and stomachs. The most distinctive strip is located on their forehead. The pattern is said to resemble the Chinese character for king (王). This block of skin is extremely desired due to its symbolic meaning. Tiger skins in general are very coveted and fetch a high price in illegal markets, but the presence of the Chinese character makes this piece of tiger skin even more desirable, valuable, and coveted than skins without the marking. Tiger skins, in general, are an example of endangered species by-products that fit the CRAVED model very well, unless the entire intact skin is being sold. Small pieces are commonly sold, thus making them concealable. Their small size also contributes to the ease of removal. Poachers cut the skins into any size of pieces, which can then be easily removed from the point of processing to the final point of sale. Usually the pieces are small enough to fit into a pocket. The extent to which the item's characteristics fit the CRAVED model is in direct proportion to the risk the item has for entering the illegal trade—in other words how "hot" it is.

Habitat and Range States

Studies show that tigers currently occupy only about 7 percent of their historic ranges, which is roughly 40 percent less than what they occupied in 1995[5] (see Figure 5.1). Currently, there are 14 range states for tigers. These are all located in southeast Asia: Bangladesh, Bhutan, Cambodia, China, India, Indonesia (Sumatra), the Lao People's Democratic Republic, Malaysia, Myanmar, Nepal, North Korea, Russia, Thailand, and Vietnam. The type of habitat varies within each of the regions, but largely consists of subtropical, tropical, and moist broadleaf forests.

Tiger experts worldwide believe that the shrinkage of hospitable land scientifically endangers the ability of the big cats to procreate due to its diminishing gene pool. The exact number of tigers in India is not known, but India is believed to host 80 percent of the world's remaining tiger population. Only two genetically viable populations of Bengal tigers live in the Corbett Tiger Reserve in Uttaranchal and the Kanha Tiger Reserve in Madhya Pradesh, India.[6] Unfortunately, poachers killed all the tigers in Sariska Tiger Reserve in Rajasthan in February 2005. In late 2007, 20 tigers were reportedly seen in the mountains of Maharashtra.[7]

The WWF, Save the Tiger Fund, Wildlife Conservation Society, and the Smithsonian National Zoological Park in Washington, D.C., undertook a

Figure 5.1 Current Tiger Range Map in Relation to Historic Distribution. (Save the Tiger Fund)

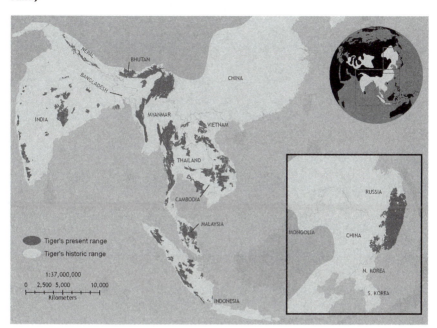

comprehensive scientific study of tiger habitats[8] in order to provide guidance for conservationists, practitioners, development agencies, and governments in their efforts to save the tiger. Across Asia, 76 areas were suitable for tiger conservation locations. They were prioritized by using three databases: (1) land cover, measured from satellite images; (2) human interference, determined from previous human footprint analysis; and (3) tiger distribution records. Several "stronghold" areas were deemed suitable for hosting more than 500 tigers. These included the Russian Far East/Northeast China, Terai Arc Landscape of India[9] and Nepal, Northern Forest Complex-Namdapha-Royal Manas (Bhutan/Myanmar/India), and Tenasserims of Thailand and Myanmar.

Threats

Wildlife workers estimate that tigers are being killed at a rate of one per day. The main threat to tigers is poaching (see Figure 5.2) followed by their loss of habitat due to human encroachment into their environment. In terms of poaching, the animals are desired for their skins, bones, teeth, and claws (see Figure 5.3). Skins are used for ornamental decoration (see Figure 5.4), as are the teeth and

Figure 5.2 Tiger (Farmed) Cut in Half by Smugglers, Caught by Thai Highway Police, May 2004. (FREELAND)

claws, which are used for jewelry. Bones have a number of uses including magic and healing. Primarily, tigers are hunted for their usefulness in TAM; ingesting or adorning oneself with parts of the tiger is believed to bring good luck and protective powers. Each part of the animal has its uses:[10]

- Canines: bring good luck;
- Claws: protect those who wear them;
- Skins, whiskers, eyebrows, or tails: protect the bearer from malicious curses;
- Skins from the Forehead: alleged to bear the Chinese character of royalty and possessing it will bring good luck and prosperity;
- Penis: used in TAM as an aphrodisiac;
- Gall: used in TAM to cure bone disease;
- Flesh: used as TAM by cooking and eating it to treat skin diseases. It also provides protection from wild pigs when strips are laid around crops;
- Milk: used in TAM and has many medicinal qualities;
- Bone: used in TAM by crushing into powder form. When mixed with warm water, it treats rheumatism and headaches. It is also made into wine (see Figure 5.5);

Figure 5.3 October 2003 Bust by Thai Police of Wildlife Slaughter-house outside Bangkok. (c/o Royal Thai Police)

- Right front paw bone: used in magic and in TAM. These bones are considered the strongest in terms of remedy, as they are the ones used to pull down prey. Tonics with this bone treat headaches and also drive away malicious spirits.

All of the items listed above easily fit Clarke's CRAVED model (see Box 5.1). Teeth, whiskers, skins, powders, and organs are easily concealable, removable, valuable, enjoyable, and desirable. The variability of uses increases the degree to which these parts and others like them become "hot." Officials must remain vigilant in monitoring what parts are being seized and available through illegal means.

The WWF report, *Conserving Tigers in the Wild*, identified poaching as a main threat in five of the six priority tiger conservation landscapes. A constant theme in the description of that threat is the killing of tigers for the illegal trade in their parts. Two of the six landscapes had what were described as "strong anti-poaching" programs in place, but the slaughter of these animals continued to be a significant problem. For the other areas, weak law enforcement stemming from the lack of proper government support was thought to contribute to the proliferation of poaching.[11]

Figure 5.4 Tiger Skin Costume at Litang Horse Festival, Aug 2005, Sichuan Province, China. (Environmental Investigation Agency, http://www.eia-international.org/)

   Another threat to the great tiger is the loss of habitat. Large-scale mining and land clearing, both legal and illegal, has disrupted the lives of these large cats. Encroachments by humans can have deadly consequences. For example, research shows that when tigers and humans interact, death to humans by tigers occurs. Because of the loss of natural prey, tigers are forced to hunt domestic livestock, which are usually located in close proximity to human settlements. Furthermore, this increases human-tiger interaction and thus, contributes to the increases in either the loss of human life or that of the tiger. Moreover, the killing of domestic animals by tigers threatens human subsistence, further affecting human survival.[12]

Trafficking in Tigers and Tiger Parts

Much of what we know about the illicit trade in tigers stems from three studies[13] that examine activities in Sumatra, Indonesia, and one that examines the wild and captive trade in China since the trade ban there in 1993. The information gained from these studies has no doubt helped to develop a clearer picture of how the trade operates.

Figure 5.5 Vat of Tiger Bone Wine, Harbin China. (Save the Tiger Fund)

Box 5.1 Hot Products and CRAVED

In the 1990s, researchers began acknowledging that crime is not evenly distributed throughout society. New technologies began to make mapping of crime much easier than in past. Crime maps visually depict where crimes are concentrated, and therefore indicate where police forces should deploy their officers. As crime reduction became a more fashionable perspective, theses crime maps helped discern where prevention efforts could be useful. In conjunction with research on the distribution of stolen goods markets, theft, and burglary, Professor Ron Clarke began to think of stolen *goods* and how some products were more vulnerable than others. Once it could be determined which goods were most at risk of being stolen, (i.e. hot products), interventions could be designed to protect those products, effectively reducing theft levels.

From his research, Clarke determined that hot products have several common characteristics: value, size, and portability. CRAVED is a model that helps to assess the risk of a product becoming hot. Specifically, items that were most at risk were those with certain attributes: Concealable, Removable, Available, Valuable, Enjoyable, and Disposable. This model has been successfully applied to the identification of hot traditional products. There is utility in applying this model to nontraditional hot products, such as those derived from endangered species.

Source: Ronald V. Clarke, "Hot Products: Understanding, Anticipating, and Reducing Demand for Stolen Goods," *Police Research Series* Paper 112 (1999).

Indonesia   The Red List classifies the Sumatran tiger as critically endangered. The population of this species of tiger has plummeted over the years with reasons that are the same as the other tiger subspecies—poaching, loss of habitat, deaths due to human-tiger interaction, and loss of natural prey. The trade in these animals was studied in 1995 and again between 1999 and 2002.[14]

Researchers in both the 2004 and 2007 studies posed as potential buyers of tiger parts in northern Sumatra, particularly near the city of Medan.[15] Prior to undertaking the studies, tiger bones were studied by researchers so that they could be more easily identified in the field. It is important to note that at the time of the research, the tiger was protected fully in Indonesia by national legislation, which was first enacted in 1972. In 1990, the passage of the Act of the Republic of Indonesia on the Conservation of Living Resources and Ecosystems (Conservation Act No. 5) updated the earlier legislation, granting the tiger full safeguards. Further, efforts to protect the species involved mandatory registration of tiger trophies or other body parts that were acquired prior to the new legislation going into effect. Indonesia is also a signatory country to CITES (signed on December 28, 1978). As such, all commercial trade in tigers was made illegal under CITES when the tiger became listed in Appendix I. CITES states that Indonesia's Conservation Act No. 5 amply implements the tenets of CITES.

The study conducted in 2004 was one of the first comprehensive studies[16] on the plight of the tiger and the illegal trade in Indonesia. The trade involved 88 outlets (including goldsmiths, traditional and western pharmacies, and souvenir shops) and a number of outside stalls were identified and visited with the aim of seeing if tiger parts were for sale in those operations—overtly or covertly. Ten outlets (11%) offered tiger parts for sale. These parts were verified to be actual tiger remains, including bones, claws, teeth, and a pelt, all of which fit the CRAVED model. Three additional outlets claimed that they had bones for sale, but the researchers did not actually see the bones offered.

There was an interesting mix of the types of shops that sold the parts in Medan. The types of shops visited included western-style pharmacies, traditional Indonesian pharmacies, TAM shops, souvenir shops, gold stores, and local tent-markets.[17] Interestingly, only one TAM shop actually had products containing tiger products. Gold shops appeared to be, by far, the most important outlet for illicit tiger parts. Farther afield, the total weight of tiger bones for sale in Blankejeren and Takengon, southeast Ache, and Sumatra, Indonesia was 79 pounds (35.90 kg), with price estimates ranging from US$6.80/kg to US$45.45/kg. Prices for bones in Medan were approximately US$45.45/kg for retail establishments and US$125/kg for export.[18]

The illicit market always begins with a demand for the commodity, which in this case is tiger parts. The methods for collecting tigers in early studies were very simplistic. They did not find evidence of professional poaching; rather those mainly responsible for killing the tigers were local farmers and villagers. Accounts from the illegal handlers/traders outlined two ways in which tigers met their demise: poisoning and snaring. The process begins when a tiger kills a domestic animal. After the tiger's first feeding, the farmer spreads poison on the kill so that when the tiger returns for a second meal the poisoned meat is ingested. Once dead, the tiger is stripped for the desired parts. Snares are usually set for catching wild pigs, but they obviously can catch tigers. When one is caught, it is harvested for the most valuable parts, which are then taken to various outlets that will offer to sell them on to customers or other retailers. Finally, those who sell the tiger parts admitted knowing that it was indeed illegal to do so; however, they did not express any concern or fear of authorities or punishment.

A second of the two TRAFFIC studies was conducted between 1999 and 2002. Like the previous study, they sought to identify outlets for the illegal selling of tiger parts.[19] They examined 43 retail shops in 24 towns and cities in Sumatra. Of the 453 shops, about one-fifth had tiger parts for sale to the public. All related information to the illegal sale of tiger parts was given to authorities in hopes that action would be taken. Regrettably, the authorities did not take this information seriously and did virtually nothing to intervene. TRAFFIC published the findings in both English and Indonesian in order to facilitate the dissemination of the information. Additionally, training sessions were conducted with local officials in order to help raise awareness of the plight of the tiger.

TRAFFIC conducted a follow-up study on the Sumatran tiger trade.[20] Again, 28 cities and towns were surveyed in seven provinces and in seven seaports in Sumatra. Earlier research guided the choice of outlets for investigation.[21] The latest research studied a total of 326 retail outlets[22] to include goldsmiths (272), souvenir shops (15), traditional medicine shops (8), antique dealers and jewelers of precious stones (31, combined). What is not known is the total number of retail establishments in the area so that we can determine proportions of those partaking in illegal activities.

As in previous years, goldsmiths played a prominent role in the trafficking of tiger parts.[23] Of the 272 goldsmiths surveyed, only 20 actually had tiger parts for sale. Antique dealers and jewelers that sold tiger parts numbered 31, followed by 15 souvenir shops, and only eight traditional medicine shops selling tiger products. A critical failing of these findings is that the number of goldsmiths or other types of establishments in the study area was not known. Before any targeted intervention strategies could be designed or implemented, the total number of goldsmiths in a given area would need to be identified so that the proportion of those that actually deal in banned products can be determined. Practitioners cannot know from the findings published in the TRAFFIC study, with any degree of certainty, which outlets do indeed play the most prominent role in the trafficking of these animals.

In the 2007 study, tiger parts for sale included CRAVED products like skins, canines, claws, and bones. The majority were found in shops in Medan. One traditional medicine shop had 5 pieces of tiger skin (5 × 5 cm); 8 gold shops had 11 canines; 2 souvenir shops had 1 canine and 1 claw; and 4 jewelry shops had 36 tiger canines, 6 pieces of tiger skins (3 × 3 cm), and about 15 tiger skins (3 × 6 cm). In the Riau Province, one jewelry shop in Dumai had one canine and in Duri, 2 traditional medicine shops had 3 canines, 2 claws, and 2 skins (3 × 7 cm). In Jambi, Jambi Province, 1 traditional medicine shop had 4 canines, 3 skin pieces, and 2 bones. In the South Sumatran Province of Palembang, 1 goldsmith had 1 claw; 1 medicine shop had 1 skin piece; and 1 jeweler had 1 canine. Finally, in Padang, West Sumatra Province, 2 skin pieces were found in a jewelry shop and in one souvenir shop, 2 canines were located.

While prices for the tiger contraband varied, tiger bones fetched the most money except in instances when the whole pelt was sold. Prices for entire pelts were estimated to be as high as US$10,000.[24] The highest price was US$116/kg. This price increased from the first trade study, which reported the cost of bones between US$12 and US$61/kg. Canines were the second most costly body part, realizing up to US$88 per tooth. The average canine price was US$50 while the average price for a tiger's claw was US$14. Both of these represent an overall decrease in the prices reported by Shepherd and Magnus in 2004. The price of tiger skin varies by the size of the piece; in this study, the prices ranged from US$4 to US$17.

The market for endangered tiger parts was described in the 2007 study, but only in the most vague terms.[25] (For research on traditional stolen markets see Box 5.2). There is no doubt that information about these markets may be as scarce as the animals themselves. Middlemen traveled to Jambi and Bengkulu province trying to buy tiger parts. The remaining information is based on anecdotal evidence, which is problematic when trying to design interdiction mechanisms. Basically, there are two models that depict the illicit trade in tiger parts in Sumatra. The first shows that hunters have several outlets to which they can sell the tiger and/or its parts: (1) to a dealer who will sell to an exporter; (2) to the end user directly; (3) to a middleman who will get the parts to either dealers or to end users; or (4) directly to manufacturers of traditional medicines. In this model, dealers are responsible for getting the goods to the exporter or directly to end-users. The second model is less complicated. The hunter has three options: (1) to sell to manufacturers of traditional medicines; (2) to sell directly to end-users; or (3) to sell to a trader who will then move the tiger parts to exporters.[26]

Punishments for participating in illegal buying/selling of this protected species vary. This is most likely due to the variation in domestic laws aimed at protecting the tiger species, as well as the level of importance placed on this crime. Furthermore, the level of enforcement obviously plays an important role by bringing offenders to the notice of the criminal justice process. Without strong legislation that is enacted and enforced, intervention efforts will be moot. Statistics from the Directorate of Investigation and Forest Protection

Box 5.2 Traditional Stolen Goods Markets

Research on stolen goods markets is sparse, especially when compared to the volume of work on theft-related crimes such as burglary and shop theft. In the 1990s and the first decade of 2000, the small body of literature expanded with research conducted in the United Kingdom. In 1993, Sutton began looking at how stolen goods markets keep theft levels high. Later in 2003, Schneider examined how stolen goods operate and what types of property were hottest. Simply put, stolen goods markets exist because thieves know that they can easily sell the goods they steal. Handling stolen goods is a serious crime, whereby thieves sell goods to people who either use the items or who sell them on to others. Handling can be extremely complicated due to the number of handlers involved in the illegal chain. It is difficult to curtail because consumers of stolen goods turn a blind eye to their involvement in the crime. Rather they rationalize their purchases as simply "getting a good deal." Regardless, their participation helps to keep theft levels high.

Before specific interventions can be designed to combat the existence of stolen goods markets, police and researchers must analyze (1) what markets are operating and (2) what goods are most at risk or hot. Interventions must be designed with a particular market in mind along with knowing what products are hot. Markets are constrained by geography and by time. In other words, conditions change over time and how goods are bought and sold will vary by the cultural constraints of a given area.

See: Sutton, 1995, 1998. Also see: Jacqueline L. Schneider, "Stolen Goods Markets: Methods of Disposal," *British Journal of Criminology* 45, no. 2 (2005): 129–140.

---

and Nature Conservation, Ministry of Forestry, Indonesia report that there were 12 criminal court cases from 2004 through 2006 in the six provinces in the Ng and Nemora 2007 study. Goods seized as part of these cases included a dead tiger, complete and partial skeletons, which included individual bones, skins, and canines.

Jail time for the offenders resulted in all of the cases[27] with sentences ranging from eight months to three years. Fines also accompanied incarceration. To the reader, fines may seem farcical when compared to Western punishments. However, it is important to situate these fines within the income levels of the country, which is among the poorest countries in the world. The average monthly income reported in Indonesia in the first quarter of 2001 was 420,000 Indonesian rupiahs (US$41.44);[28] therefore, some of these fines may be onerous to offenders. In 2006, the monthly average wage was around US$73, and most people have to survive on less than US$3.50 per day. Reported fines[29] are as follows: 25,000 Indonesian rupiahs (US$3) for possession of two swatches of tiger skins along with pieces from a Barking Deer; 500,000 Indonesian rupiahs (US$55) for possession of one tiger skin, bones of one tiger, and the skull of a second one; 500,000 Indonesian rupiahs (US$55) for having one tiger skin and bones from not less than three tigers; 1 million Indonesian rupiahs (US$110) for possession of two whole tiger skins and one tiger skull.

Enforcement of laws protecting the critically endangered tiger in Indonesia was not consistent across the provinces under investigation.[30] There was no explanation offered by the researchers for this variation. This may be attributed to differences in the characteristics of the provinces—rural versus urban, which may influence the amount of resources available for enforcement practices. Variation may also exist in the level of commitment of the regional provinces to the protection of the species, as well as the level of competence of those responsible for enforcing both domestic laws and CITES regulations.

Figure 5.6 depicts a poacher arrested in Indonesia. Tiger researchers there explained that the man received jail time for his poaching crimes; however, that was not his only punishment. The man proudly displaying the tiger's head was being mentored by a more experienced poacher in the area. The mentor, upon hearing of this student's hunting success, became extremely upset as the student killed the tiger without the mentor's permission or input. The villagers in

Figure 5.6 Tiger Poacher Arrested in Sumatra (May 2005), Holding Fresh Tiger Skin—Apparently His Fourth Tiger. (FREELAND)

the area were also angry with the poacher because his arrest brought unwanted police officials into the area. The presence of the police in the area also disrupted the illegal logging that was also taking place! Upon the poacher's release from jail, the entire village shunned and banished him from the community, and his wife divorced him.[31]

China   China is the largest consumer country of tigers and their body parts.[32] The primary reasons for this are the use of tiger bones in TAMs and the use of skins in ornamental clothing. The tiger, in Chinese culture, is said to represent strength; therefore, a person seeks to ingest parts of the tiger in order to receive some of the great cat's strength. Bones are milled into ingredients of TAMs, and tiger blood or bones are used in wine production.

China became a party to CITES in 1981, but it was not until 1993 that the country instituted a complete ban on trafficking in the tiger and its parts. The effect of the 1993 complete trade ban on the availability of wild tiger parts and on the existence of illegal markets in China was examined.[33] Very little evidence was found to support claims that shops were trading wild tiger parts. Of the 663 medicine shops and dealers that claimed to stock tiger products in 26 cities, less than 3 percent actually did have products available for purchase. This is due to the government's campaigns to make the public aware of the ban and the need to conserve the big cat.[34]

What the study cannot tell us is whether the compliance with government policy merely forced the trade underground—allowing the illegal markets to flourish. One unanticipated consequence of the complete ban on the tiger trade is the increase in demand for other big Asian cats such as the snow leopard (*Panthera uncia*, IUCN status: endangered), leopard (*Panthera pardus*, IUCN status: near threatened), and clouded leopard (*Neofelis nebulosa*, IUCN status: vulnerable).[35]

In order to comply with CITES, Chinese seizure records pertaining to tigers were submitted. According to China's CITES Management Authority, authorities seized 80 tiger skins and 30 bones/skeletons from 1999 to 2005.[36] None of the reported seizures were said to originate from India, which is a range area for tigers. China is considered to be the main destination for tiger parts that do originate from the Southeast Asian area. A large seizure of leopard and tiger skins occurred near the Purang Pass on the China–Nepal border (31 tiger skins and 881 leopard skins); however, Tibet is not considered to be a large consumer of these products, so it is believed that China was the final destination for the skins.

The international conservation community recommended maintaining a total domestic trade ban, cessation of intensive captive-breeding programs and the destruction of remaining carcasses, and continued public education about conservation and awareness of the consequences of the illicit trade. China's laws are rather strict and violators have been met with very hefty penalties for infractions; enforcement is said to be strong. Cases of illegal hunting of protected species have resulted in long prison sentences, including life imprisonment and execution.

Tiger Farms

Part of China's conservation strategy is captive breeding (tiger farms) which is illustrated in the Chinese government policy entitled, The 1988 Wildlife Protection Law, Article 17, which states that, "the State shall encourage the domestication and breeding of wildlife."[37] As late as 2006, there were 14 registered tiger farms in China. These farms are tourist attractions, as well as breeding grounds and a place where tigers are easily slaughtered for the production of various products, including TAM.

The impetus behind the concept of tiger farms was the belief that the demand for wild tigers would decrease once the market was open to trade in captive animals. Conservationists worldwide refute this claim. It is impossible to distinguish between tiger products derived from wild tigers and farmed ones. If farmed tiger parts begin to appear on the market, it most probably will send a message to hunters that it is acceptable to hunt wild tigers.

The owners of the tiger farms say that they will donate some of their profits to conservation causes, but conservationists do not believe this happens. Animal welfare experts are appalled by the conditions in which these majestic animals live and die. They are calling for the farms to be closed due to the inhumane conditions under which these animals are kept, as well as the effects they have on the illicit markets. The animal farms are not, however, designed with conservation in mind; rather they are commercial enterprises that are known for their inhumane conditions. In 2005, the Chinese government sought to lift the ban for products made from captive-bred tigers, but efforts were not supported, leaving the ban in effect.

Conservation

The main focus of literature on tiger conservation pertains to habitat rehabilitation/restoration, even though poaching is the immediate threat to the big cats. The earliest efforts focused on tiger ecology. This work provided a strong foundation from which the next generation of researchers could build. In the 1990s, an increase in interest in the fate of the tiger and an increase in funding became evident. Exxon Mobil Corporation, whose mascot is a tiger, partnered with the U.S. National Fish and Wildlife Foundation to create Save the Tiger Fund.[38] The purpose of the Save the Tiger Fund is evident in the organization's title. Areas of the Fund's work include scientific inquiry of tiger ecology, education and outreach programs to build public support, antipoaching patrols, market reduction activities to combat global supply and demand, rehabilitation of tiger habitats, sustainable development projects in those areas where tigers and humans interact, zoo breeding programs, and programs aimed at reducing human-tiger conflict.[39] Part of their work involves the identification of the routine activities of tigers, as well as those of humans. This knowledge is critical when developing an understanding of how victims (tigers) come together with offenders (poachers) in the absence of capable guardians (villagers, antipoaching patrols, and conservationists). Once this is known, intervention strategies can be tailored in order to have the best possible chance of success.

While it is obviously acknowledged that the tiger is valued because of its skin and bones, it is somewhat difficult to find information on programs that prevent the slaughter of the species. Mainly, antipoaching teams are in place in conservation landscapes, national forests, and preserves, but these teams are significantly understaffed and underfinanced. These teams help identify patterns of behavior that assist in the development of strategic interventions. However, given the vast areas that tigers roam, the utility of these teams is questionable. This is not to say, however, that antipoaching patrols are unsuccessful. In some locations where these patrols exist, there are success stories of capturing poachers. The most recent capable guardians are the "Green Army," a team of women who have decided to organize female patrols into the forests of the Periyar tiger reserve in Kerala in order to catch poachers.[40] The enforcement of laws is patchy at best. The countries in which tigers live have competing policy demands for financial support. Countries, especially those with economies in transition, are in need of social and economic programs that will enable them to divert funding toward sustainable development programs. Money needed to save the tiger oftentimes is allocated to the programs that hold higher priority.

Much of the world's remaining tiger habitat is situated in countries that are indeed parties to CITES, but also where economic and social development lags behind the West. Law enforcement efforts are hampered by weak domestic laws regulating the killing of protected species, as well as extremely underfunded enforcement agencies. There are only a small number of antipoaching patrol programs in existence throughout tiger habitats. Antipoaching seems to be the only enforcement-related activity aimed at reducing and disrupting the illegal trade of these cats.

The Tiger Study[41] identifies two main ways in which to protect and conserve tigers. The first is to develop and support numerous tiger reserves where the cats are isolated into particular regional areas. The second, which is preferred by conservationists, is the creation of tiger conservation landscapes where there is enough land area to support at least five tigers and where tigers have been confirmed to exist during the last 10 years. Identifying only these two ways to protect and conserve the species is indicative of the prevailing inclination of conservation efforts. There is perhaps a third way to protect and conserve the animals—

to design and implement innovative crime reduction strategies aimed at reducing the illicit markets that deal in endangered species.

The predecessor to the tiger conservation landscapes were tiger conservation units, which were defined as blocks of existing habitats of tiger populations or those that are favorable to hosting them. In the years since the tiger conservation units were identified, research has moved to identifying tiger conservation landscapes. These landscapes are identified through complicated mapping techniques that identify suitable habitats where tigers can flourish. Ideally, land corridors are created in order to link tiger conservation landscapes together so that genetically diverse tiger populations can interact enabling genetic viability to increase. However, only 26 percent of the 76 identified areas are protected, which is problematic. *The Tiger Study*[42] recommends the creation of human–tiger friendly landscapes, containing core-protected areas where breeding can take place unencumbered by human interference. Perhaps more important is the concentration on the tiger, its reproduction, and the maintenance of the tiger's prey. However, it must be noted here that with the creation of human–tiger friendly landscapes comes increased opportunities for tigers to be harmed.

Each country that hosts tiger populations through tiger population units or landscapes works to ensure the recommendations are enacted. Information on conservation, including habitat rehabilitation and enforcement and the efforts in India and far eastern Russia are described next. These are perhaps the most comprehensive programs in existence today.

India

The largest population of tigers resides in subcontinent India. Perhaps the evolution of conservation efforts for the tiger began because of the work of Jim Corbett.[43] From 1906 to 1941, Corbett was called on to hunt and kill man-eating tigers and leopards. While humans are not part of the natural diet of tigers, man-eaters do exist when they are forced to adopt an alien diet—humans. Corbett alone was responsible for killing twelve tigers responsible for over 1,500 human deaths. He only agreed to hunt the animals if all other hunters were ordered out of the area for his personal safety and if the rewards being offered for the cats were removed, as he did not want to become known as a reward-hunter.

During the 1920s and 1930s, tiger hunting was big business. The popularity of the big hunt made Corbett fear for the viability of tiger species in India. As a result, he established two organizations in India dedicated to the preservation and conservation of wildlife, especially tigers. The Association for the Preservation of Game was located in Uttar Pradesh and came under the auspice of the All-India Conference for the Preservation of Wildlife. In 1936, the Corbett National Park[44] was established for the preservation of wildlife. For his dedication to the species, the Indo-Chinese tiger (*Panthera tigris corbetti*) is named after him.

Despite Corbett's work in India, hunting tigers was still legal as was the exportation of their skins and other parts as recently as the 1970s. India's

Prime Minister Indira Gandhi (1966–1977 and 1980–1984) elevated the status of the tiger by making it India's national symbol.[45] By doing so, Mrs. Gandhi reminded India that the tiger was an important cultural treasure and because of the declining numbers, she declared it a protected species. Gandhi established Project Tiger in 1972, which was launched fittingly at Corbett National Park in 1973. The aims of the project are many; however, the main goal is to ensure the maintenance of a genetically-viable tiger population in India. Project Tiger initially established nine tiger reserves throughout India. These reserves sought to preserve the tiger by reducing or eliminating its biggest threats: habitat destruction, forestry disturbance, loss of natural prey, and poaching.

Unfortunately, Project Tiger fostered a rash of tiger killings before the law went into effect.[46] Once the law was enacted, specific areas on the reserve were designated breeding grounds, which were strictly out-of-bounds to the public. The premise was to allow the cats to breed and migrate into other hospitable grounds. In order to accommodate this, travel routes that excluded humans were established for the tigers. Other efforts included the relocation of human settlements and their domestic animals. Additionally, forest harvesting was stopped in order for the tiger habitat to thrive. Initially these efforts appeared to yield increases in tiger populations; however, after the death of Prime Minister Gandhi, the tiger census was questioned. The numbers were found to significantly overestimate the counts, but there can be no doubt that the Tiger Project increased populations.

The death of Mrs. Gandhi in 1984 also brought with it a return to the old ways and thoughts in India. Tigers and their preservation were no longer seen as a high priority for government intervention. The needs of local farmers and villagers took precedence, resulting in the migration routes and core breeding grounds of the tigers being encroached. This, of course, brought about the loss of habitat and natural prey. Moreover, tiger poaching took a stronghold once again, with body parts being illegally exported to China and other Southeast Asian countries.

Today, there are between 23 and 28 tiger reserves (depending on the source[47]) that cover about 12,741 mi^2 (33,000 km^2). The original objectives remain intact, with an additional goal of moving those currently living inside the conservation area to a more suitable area outside in order to further reduce human-tiger interaction and conflict. A major obstacle faced by the Tiger Project is adequate funding and equipment needed for antipoaching patrols.

In 2003, India Wilderness Project[48] developed an interesting program whereby former poachers were hired to catch current poachers. The former poachers, called tribal trackers and guides, make up teams of antipoaching patrols. The rationale behind the project was twofold: (1) the poachers were familiar with the process of poaching and smuggling, and (2) they knew the terrain extremely well as it served as their former hunting grounds. A grant totaling US$10 million from The World Bank helped the Kerala Forest Department develop the program, which was part of The World Bank's ecodevelopment initiatives that aimed to conserve areas in the Periyar Tiger Reserve.[49] Many of the poachers were wanted criminals for previous poaching activities, but amnesty for their past was granted in exchange for their participation in the project. More than 80 poaching cases (not just of tigers) resulted from their efforts. The initiative is considered to be successful not only in helping to reduce poaching, but also in the development of ecotourism in the area.

Russia

The Russian Far East is the home of the Amur (Siberian) tiger. Specifically, the tiger inhabits Sikhote-Alin Zapovednik, a World Heritage site, a mountain range that stretches from the mountains' peaks to the Sea of Japan. This mountain range is approximately 156,571 mi^2 (405,517 km^2) and is located in the Primorye of the Russian Far East. There are between 429 to 502 Amur tigers living there at any given time; however, within the area about 25 to 30 tigers are killed each year.

The Siberian Tiger Project[50] is probably the most well-known of Russia's conservation efforts. In place since 1992, the Wildlife Conservation Society's Hornocker Wildlife Institute has undertaken a thorough study of tiger ecology within Sikhote-Alin Zapovednik. The project seeks to understand the role of the tiger in this ecosystem, as well as to gain an understanding of the Amur tiger itself. The study uses radio-fitted collars that are placed on cats that are captured and then released. The data drawn from the collars have enabled researchers and conservationists to gain information about habitat, reproduction, and mortality rates, among other topics.

There are six nature reserves (zapovedniks) and a number of protected areas (cakazniks) where hunting, mining, and logging are forbidden, either temporarily or permanently. It is these areas where the big cats roam. The Siberian Tiger Project[51] also seeks to determine the correlation between multi-use areas and tiger mortality. In other words, researchers are trying to demonstrate the impact on tiger survivability when humans use managed land.

As with other subspecies of tiger, the Amur's main threats are loss of habitat, poaching, and depletion of natural prey.[52] Findings from the study show that Amur tigers require an enormous amount of land upon which to live. For example, a female tiger needs approximately 174 mi^2 (450 km^2) in order to successfully rear her cubs. Proper land management is, therefore, crucial to survival. These tigers, as well as all tiger breeds, are hunted for the value of their skins and body parts, but also because they are a threat to the domestic livestock of the local communities.

Researchers on the Siberian Tiger Project wrote a very disturbing account of their work in 2002.[53] A poacher slaughtered a radio-collared tigress; her skins, legs, spine, ribs, and head were scattered in pieces at her kill site. Before her death, Nadia provided her human colleagues valuable data about patterns of poaching. The main finding was that tigers have a higher mortality rate where roads exist. Where there are roads, there are people and where there are people, there are poachers. A corroborating finding was that there where there were no roads, tigers died from natural causes. The Siberian Tiger Project's research provides a simple solution—separate humans from tigers. Of course, this is not realistic in some instances, nor is it easy to accomplish. As in India, conservation policy must strike a balance between the endangered cat's need for survival with the needs of humans for that same reason. Humans need access to forests and remote areas in order to collect food and wood in order to survive.

The project examined three types of remote areas:

- Sikhote-Alin Zapovednik that has no roads;
- Areas around Zapovednik where there are secondary roads that are only maintained for access to the forest by off-road vehicles; and
- Areas with primary roads that are maintained year-round so that vehicles can move quickly.

These areas were monitored between 1992 and 2000 by following 10 tigresses and their 37 cubs coming from 15 litters. Where there were no roads, the tigresses had 100 percent survivorship and the cubs had 90 percent. In areas with secondary roads, survivorship decreased to 89 percent for the female tiger (data were not available for cubs). Primary roads sealed the fate for the big cats. Survivability for tigresses was only 55 percent and their cubs only 40 percent.[54] Tigresses died as a result of poaching, which left their cubs extremely vulnerable because they were too young to fend for themselves. Cubs died at either the hands of the poachers or by encounters with motor vehicles.

Another project, Inspection Tiger,[55] is a multiregional antipoaching project funded by Phoenix Fund, the Save the Tiger Fund, and the David Shepherd Wildlife Foundation. However, because of Russia's ever-changing policies and weak environmental laws, it is very difficult to sanction poachers. Regardless, there have been successful interventions. For example, the Phoenix Fund[56] reports that in 2004, a poacher was found guilty of killing a tigress, who had two cubs—one who died and another that is being cared for by conservationists. The offender was fined 130,000 rubles (US$4,500). In addition to the antipoaching efforts, interregional teams also conduct training for government and local law enforcement agencies on how to patrol effectively. Additionally, the teams do numerous public service announcements via television, radio, and community presentations.

Between the years 1994–2006, WWF's antipoaching activities yielded the following results:[57]

- 78 Amur skins confiscated;
- 12,898 poachers detained;

- 3,582 weapons confiscated; and
- 471 criminal cases pursued.

The numbers of poachers detained can only be described as a roller-coaster ride. The number has fluctuated over time, with peaks in 1998, 2000, and 2006. The lowest number of poachers detained occurred in 1995 (n = 326) and the highest in 2006 (n = 2,313). In the intervening years, the number of poachers detained varied significantly year to year: 1996 (n = 507), 1997 (n = 770), 1998 (n = 1,425), 1999 (n = 1,011), 2000 (n = 1,371), 2001 (n = 712), 2002 (n = 371), 2003 (n = 840), 2004 (n = 32), and 2005 (n = 712). There is no recorded explanation as to why such significant peaks and valleys exist in these numbers. One possible reason might be the increases or decreases in funding or the changes brought about in governmental environmental or conservation policy. The Russian government has not been consistent in its efforts to protect this critically endangered animal. As with the numbers of poachers detained, there are noticeable fluctuations in the number of weapons seized during antipoaching activities: 1995 (n = 128), 1996 (n = 242), 1997(n = 302), 1998 (n = 488), 1999 (n = 301), 2000 (n = 369), 2001 (n = 200), 2002 (n = 168), 2003 (n = 170), 2004 (n = 153), 2005 (n = 104), and 2006 (n = 405).

Conservation efforts in Russia have seen many successes, but there remain just as many obstacles. The main accomplishments, as reported by WWF,[58] include the creation of antipoaching teams, ecological education programs about Amur tiger conservation, the development of protected area network, the creation of Conflict Tiger Response Team and Wildlife Rehabilitation Centers, the creation and maintenance of an extensive database of valuable information about the Amur tiger, and regular monitoring and inventory activities.

In order to move forward, Russian legislation needs to be rationalized regarding protected areas, including the need for increased penalties for poaching tigers and their natural prey. Government funding is lacking for the conservation of tigers. Furthermore, land management decisions must be made with the conservation of Amur tigers in mind.

GORILLA (*Gorilla gorilla* subsp.)

Discussions exist among the taxonomists regarding the classification of the gorilla species. Some recognize two species (*Gorilla gorilla* and *Gorilla beringi*) with four or five subspecies, while others maintain the existence of only one species (*Gorilla gorilla*) and three subspecies.

Following the IUCN's classification, the subspecies of gorilla are categorized into two main groups. The Western subspecies include the western lowland gorilla (*Gorilla gorilla gorilla*) and the Cross River gorilla (*Gorilla gorilla diehli*). The Eastern subspecies include the mountain gorilla (*Gorilla beringei beringei*) and the eastern lowland gorilla (*Gorilla beringei graueri*). A newly identified species of gorilla, the Bwindi gorilla,[59] is a subspecies of the mountain gorilla; however, there is some contention about the genetic differences between the mountain gorilla and the Bwindi mountain gorilla of the Impenetrable National Park in Uganda, so no scientific name has yet been given.

All subspecies population estimates are in serious decline. The western lowland, Cross River, and the mountain gorillas (including the Bwindi) are classified by the IUCN's Species Survival Commission as critically endangered and listed on CITES Appendix I. It classifies the eastern lowland gorilla as endangered. The most threatened of all gorilla species is the Cross River gorilla, with estimates of only 300 left in the wild. There are an estimated 720 mountain gorillas alive in the wild. The western lowland gorilla population is commonly numbered at 95,000, but it is noted that these estimates are based on assumptions that their habitat remains at densities that were typical in the early 1980s. There are no accurate estimates of the eastern lowland gorilla population today.

Characteristics[60]

Gorillas are the largest of the primates. There are slight variations in characteristics of the subspecies. Generally, gorillas have arms that are longer than their legs and are covered with hair except on their fingers, palms, bottoms of feet, and faces. Their heads are extremely large with a bulging forehead. All gorillas have a sagittal crest, which is a ridge that extends from the front to the back of the skull. The sagittal crest supports powerful muscles along the side of the skull. They have tiny ears, small dark eyes, and no tails. They do not use their legs to walk upright; rather they walk with both their arms and legs in a position known as "knuckle-walking." They have 32 teeth with large flat molars and large canines, which are more prominent in males. Their nose prints, like the human fingerprint, are unique to individuals.

Gorillas vary in size by species and gender. They are said to reflect sexual dimorphism, which occurs when the same species reflects two distinct forms that differ in one or more characteristics such as color, size, or shape. Male gorillas are significantly larger than their mates, sometimes weighing as much as twice that of the females. The weight and height are subspecies dependent, but generally females are approximately 4.5 feet tall (1.37 m) and weigh up to 300 pounds (136 kg), while the males are over 5.5 feet (1.68 m) tall and can weigh up to 600 pounds (272 kg).

The western gorillas have a characteristic body shape with a broad chest, heavy neck, and strong hands and feet. They have a fine, brownish coat with a red tint on the crown. The western lowland gorillas have a wider skull and a more pronounced brow than other subspecies of gorillas. The eastern gorillas are darker, with black coats. Mature males in both species and their subspecies are given the name "silverbacks" because of the silvery-white saddle of hair apparent on the back around to the rear and thighs.

Much of the information that exists on the social interaction patterns stemmed from the work of Dian Fossey, who began studying mountain gorillas in the wild in 1966.[61] Her work indicates that gorillas are generally quiet and peaceful animals. They have longer life spans in captivity (50 years) when compared to those living in the wild (35 years). Gorillas communicate through a series of sounds and gestures; scientists have recorded at least 25 different vocalizations and a variety of bodily movements that include chest-beating, lunging, slapping, and sideways running, among others. While there is slight variation in the diets of the subspecies of gorilla, they are mainly herbivores that feed on fleshy fruit that are in season—seeds, plants, shoots—but they are classified as omnivores due to occasionally eating grubs, ants, and termites.

Gorillas have an extremely low reproductive rate, with an estimated maximum intrinsic rate of increase of about three percent.[62] Mountain gorilla females, for example, may only have two to six live offspring. They give birth for the first time at about age 10 and will do so about every four years. Males mature more slowly than the females. The males do not breed until they reach between 15 and 20 years of age. Infant mortality is high in the first three years of life. The gestation period is between 251 and 295 days resulting in the birth of a baby gorilla that weighs between 4 to 4.5 pounds (1.8 kg–2 kg). Mating patterns and infant mortality rates have serious implications for the recovery of the species because the rate of killing will far surpass the ability of the species to generate population increases.

Habitat and Range States

Gorillas are forest dwellers. They subsist in lowland tropical and subtropical forests, especially in areas of dense ground cover with herbaceous growth. There are eight range states for western lowland gorilla:[63] Cameroon, Central African Republic, mainland Equatorial Guinea, Gabon, Nigeria, Republic of Congo, Cabinda (Angola), and possibly the Democratic Republic of the Congo. The core of the population lives in a continuous habitat from southern Central African Republic. There is a small population that lives on the border of Nigeria and Cameroon near the Cross River and also in the Ebo-Ndokbou forest in Cameroon. For the past several decades, the Cross River gorillas inhabited forested areas that spanned about 8,000 km^2 and today are found in at least 10 areas that are geographically different, yet connected. Primarily, they live in forest patches in southeast Nigeria and western Cameroon. The eastern lowland gorilla lives in the tropical forest of eastern Democratic Republic of the Congo.[64] The mountain gorilla lives at high altitudes of 5,413 to 12,434 feet (1,650–3,790 m) in Uganda's Impenetrable National Park and in the Virunga Volcanoes on the borders of Uganda, Democratic Republic of the Congo, and Rwanda. The Bwindi gorillas live in the rainforest of the Bwindi Impenetrable Forest.

Threats

Like so many other species, there are a number of factors that contribute to the demise of this great ape. Threats include loss of habitat, commercial hunting, disease, and civil unrest. The loss of habitat is primarily due to increased and competing demands on the use of land. Logging, subsistence farming, road works, and illegal charcoal production all negatively impact the survivability of gorillas.

Commercial hunting of the species is prohibited strictly by CITES, which lists all the gorilla subspecies in Appendix I.[65] This practice is related, in part to the logging industry and to the bushmeat trade. Because these are so interrelated, it becomes difficult to describe the situation adequately. The trade in bushmeat will be discussed first, followed by a description of how logging and other industry plays a part.

The Bushmeat Trade

The bushmeat crisis is defined as being a global problem characterized by unsustainable and indiscriminate destruction of wildlife and ecosystems for short-term economic gains.[66] There are a number of reasons for the extent of this crisis: weak or nonexistent effective wildlife conservation policies, the failure or absence of government controls, and the failure of local communities to develop alternative mechanisms that are aimed at economic growth in order to fosters holistic wildlife conservation.

It is difficult to determine what proportion of bushmeat is consumed at the site of the kill or sold for profit, but what is clear is that after the kill is used for food, body parts are used for trophies, medicines, or magical charms. In some instances, the animals are kept for pets. As with products made from tigers, gorilla by-products also fit the CRAVED model. Unless the entire animal is kept for sale as a pet, smaller portions can easily be concealed, transported (removable), and disposed. Furthermore, due to the scarcity of gorillas, they are extremely valuable and desirable. The notoriety of the species has helped to develop a number of capable guardians—ecotour operators, conservationists, biologists, and strangely, rebel fighters, although there has been some speculation that rebels are responsible for recent slaughters.

Workers from the Last Great Ape Project and a television journalist traveled to Cameroon. Hunters[67] offered to kill gorillas for them because they argue that gorillas make for the best bushmeat. Their fee for the slaughter was the cost of the ammunition and the meat. The project workers and journalist were offered the skull, palms, and legs free of charge. According to the workers, abject poverty forced hunters to kill any animal.

Bushmeat, or *night-spinach* in Swahili, is defined as any nondomesticated terrestrial mammal, bird, reptile, and amphibian harvested for food.[68] Those living in or near the forest have depended on the land for sustenance, whether it has been for plants or animals. At issue is the rate at which natural resources are used and consumed. Article 2 of the Convention on Biological Diversity[69] stresses the importance of sustainable use of all natural resources economically, socially, and ecologically. To ignore the sustainability issues runs the risk of decimating a variety of species. Increases in hunting pressures and the loss of habitat greatly impact larger species that have low reproductive rates, like the gorilla.

Studying the bushmeat trade is critical to understanding its impact on the health and welfare of communities. There are issues surrounding this trade that require examination. First, the scale of hunting poses a real threat to many tropical forest species. Second, the depletion of wildlife and forests is closely linked to food security and the economic stability of indigenous people who have extremely limited alternative sources of income and sustenance.[70] Third, research is now demonstrating the health risks surrounding the consumption of and exposure to bushmeat.

Bushmeat is currently not just for local consumption. The commercial trade is supplying the meat to cultures in regional urban areas, as well as to the global market. The bushmeat trade is the biggest threat to primates.[71] The trade is not isolated to range countries where the meat provides sustenance to local communities; the National Geographic Society[72] reports that researchers from the University of California at Berkeley found illegal meat has been discovered in markets in Paris, Brussels, London, New York City, Montréal, Toronto, and Los Angeles. Some species of bushmeat are seen as a necessity for rural villages in some countries, but farther afield it is seen as a luxury item. Expatriates merely believe it to be "home cooking." Urban families consume less bushmeat than their rural counterparts; however, the supply of bushmeat to areas outside rural communities strains the viability of the species. In short, the demand for bushmeat in urban areas worldwide far exceeds rural demand.

Forest dwellers value bushmeat for the protein it provides to their diet, as well as the money they can generate from its sale and trade. Bushmeat has more protein and less fat than most domestic meat. In the Congo Basin, bushmeat hunting contributes between 30 and 80 percent of protein for forest dwelling families.[73] While the majority of calories is provided through agriculture, there is no question regarding the importance of protein in diets. Nowhere is this more evident than the refugee camps in Tanzania, which are filled with displaced citizens from Rwanda, Brundi, Democratic Republic of Congo, and Uganda. Aid agencies estimate the population of these camps to be near 548,000.[74] In the camps, people are turning to bushmeat due to the absence of meat rations that are provided by the international aid agencies. Because meat is lacking in the refugees' diets, many are turning to poaching and the consumption of bushmeat as a solution.

Southwest Cameroon is an extremely complex ecosystem and is home to some of the most endangered species on the globe. Bushmeat consumption in the Congo Basin, while impossible to definitively ascertain, is estimated to range between 1 million to 3.4 million tons per year. It is also estimated that approximately 60 percent of species taken are done so at unsustainable rates.[75]

The bushmeat trade is not yet as lucrative as the overall trade in endangered species, but it is growing, especially in areas with a large expatriate population. Bushmeat derived from endangered species is desired because of the status it carries, thus making it an extreme luxury food item. It demonstrates wealth and connections to those who can obtain it. Estimates of the bushmeat trade value is between US$42 and US$205 million across the West and Central Africa range.[76] From 1995 and 1996, approximately 79 to 90 tons of bushmeat were sold monthly in the areas around the capital of Cameroon, Yaoundé.[77] The overall trade in wild fauna, which includes both legal and illegal varieties of species, is estimated at US$3,581 million.[78] CITES regulates the trade in protected species; however, these are largely traded through the black markets, but endangered species have also been offered openly in various local markets. This practice occurs because there is low risk of enforcement or apprehension. The extent to which bushmeat trade exists worldwide is incredibly difficult to estimate. In the United Kingdom, approximately 12 tons of all types of illegal meat are smuggled into the country each year. Authorities believe that a "significant" proportion of those seizures were from shipments of bushmeat.[79]

The timber and charcoal trade are commercial activities most closely aligned to the illegal trade in bushmeat.[80] The scale of the trade for these two commodities is dependent on the infrastructure. Where logging roads exist, transportation of the bushmeat internally or across borders is much easier—either in concert with logging employees or independent hunters using the roads in an unobstructed manner. This means that the scale of the bushmeat trade can be much larger.

The influence of logging on illegal trade in bushmeat is notable. Habitat is destroyed while providing the mechanisms (roads) by which hunters can get access to animals and the means to transport their kills. Workers in the logging industry fuel the bushmeat trade by either consuming or participating in the trade by offering assistance in the transportation of the goods. These workers are "cash-rich" and can offer local hunters a hefty sum for their meat.[81]

Karl Ammann is a photojournalist who has devoted a large portion of his career trying to raise awareness of the impact of the bushmeat trade on the sustainability of gorilla. He states that, in the Democratic Republic of Congo, logging company employees supply weapons and ammunition to the locals so they can hunt gorilla.[82] In turn, the carcasses are transported to markets via logging company trucks and boats. Additionally, the meat is sold to employees of those companies. The employees of the largest logging company (Société Industrielle et Forestière Congo Allemand, SIFORCO, a subsidiary of Danzer, a large German company) are complicit in these illegal activities. Captains of their watercraft permit the transportation of the illegal bushmeat on their boats. Wives of employees became bushmeat traders, thus perpetuating this illegal activity.

Roads and associated hunting have been shown to reduce the abundance of the number of species, including the lowland gorilla. Male lowland gorillas, the silverbacks, yield the most money to poachers, but their loss is even more devastating to their remaining families. Three silverbacks were found chained at a logging camp, thus depriving their family's protection and breeding capabilities. They were first used as entertainment, then for food.[83]

Ammann's interviews with loggers and hunters in Cameroon revealed that illegal bushmeat is transported via express trains from the north of the country. Stops along the way allowed bushmeat traders to load meat.[84] Along the trek, engineers were coerced to stop before arrival at major cities so traders could unload their goods to be sold at nearby bushmeat markets. Government officials, according to Ammann, went on the record stating that police and Army personnel are involved in the bushmeat trade. Part of their role was to rent weapons to commercial hunters and poachers. Gorilla meat was reportedly eaten weekly and for feasts. One hunter admitted to shooting three gorillas in one morning. Representatives of IUCN at the Dja Reserve, a World Heritage site, confirmed hunters in the southeast Cameroon entering the park and hunting at unsustainable rates. One hunting camp alone supplied 330 pounds (150 kg) of bushmeat within one week. There are approximately 100 of these types of camps inside the park reserve.[85]

The overlap of industries with the illegal bushmeat serves as an example of how routine activities support illegal activities. The daily activities of boat captains, employees, and their wives provide various opportunities for crimes to occur, especially the illegal transportation of illicit goods like bushmeat. These individuals do not have to go out of their way to participate in the illegal trade; rather, their daily routines support their criminal activity. The ease with which bushmeat is transported either via roadways, waterways, or railways provides officials an opportunity to design strategic responses to their illegality.[86]

Because gorillas and humans share approximately 97 percent of the same genetic material, diseases that infect humans can also be transmitted to gorillas. The common cold, while a human nuisance, can be fatal to gorillas. In recent years, reports of groups of gorilla contracting Ebola hemorrhagic fever have been reported.[87] The outbreaks coincided with human infections. Large-scale deaths of the animals were reported in the north of the Congo on the border with Gabon.

In 2004, researchers at Johns Hopkins University[88] released health warnings regarding the consumption of bushmeat. The University's study of bushmeat hunters documented a virus similar to Human Immunodeficiency Virus (HIV) passing from apes to humans through the consumption of bushmeat. Researchers tested over 1,000 hunters and found the retrovirus from the same family of HIV in a large number of the hunters. This study supports previous research hypothesizing that consumption of bushmeat is the likely mechanism by which HIV infiltrated the human population.

More recently, in August 2008, the independent African news agency (*afrol*) reported that the consumption of bushmeat, particularly from great apes, is responsible for breeding a new strain of HIV among humans in Cameroon.[89] According to scientists, viruses can move between the species (primate to human) because of blood contact directly or through consumption of improperly cooked bushmeat. Simian Immunodeficiency Virus (SIV), the primate equivalent to HIV, is said to have mutated into the HIV. Furthermore, warnings were posted about an incident in which a bushmeat hunter tested positive for SIV. This is the only documented incident of its kind and is alarming scientists to the potential for eruption of an entirely new human virus for which there is no existing research or cure.

The Illegal Charcoal Trade

In 2002, mountain gorillas in Rwanda's Volcanoes National Park were violently slaughtered.[90] Two mothers were shot dead for their babies; one of the babies was found lying next to its dead mother and the other one was not found. It was speculated that if the baby was sold, it could fuel the endangered species trade. Before this incident, no killings of mountain gorillas in Rwanda had been reported for the previous 17 years. As a result of these killings, the head of the WWF–UK called for greater penalties for those who hunted and killed the protected animals. The agency also called for more stringent enforcement of CITES in order to curb international trafficking and trade in species. The poachers caught were all from Uganda and were said to be helping the government with the identification of middlemen.

In 2007, news agencies worldwide[91] carried the story that eight mountain gorillas were shot dead in Virunga National Park, a World Heritage site that is situated in the mountainous areas between Rwanda and the Democratic Republic of Congo.[92] This Park is not, however, new to poacher encroachment problems. In 2004, nearly 4,000 acres of prime mountain gorilla areas were cleared by illegal settlers in the same park. In 2006, Congolese militia killed more than 400 hippopotamuses over a two-week period. The Park is home to two rival groups of militia who are engaged in a guerilla war with the Congolese Army. It is also home to poachers and traders in endangered species and in illegal charcoal. The killings prompted UNESCO to send support to the people charged with protecting Virunga National Park and its natural resources.[93] Rangers from the Congolese Wildlife Authority found the animals that were part of a 12-member troop known as the Rugendo Family.

Because none of the body parts were removed from the animals, either for food or trophy, the slaughter was seen as a warning to local conservationists rather than the work of poachers. Rangers and conservationists believed that the slaughter was related to the illegal trade in charcoal (makala), which is used for heating and cooking by millions in the region. Unfortunately, the presence of gorillas is seen as a hindrance to the illegal charcoal activities.[94]

The illegal trade in charcoal and gorillas is connected to Rwanda, which has strong influence in Eastern Congo.[95] Congo's central government is more than 1,000 miles from where the trouble exists; it, therefore, has very little control over illegal activities that are thriving in the area. Rwanda banned the production of charcoal in 2004, but the country does not have sustainable resources within its boundaries to keep up with the demand for charcoal used for cooking and heating. Emmanuel de Merode, the director of Wildlife Direct, a conservation group located in the Democratic Republic of Congo and Kenya, states that the illegal trade in charcoal is estimated to be US$30 million in Goma (population 500,000). In Goma, approximately 110,000 sacks of charcoal are consumed every month simply to prepare food, heat homes, and boil water for drinking.[96]

Director de Merode claims that Congolese military officials are behind the illegal trade in charcoal. Reports show that military members have not been officially paid a salary for many years, so illegal charcoal becomes a viable source of income. To make matters worse, park rangers are driven out of their patrol areas because "military maneuvers" are taking place. Paulin Ngobobo, a lead ranger, does not believe the stated reasons for usurping the patrol of the park rangers; rather, he believes that the rangers are prevented from performing their duties to protect gorillas because the military produces illegal charcoal and because of poaching activities.[97]

Conservation

The Bushmeat Trade

National and international laws that control the hunting and capturing of gorillas exist in all habitat/range countries. Enforcement of these laws remains a significant problem. All species of gorillas are included in Appendix I of CITES and Class A of the African conventions. Conservation areas in range states are mainly housed within the boundaries of national parks and are aimed at reducing the bushmeat trade and protecting the species from disease.

The Jane Goodall Institute[98] maintains that conservation is a complex issue requiring multinational coordination, which must include local communities within range countries, governments, NGOs, and the private sector. According to the Institute, a "conservation crisis" is occurring because of the rapid commercialization and escalation of industry, particularly that of logging and mining, in areas of inadequate local government controls. The root of the problem lies within the host countries. The solution to the "conservation crisis" includes raising awareness, increasing government support, enforcing strong and active law, and creating policy—all which are aimed at reducing illegal commercial hunting of species.

The Jane Goodall Institute has proposed a four-pronged approach in achieving this goal: (1) education, (2) field conservation, (3) public awareness, and (4) advocacy. Community involvement is crucial to the success of conservation efforts. Support from true "stakeholders" in the illegal trade of bushmeat is critical. These stakeholders include hunters, buyers, and sellers. Women play an important role in the bushmeat trade, as they are largely responsible for day-to-day household activities, which include the provision of sustenance for the family. Not only do women have access to wildlife, but they also act as the main market buyers and sellers of bushmeat.[99] It is imperative to develop an understanding of the social causes that fuel the participation of the illegal trade. The responsibility for discovering what driving forces are at play falls firmly upon the shoulders of government, industry, and local officials. Without fully comprehending the underlying causes for the problem, officials run the risk of misplacing valuable efforts and resources.

On a broader scale, the Institute believes that conservation efforts are at risk of failure if they do not address the threats inflicted by global politics, industry, exploitation of resources, population demands, economic greed, and bad/inadequate governance. Conservation efforts, in order to be successful and have impact, must take into consideration the needs of local populations so that they have access to sustainable livelihoods and development. This must be done in a way that also takes into account the heritage and culture of indigenous populations. As with any policy, it must be implemented in a transparent way so that government can be held accountable for conservation/enforcement actions.

There are calls to increase the visibility of the bushmeat trade and its negative consequences.[100] Part of these efforts call for the levels of wild meat consumption to be included in national statistics and to include bushmeat hunting and trade into national planning efforts. Some are proposing the legalization of a portion of the trade.[101] Almost everyone agrees that there must be a national review of law and policy among those countries that are range states for various types of bushmeat. In protected forest areas, rangers and conservation officers must be able to identify hot spot areas for illegal hunting, which will also drive interventions. A helpful measure would be to align the control of the bushmeat trade with other natural resources management programs.[102]

The call for the removal of the stigma associated with the bushmeat trade has been made. Researchers, on behalf of the Secretariat of the Convention on Biological Diversity stated that "the aura of illegality which surrounds all aspects of the trade is unhelpful to the policy process and is preventing a sound assessment of management requirements."[103] Their recommendations neglected to mention how to ensure a way to sustain the high pressure and stigma associated with the illegal trade of protected species that are part of the bushmeat trade. The researchers also do not suggest ways to permit the legal hunting and trading of unprotected species. They naïvely ignore the fact that endangered species are included in the bushmeat trade.

Ebola

Ebola can be transmitted to gorillas via human contact. Vaccination and/or the reinforcement of effective physical barriers can help prevent the introduction or spread of the disease. Stronghold areas not yet affected by Ebola include Dja Conservation complex, Boumba-Bek/Nki Complex in Cameroon, Loango/

Moukalaba-Doudou/Gamba in Gabon, Lac Télé Likouala complex in the Republic of Congo, Sangha Trinational complex of the Republic of Congo, Central African Republic and Cameroon.[104]

Leading conservationists and conservation agencies acknowledge that the remedies for existing threats to gorillas are complex and difficult. This is because of the transnational aspect of the illegal trade and the clandestine nature of poaching and trading. The Ape Alliance[105] recommends that in order for change to occur, retailers and consumers must only purchase timber and charcoal from companies that have their goods certified by independent sources as environmentally responsible. For example, the European Union has recently pressured European companies that have working relationships with companies in West and Central Africa to adopt a code of conduct that ensures activities do not assist in hunting, killing, and trading of protected species. Approaches such as these have the potential to make significant and positive strides in conserving our natural resources, but they must expand well beyond the boundaries of EU countries.

Efforts and Programs

There are a number of conservation tactics pertaining to the Cross River gorilla. Conservation efforts are grounded in the value of education and awareness programs; it is also believed that community involvement is important so that citizens begin to understand the value and the need to protect the species. Because the natural range for the Cross River gorilla spans country boundaries, it is imperative that cross border conservation initiatives are developed. These include joint patrols to control bushmeat trade, as well as hunting practices.

In Cameroon, the Minef-Camrail Bushmeat Project[106] is underway. It is a collaborative effort between the Cameroon Ministry of Environment and Forestry and the Cameroon Railway Company (Camrail). Enforcement of the trade in bushmeat and other wildlife via railroad transportation lines is at the heart of the project. Trade increases around urban centers and around industrial centers.

In 1979, the Gorilla Project began in order to protect the mountain gorilla population in Rwanda. Focusing mainly on antipoaching patrols, the project has evolved into one of the longest running species conservation programs, which is now known as the International Gorilla Conservation Programme.[107] This program is a joint initiative of the African Wildlife Foundation and Fauna and Flora International. The International Gorilla Conservation Programme works to protect remaining populations of mountain gorillas in Rwanda, Uganda, and the Democratic Republic of Congo. Success is dependent on strong working relationships with a number of key international agencies, as well as with the governments of gorilla range states.

The African Great Apes Programme[108] is a conservation project developed by WWF with the aim of protecting four species: chimpanzee, Bonobo, western gorilla, and eastern gorilla. The program has six objectives, which include:

1. protection and management;
2. increase overall community support, which is essential for great ape conservation and is achieved by providing incentives to local populations, as well as reducing human–ape conflict;
3. establishment of conservation policies, strategies, and laws that eliminate ape poaching and unsustainable forest practices;
4. increase capacity within range states to conserve and mange great apes;
5. reduction of illegal national and international trade in great apes and their byproducts; and
6. increase awareness of great ape conservation among community members and government leaders.

After the end of the Congolese five-year civil war (1998–2003), the most significant conservation accomplishment[109] includes the first national conference in the Democratic Republic of Congo, whose aim was to discuss great ape conservation. After the end of the conflict, 630 antipoaching patrols were in existence between May and July 2003 within Kahuzi-Biega National Park, Democratic Republic of Congo. Results included the arrest of 52 poachers and the confiscation of 3 firearms, over 700 snares, and 2 live chimpanzees. For the first half of 2004, antipoaching patrols increased by 68 percent from 238 patrols per month to 477 per month. The Institut Congolais pour la Conservation de la Nature (Congolese Wildlife Authority) had staff operating in the lowland sector of Kahuzi-Biega National Park for the first time since the civil war. Congolese Wildlife Authority recruited new personnel for new ranger posts and now controls roughly 70 percent of the park in contrast to 30 percent in 2003. Despite insecurity and rebel army activity, Congolese Wildlife Authority regularly monitors the population of gorillas.[110]

Volcanoes National Park in Rwanda also has an active antipoaching patrol program.[111] These patrols have increased in number, duration, and area coverage. Nine poachers have been convicted, with some receiving sentences of up to four years incarceration and fines totaling US$400. No incidents of poaching mountain gorilla have been reported in Rwanda since 2002.

Minkebe National Park in Gabon also has antipoaching and surveillance teams in place.[112] The presence of these teams has been reported to reduce the bushmeat trade in that region. In addition, within the Gamba Protected Areas Complex, gorilla-watching activities have been implemented in order to attract tourism to the areas, thus offsetting the loss of income from illegal practices.

In Cameroon, two additional gorilla sanctuaries, one for the Cross River gorillas in the Kagwene Mountains and one for the western lowland gorillas, have been established.[113] Wildlife and human health experts have begun working together to tackle the Ebola problem. As part of their initiatives, awareness programs that address the dangers of eating bushmeat have also been implemented.

Research and conservation depends on regional studies that document illegal trade. Communities must be informed and educated about national wildlife hunting and trading laws. Community-based action plans that address regional environment and development issues dealing with sustainable livelihoods are most successful. National governments are responsible for designing policies, drafting legislation, and developing structures that allow for the implementation of efforts aimed at conserving wildlife. The Jane Goodall Institute also calls for the development of school curriculum that addresses conservation, especially of the great apes.[114]

The illegal trade in vulnerable and endangered species has irrevocable consequences. The most significant consequence is the extinction of these species, in addition to common species becoming rare and potentially vulnerable if no intervention takes place. A second consequence is the perpetuation of illegal activities—the trade itself. Subsistence-based, indigenous communities are at risk because of the delicate balance that exists between humans and the environment. Finally, there is an increased risk of the transmission of potentially fatal disease that can pass between animals and humans.

AFRICAN ELEPHANT (*Loxodonta africana* subsp.) AND ASIAN ELEPHANT (*Elephas maximus* subsp.)[115]

Elephants are the largest land mammals on Earth and are direct descendents of the extinct woolly mammoth. The existing species belong to the *Proboscidea* order, which had about 350 members at its zenith; today, however, only two remain: African elephant (*Loxodonta africana* subsp.) and Asian elephant (*Elephas maximus* subsp.) (see Table 5.2). All others have succumbed to extinction. Unfortunately, the two remaining subspecies of the African elephant—African savanna or bush elephant (*Loxodonta africana africana*) and African forest elephant (*Loxodonta africana cyclotis*)—have been faced with the same fate.

Table 5.2 Elephant Species

Elephas maximus sumatrensis Sumatran Elephant	Habitat	Tropical and subtropical moist broadleaf forests
	Range State	Sumatra, western Indonesia
	Wild Population	2,440–3,350
	Status	Endangered
	Habitat	Tropical and subtropical moist broadleaf forests

Table 5.2 (Continued)

Elephas maximus indicus Indian Elephant	Range States	India, Nepal, Bhutan, Bangladesh, Sri Lanka, Myanmar, Thailand, Laos, Cambodia, Vietnam, China, Malaysia, Indonesia
	Wild Population	20,000–25,000
	Status	Endangered
Elephas maximus maximus Sri Lankan Elephant	Habitat	Tropical and subtropical moist broadleaf forests
	Range States	Southwestern Sri Lanka
	Wild Population	3,160–4,405
	Status	Endangered
Elephas maximus or *Elephas maximus borneenis* Borneo Pygmy Elephant	Habitat	Tropical and subtropical moist broadleaf forests
	Range States	Sabah, Borneo, Malaysia, east Kalimantan, Indonesia
	Wild Population	1,500 or less
	Status	Endangered
Loxodonta africana africana African (Savanna or Bush) Elephant	Habitat	Savanna and woodland environments
	Range States	Angola, Botswana, Burundi, Chad, Eritrea, Ethiopia, Kenya, Malawi, Mozambique, Namibia, Rwanda, Somalia, South Africa, Sudan, Swaziland, Tanzania, Zambia, Zimbabwe
	Population	400,000–600,000 (no separate counts for subspecies)
	Status	Vulnerable
Loxodonta africana cyclotis African (Forest) Elephant	Habitat	Dense broadleaf tropical forests
	Range States	Benin, Burkina Faso, Cameroon, Central African Republic, Congo, Democratic Republic of Congo, Côte d'Ivoire, Equatorial Guinea, Gabon, Gambia, Ghana, Guinea, Guinea-Bissau, Liberia, Sali, Mauritania, Nigeria, Niger, Senegal, Sierra Leone, Togo, Uganda
	Population	400,000–600,000 (no separate counts for subspecies)
	Status	Vulnerable

Due to extensive conservation efforts in recent years, the IUCN has changed the status of both *Loxodonta africana* to vulnerable. IUCN justifies the change in status because of the complexity of the species' range and the ambiguity in census taking. The level of threat, and therefore, its vulnerability status, may well differ in each range country. Populations in southern and eastern Africa have been steadily increasing, thus offsetting the declines in other regions. It is important to note that while overall numbers have increased, population distributions vary in different range states. For these reasons, the African elephant, while only classified as vulnerable, is included in this discussion.

The Asian elephant (*Elephas maximus* subsp.) is classified as endangered by IUCN.[116] This has been determined because over a time period equal to three generations, populations have declined by at least 50 percent.[117] Population trends indicate a continued decrease, which necessitates close monitoring by IUCN, especially with the growing demands for ivory. Gladly, one range area—Western Ghats, India—is showing some slight increases in Asian elephant populations due to conservation effectiveness. IUCN recognizes three subspecies of the Asian elephant: the Sumatran elephant (*Elephas maximus sumatrensis*), the Indian elephant (*Elephas maximum indicus*), and the Sri Lankan elephant (*Elephas maximus maximus*).[118] The different classifications are largely based on slight variations of body size, color, and ear size. The Borneo elephant (*Elephas maximus* or *Elephas maximus borneenis*) is only found on the island of Borneo and has been classified as part of the Sumatran elephant family or included among the Indian elephants. Recently, a discussion has begun about naming the Borneo elephant as a separate subspecies; the IUCN awaits studies that will finalize the categorization.

African Elephant (*Loxodonta africana* subsp.)

Historically, elephants inhabited most of the African continent and were adaptable to a number of diverse climates and environments. Census counts of elephant populations, as with other wild species, are incredibly difficult to conduct and to validate. Scientists believe that several million elephants were alive in the early 1900s. By the 1930s and 1940s, numbers decreased to three to five million. Nearly 80 percent of herds were lost during the 1980s, with approximately 100,000 animals being killed annually.[119] In 1989, the African elephant was placed on CITES Appendix I, thus offering the species protected status. Perhaps, this action came too late as census counts fell to a remarkable 400,000 in the 1990s. In early 2007, the last continentwide assessment was conducted, in which populations were estimated to be between 472,269 and 554,973, with the possibility of being as high as 685,000.[120] It must be said that population estimates can be misleading. As mentioned previously, while the numbers of African elephants are steadily increasing overall, the increases are not constant across all range states. Populations are increasing as much as 7 percent in southern African states such as Botswana, Namibia, and Zimbabwe, but other nations are not so fortunate.

In Africa today, some small range areas exist among larger areas of agriculture and human settlements. It is within these areas that elephant populations are most at risk. Elephants are seen both as economic assets and as detriments. They bring ivory, hides, meat, and tourism to the communities they inhabit; the elephants are used on the front lines of antipoaching patrols. Additionally, the animals are attributed for rejuvenating ecosystems by helping to maintain habitats for other species. Conversely, they ruin crops and stampede living areas, thus increasing human–elephant conflict, which periodically ends in death.

Characteristics[121]

Male African elephants (bulls) grow up to 13 feet (4 m) in height at the shoulder and weigh up to 16,535 pounds (7,500 kg). The elephant's nose develops into a trunk that uniquely identifies the animal. It has large ears and large incisors that grow into tusks in both males and females. Food sources depend on subspecies, but include a variety of plants, grasses, leaves, fruit, and tree bark. Elephants can consume up to 5 percent of their total body weight in a 24-hour period, and they drink 60 liquid gallons (225 liters).

Elephants are social animals that live in matriarchal groups consisting of a mother and her offspring (see Figure 5.7). Male elephants are forced out of the

Figure 5.7 Family of African Elephants. (Jim Gore, University of Tampa)

group when they reach between 10 and 14 years of age, after which they either live a solitary life or one with other lone males. Elephants breed all year, and females are capable of reproduction from age eight, with their fertility period lasting from days to weeks. Gestation ranges from 640 to 650 days. Typically, only one calf is born per pregnancy; however, there are rare instances of the delivery of two calves. Offspring stay with their mothers for up to 10 years. In the wild, elephants can live up to 65 years.

Elephants are highly intelligent animals with reports of them engaging in the usage of tool communication. These include sounds, the use of chemicals for signaling, and touch. One of the unique characteristics of the elephant is their ability to exhibit concern for members of their groups and to display grief for their dead along with their ability to return to distant gravesites. When members of their group are in distress, other will come to their aid.

Habitat and Range States

Today, African elephants exist in 37 range states on the African continent (see Table 5.3). The environment in which these species live varies significantly, and therefore, becomes difficult to catalogue. Generally, savanna elephants live in the savanna and woodland environment, grazing on grasses. Forest elephants, on the other hand, live in dense tropical surroundings. Elephants play both a destructive and productive role in their habitats. Due to their sheer size, they destroy trees, either by stripping them of their bark, leaves, and fruit or by trampling vegetation as they move through an area. The dung left by the animals—an average of 500 pounds per animal each day—is rich in seeds, which are carried by birds to resow the land, enabling vegetation to re-establish. Additionally, in Sri Lanka elephant dung is being collected and processed into stationary paper. Sales from the dung-based paper help to support local farmers, who have been at risk of human–animal conflict.

Table 5.3 African Elephant Range States

Central	Cameroon, Central Africa Republic, Congo, Democratic Republic of Congo, Gabon, Equatorial Guinea
Eastern	Eritrea, Ethiopia, Kenya, Rwanda, Somalia, Sudan, Tanzania, Uganda
Southern	Angola, Botswana, Malawi, Mozambique, Namibia, South Africa, Swaziland, Zambia, Zimbabwe
Western	Benin, Burkina, Faso, Chad, Côte d'Ivoire, Ghana, Guinea, Guinea Bissau, Liberia, Mali, Niger, Nigeria, Senegal, Sierra Leone, Togo

Asian Elephant (*Elephas maximus* subsp.)[122]

The differentiation between the various subspecies of *Elephas maximus* is based largely on body size and slight color variations. In 2008, the Red List classified the Asian elephant as endangered. Main threats to wild and domesticated Asian elephants are exactly the same as their African cousins: disappearing suitable habitats, poaching, and human–animal conflict.

Characteristics

Asian elephants are the largest land mammal in Asia, but smaller in stature than their African cousins. Their ears are smaller with pink patches, while the rest of their body is dark gray to brown with additional areas of pink on their head, chest, and trunk. The head is the highest point of their frame. Both male and female Asian elephants grow tusks; however, the tusks in females are extremely small and largely unnoticeable. A significant number of males do not carry tusks, but this varies by region. For example, 90 percent of males in southern India carry tusks, but only 5 percent in Sri Lanka do. Bulls weigh up to 11,000 pounds (4,990 kg) and stand 8 to 10 feet (2.4 m–3 m). Asian elephants have acute senses including superb hearing, vision, and smell.

Like their African cousins, Asian elephants are extremely sociable, forming groups of six to seven, all of whom are related to the oldest matriarch. Different groups join together to create herds, but these unions are never permanent. The majority of the animals' day is spent foraging for grasses, tree bark, roots, leaves, small stems, fruit, sugar cane, and rice. Their daily intake is approximately 330 pounds (150 kg). The animals always stay near to water, as they need to drink a minimum of once per day.

Both males and females are sexually mature by nine years of age, although females do not engage in sexual activities until age 14 or 15. Because the young female is not dominant in her group, she may not have the opportunity to mate until much later. While conditions dictate actual occurrences, births can take place every 2.5 years to four years if conditions are favorable. If they are not, the time frame can be as long as eight years. Elephants can live to be 100 or more years old.

Habitat and Range States

The Asian elephant's ancestors originated in Africa nearly 55 million years ago. Their original range extended from Iraq/Syria to the Yellow River in China. Today, their geographic region is significantly smaller—ranging from India/Vietnam, with a small population in China's Yunnan Province. Asian elephants are now extinct in most of China, Java, and west Asia.

Asian elephants populations are critically low, with only 25,600 to 32,750 in the wild. The IUCN reports disagreement within the scientific community about the population counts. The research from the IUCN estimates the population to be between 41,410 and 52,345, while other research claims 40,000 to 50,000.[123] There are approximately 16,000 domesticated elephants in Southeast Asia that are used in farming and logging, but they are faced with extinction in the wild. Their habitat consists of fragmented tropical and subtropical moist and dry broadleaf forests. Because of their relatively small frames, these elephants are unable to migrate the expansive distances between their landscapes. There are 13 range states: India, Nepal, Bhutan, Bangladesh, Sri Lanka, Myanmar, Thailand, Laos People Democratic Republic, Cambodia, Vietnam, China, Malaysia, and Indonesia.[124] The Asian elephant is extinct in Pakistan.

Role in Society

This elephant species has a unique role to play in Asian cultures as the actual animals are used in religious and cultural ceremonies. The elephant has spiritual significance in the Buddhist religion where legend states that the mother of the Buddha was only able to conceive after dreaming of a white elephant entering her.[125] This legend provides the foundation for today's practices involving the extremely rare white elephant, which upon certification by Thailand's Ministry of Interior and the Bureau of the Royal Household, elevates the animal to royal status, thus requiring it to be honored as prince after certain ceremonies are performed. The elephant is the symbol of Thailand.[126]

In addition to ceremonial duties, the Asian elephant is extremely important to life in Thailand. India also reveres the Asian elephant.[127] In Indian mythology, gods and demons searched the oceans for the elixir of life in order to become immortal. Through their efforts, nine jewels surfaced that required protection with the elephant being one of those jewels. The elephant is worshipped as Lord Ganesha—the God of Success—to whom people pray for the removal of obstacles in their lives.

Threats—African and Asian Elephants

Threats for both the African and Asian elephants are similar to other species: loss of habitat, poaching; and human–animal conflict.[128] Loss of habitat for both species involves deforestation due to the illegal timber trade, but for the Asian elephant, additional threats exist. Loss of natural land is attributable to competition for scarce resources. Range fragmentation, typical to most endangered animals, is also affecting roaming areas of the elephants. The manmade barriers reduce the gene pool among herds, thus impacting the survivability of the species. National parks and reserves are often too small to sustain a viable population of elephants. Additionally, these parks and reserves meet with human encampments where crops are raided by elephants. As a result, angry farmers kill the offending elephants.

In Asia, the illegal cultivation for Robusta coffee and legal palm oil planta-tions are also robbing the animals of their land.[129] Human–animal conflict is a byproduct of illegal and legal farming practices. As humans encroach into elephant ranges, the animals must explore for replacement food, which results in crop raiding and stampedes on local communities.[130] However, poaching for ivory is the most significant hazard for both the African and Asian elephant.

In the last half of the 20th century, African elephant populations—both the savanna and forest—were decimated, with losses of nearly half their estimated populations in Africa. At that time, the main reason reported for the decline was hunting—both legal and illegal.[131] Elephant meat is rarely eaten. Rather, they are hunted for skins—for leather, and hair—which are used for decorative items such as rings. By far, the most desired commodity offered by the elephant is its ivory, which has been used for a number of centuries for decorative carving and trophies. The ivory trade has been regulated since the elephants' placement on CITES Appendix I and/or II. However, not all trade has been legal, which accounts for the levels of increased poaching since the protective status was issued by CITES.

Elephant by-products do not fit the CRAVED model. Concealing, removing, and disposing of tusks, or unworked ivory is difficult without taking considerable risk. However, once the ivory is worked into figurines, trophies, jewelry, or other desirable items, CRAVED becomes an important component in the analysis of the illegal markets. Elephant hair and meat also fit CRAVED. It must be noted and acknowledged that worked or carved ivory is particularly desired, but ivory in any form keeps the elephants at risk of poaching.

Each year in India, Asian elephants kill approximately 300 people as a result of increased interaction between animals and humans. The WWF estimates that roughly "20% of the world's human population lives in or near the present range of the Asian elephant."[132] Because humans impinge on the land, the habitat of all animals is affected; creating competition for food sources between and among species. The reason for the increase in conflict is relatively simple: human settle-ments are encroaching on the natural rangeland of the elephants. As the animal's food and habitat are diminished, they will naturally search out sustenance, which is most often located within the local boundaries of the communities. Addition-ally, humans become openly aggressive toward intruding elephants. The conse-quences for the elephant of this interaction can be dire. As an example of retaliatory action, in May 2002, a herd of 17 elephants was poisoned after invad-ing an oil palm plantation.[133]

The practice of capturing wild elephants for the purpose of domesticating them for use in industry is not new. Domesticated elephants have been used in Thailand's logging industry for many years.[134] The conditions in which the elephants are kept and within which they work are most accurately described as brutal and inhumane. Accounts of elephants being drugged with amphetamines in order for them to work longer shifts are common.[135] Since the 1998 total ban on logging in Thailand, the practice of drugging elephants to work longer and harder has curtailed, but has not completely stopped. Importantly, Thailand is not the only country that uses elephants as part of the labor force. One saving grace for the animals is ecotourism. Officials are realizing that, rather than working the beasts to death, there is much to be gained by allowing travelers to ride them during their excursions. Moreover, the animals are being used on the front line of the battle to stop illicit trafficking of endangered flora and fauna.[136] For example, ABC News ran a story[137] in 2007 about the impact of the illegal coffee crops on the mortality of wild Sumatran elephants. As a result, the "Flying Squad," a partnership between elephant and man, patrols the edge of the Tesso Nilo National Park in Sumatra. The teams help protect local communities that rely on agriculture, including coffee crops, for their sustenance and income. These patrols help to reduce human–elephant conflict, which in turns help preserve the species.

Live elephants are valuable commodities. Reports indicate that they are exported from Myanmar to other Asian countries, particularly Thailand.[138] However, no official documentation or CITES permits condoning the trade are on record. The process of capturing wild elephants is very dangerous to the animal. A recent WWF study reports that between 1970 and 1993, a total of 2,122 elephants were captured and 18.6 percent of those captured died in the process.[139] Military forces were also cited with capturing wild elephants without obtaining proper authorization.[140] Originally the calf was seen as a financial burden to owners, but today they draw a large number of tourists in Thailand. The price for calves has risen well beyond that for adults, and as such, approximately 50 are trafficked each year.[141] The latest available figures (1997) record the price of a calf as being 125,000 to 150,000 Thai bhats (US $6,000),[142] whereas an elephant that can perform tricks is worth 200,000 Thai baths (US$8,000).[143] The CITES Secretariat recommends to Parties that they not accept imports from Myanmar because the country cannot prove the provenance of the animal or its parts. In other words, officials cannot authenticate that the items are derived from domestic animals rather than those in the wild.[144]

Unfortunately, when privately owned elephants die, they are dissected for their valuable parts. Accounts also exist that healthy animals are killed for the money gained by selling their parts. Still others say that only terminally ill or severely wounded elephants are killed because healthy animals are too valuable for work. Some owners have been known to cut off between 4 and 7 inches (10 to 15 cm) of the animal's tusks in order to protect it from other hunters and to earn extra money from the cut ivory.[145] This, however, is extremely dangerous to the elephant because of the high risk of infection. The important fact to be noted is that banned elephant products are still finding their way into illegal markets, which further increases demand that, in turn, facilitates more killing of the animals. In many Asian countries, there is no domestic legal protection for the elephants. Indeed, some hunters are reported to believe that products derived from domesticated animals are perfectly legal and acceptable.[146]

The Role of Deforestation

Clearing the natural habitat of the elephants presents a real and present danger to their survivability. The main culprits behind deforestation are the international timber trade, the palm oil industry, and illegally cultivated coffee.[147] The international timber trade is exacerbating the lives and well-being of elephants and other species in their respective range states. These animals were initially visible throughout the forests of Central and West Africa, but populations in these areas have seen a decline since colonial times. Remaining numbers are found in small land tracts in protected areas, but are separated from others due to the fragmentation caused by road development. Each year, approximately 4 million hectares of the forests of the Congo are lost due to illegal forest practices including prohibited logging, mineral and oil extraction.[148]

In Asia, domesticated elephants are beasts of burden in farming, the logging industry, and as mounts for antipoaching patrols. The techniques used in capturing the animals in the wild are very crude. As a way to conserve the species, Vietnam, Myanmar, and India have banned the capture of wild elephants for domestic use.[149] The practice, however, continues within the timber industry, with workers capturing elephants to trade on the black markets. Furthermore, the captors badly mistreat the animals when at work in the timber industry even to the point of death.[150]

A considerable problem exists in Indonesia and, perhaps, the problem is no greater than within the Tesso Nilo Forest complex. This area is one of the richest and most diverse in the world. Indonesia, specifically Tesso Nilo, loses about 51 million cubic meters of wood per year, in order to meet demand for plywood.[151] Two large pulp and paper mills exist in the area, and WWF–Indonesia estimates that a significant amount of the timber used in them was illegally harvested. The elephants that inhabit the Tesso Nilo rely on the ecosystem for survival. The destruction of the forest is a virtual death sentence to the herds still remaining in the national park.

China is the world's leader in the consumption of timber and wood-based products. China imports approximately US$20 billion of wood-based products each year.[152] China passed legislation that severely restricts domestic logging in order to protect their natural resources. The legislation, while positive for the Chinese landscapes, has forced China to import timber to meet the country's demands. Unless sustainable use programs are implemented, the demand for timber in China will continue to endanger forests globally.

Additional deforestation problems arise from palm oil production. Palm oil plantations are encroaching on the elephants' natural habitat and, therefore, put the animal at risk on two fronts: (1) the removal of a food source and (2) the decrease of distances between human and animal, which increases the likelihood of human–animal conflict. Human–elephant conflicts occur each day in the areas surrounding the Kinabatanga plantations.[153] Most often, the elephants are either shot or poisoned. For example, Malaysia earns about US$4.5 billion annually from its production of palm oil, which is the largest export business in the world. Palm oil production appears to be far more important to Indonesian authorities than the conservation of the elephant species.

Like the illegal charcoal trade and its negative effect on the tiger population, illegally grown coffee has similar effects on elephants, not to mention tigers and rhinoceroses. Currently, coffee is being illegally grown in Bukit Barisan Selatan National Park, a UNESCO World Heritage site and one of the most important national parks for these animals. The park is located on the southernmost tip of Sumatra Island. According to a report by the WWF,[154] the park has lost nearly 30 percent of its land to illegal Robusta coffee cultivation. Robusta beans are used in European and North American instant coffees. It is estimated that about 20,000 tons of coffee are grown each year. The coffee finds its way into the stocks of multinational corporations, especially if their local traders are not con-scientious about the trade and its implications.[155] In 2004 and 2005, the United States, Germany, Japan, and Italy were the largest importers of coffee tainted with illegal beans. The top three offending companies include Kraft, Taloca, and Nestlé. Because of the illegal practices, a herd of 60 elephants has been decimated to only four. As a result of WWF–Indonesia's report, Nestlé has begun efforts to pay more attention to its supply chain in addition to working with local legal farmers to produce higher quality beans.[156]

Ivory Trade

The demand for ivory is the most readily recognizable threat to both African and Asian elephants. Elephant ivory has been discovered at archeological sites on the Asian and African continents, as well as in Europe, for the past 5,000 years.[157] Today, people worldwide covet the precious ivory, which is why the elephant remains threatened. Most of the illegal ivory seems to come more from African elephants more so than Asian elephants. However, in India and Myanmar, illegal ivory has surfaced in domestic markets to the point that in 2008, Myanmar was named as a main "hot spot" for smuggling.[158] The smuggling, which includes live elephants as well as their parts, is occurring between Myanmar and China and Thailand. Initially, WWF thought that illegal domestic markets, rather than international ones, posed a more substantial threat to the wild elephant popula-tions, but the continuing contravention to CITES may well refuel the international market demands.[159]

Male Asian elephants continue to be hunted illegally for their ivory. Poach-ing remains a very serious threat to the elephants, especially in southern India, where roughly 90 percent of bulls are tuskers, and in northeast India where meat is eaten. Killing large, tusker males and less mature males leaves elephant popu-lations at risk.[160] This selective culling of males interrupts mating opportunities by reducing the number of males necessary to ensure the genetic viability of the herd. A highly skewed male-female population leads to inbreeding, high juvenile mortality, and low breeding success. These critically harm population recovery efforts. For example, in the Periyar Tiger Reserve in southern India, there is one bull to 120 females; as a result, fewer than 30 percent of adult females give birth to a calf.[161]

Myanmar became a signatory party to CITES in 1979. The country has a long history of ivory working. More importantly, Myanmar allows for trade in elephant products derived from domestic elephants.[162] This creates a legal loophole because wild elephant products can be filtered or laundered through legitimate markets. There currently exists no scientific way to distinguish between the legally marketed elephant products and the illegally marketed ones.

Studies conducted in Myanmar on the ivory trade revealed interesting findings.[163] In spite of the various bans on the trade in ivory, domestic and international ivory trading continues. Ivory traders in Myanmar state that their ivory source is India with demand for carved products in Thailand, a major consumer of ivory, largely due to the tourism trade. Weak enforcement controls along the borders of Thailand, Bangladesh, and Lao People's Democratic Republic further promote the illegal importing of ivory from Myanmar.

In 2002, multiple outlets were visited in 11 study sites[164] across Myanmar to determine the extent and nature of the illegal ivory trade. In each of these outlets, ivory and other elephant products were openly traded, and in some locations, live elephants were offered for sale. Border crossings were found to be negligent in their inspection of cargo and in their enforcement of laws protecting elephants. Border points were located at the borders of Thailand, Laos, China, Bangladesh, and India. Consumers vary, but include Thai, Taiwanese, and Japanese tourists who purchase ivory chopsticks because they are believed to be able to detect poisoned food and military officials purchasing carved ivory for gifts.

A 2008 TRAFFIC study[165] of the ivory and elephant trade in Myanmar showed similar findings to the 2002 study. Illegal practices are widespread throughout Myanmar. Local ivory traders are well aware of the legislation and its loopholes; consequently, they are able to exploit the weaknesses of the legislation, as well as those of law enforcement to further their interests.

Ivory trade is not isolated to Myanmar. As with other countries, the wild elephant populations are at risk in Vietnam for the same reasons as with other countries.[166] Vietnam banned the hunting of elephants in 1960 with Directive 134/TTg, and the trade of the animals or their parts with Decree 18/HDBT. The country has been a CITES signatory party since 1994; however, there is no accurate census of elephants in Vietnam.[167] In 1997, Fauna and Flora International estimated the wild population to be approximately 100–160 and the domestic population at 169. These figures represent declines for both wild and domestic elephants. Table 5.4 shows the number of known elephant killings from 1988 to 1999.[168] It must be noted here that, while the quest for ivory is by far the most significant reason elephants are killed, the Asian elephant, like its African cousin, is also killed for other reasons. Table 5.5 describes the medicinal uses of elephants in Asia.

Table 5.4 Vietnam's Wild Elephant Killings, 1988–1999*

Date	Location	Number/Sex	Cause	Case Settlement
1988	Kon Plong	1 female	Illegal hunting	No
	Kon Plong	2 unknown	Illegal hunting	No
1989	Tanh Linh	1 unknown	Human–elephant conflict	Military fine
1990	Que Son	2 males	Illegal hunting	2 year prison
	Duc Lihn	1 male	Human–elephant conflict	No
1991	Que Son	2 males	Illegal hunting	No
	Tan Phu	2 unknown	Human–elephant conflict	No
	Vinh Son	1 male (youth)	Illegal hunting	Community imposed fine
	Tanh Linh	1 male	Human–elephant conflict	No
1992	Xuyen Moc	3 unknown	Illegal hunting	No
1993	Xuyen Moc	1 female	Human–elephant conflict	No
1994	Quy Hop	5 unknown	Human–elephant conflict & Illegal hunting	No
	Thanh Chuong	2 unknown	Human–elephant conflict	No
1996	Tra Mi-Tien Phuoc	1 male	Illegal hunting	No
1998	Tra Mi-Tien Phuoc	1 male, 1 female	Illegal hunting	No
	Krong Bong	1 unknown	Human–elephant conflict	No
1999	Vu Quang	1 unknown	Unknown	No
1999	Cu Jut	1 unknown	Unknown	No

*Reproduced from The Viet Nam Ecological Association, TRAFFIC Southeast Asia, Indochina Office and the Forest Protection Department of the Ministry of Agriculture and Rural Development, "An Assessment of the Illegal Trade in Elephants and Elephant Products in Viet Nam," *TRAFFIC International* 2 (July 2002): 5.

Table 5.5 Medicinal Uses of Elephant Parts

Part	Medicinal Use
Sole of foot	To treat hernias by making a paste from fine pieces when added to water.
Skin	To treat fungal infections by making a paste from fine pieces when added to water.
Tail hair	Made into rings to wear to ward against supernatural attacks. Men can wear to assist in attracting women.
Leg bones	To treat piles when ground and mixed with water to make a paste.
Ivory dust	To treat intestinal diseases when ground into powder and mixed with water.

Chris R. Shepherd, "The Trade of Elephants and Elephant Products in Myanmar," *TRAFFIC International*, no. 5 (August 2002): 1–16, http://www.traffic.org/; and Anon, "An Assessment of the Illegal Trade in Elephants and Elephant Products in Viet Nam," *TRAFFIC International* (2002).

China has long been an avid consumer of ivory, which has been a large part of the country's grand history. The Asian elephant was designated an Appendix I animal in 1976. When the African elephant was upgraded in 1989 to CITES Appendix I creating, in effect, an international trade ban in elephants and their products, China registered a reservation with the CITES Secretariat in order to protect its ivory carving industry.[169] China claimed that the vast majority of their ivory was pre-Convention stock and therefore legally obtained and available for trade. In 1989, China's CITES Management Authority registered 110 importers, exporters, and ivory carving workshops in addition to 110 long tons of raw and worked ivory, which they claimed were pre-Convention stockpiles. In 1991, China rescinded its reservation, which resulted in a total trade ban on elephants and their respective parts.[170]

CITES shows that despite the international ban on ivory, China continues to import, export, and re-export ivory. Between 1991 and 1999, China exported 571 tusks of which 554 were pre-Convention, 1,006,111 ivory carvings, as well as 761 pounds (345 kg) of ivory carvings. In 1990, CITES also reported exports of 9,442,401 ivory carvings. Further, with the increase in the number of safari parks worldwide, the demand for live elephants increased. Table 5.6 shows both exports from and imports of ivory to China. Not all imports were in-line with CITES requirements and incidents were reported of live animals smuggled from Myanmar. Other accounts were deemed to be questionable due to the problematic rationalizations for the export, for example, a shipment of 20 wild elephants from Malaysian "zoos" to outside destinations.[171]

Ivory must be proven to be pre-Convention ivory before it can be imported legally into China. Table 5.7 shows country destinations for both the Asian and African ivory.[172] Data show inconsistencies in what was reported by the various

Table 5.6 Gross Ivory Imports into and Exports from China

Imports	Carvings	Carvings (kg)	Trophies	Tusks	Tusks (kg)
1990	12	9,095	0		
1991	3	0	0		
1992	14	0	0		
1993	4	0	0		
1994	109	0	0		
1995	52	0	0		
1996	4	0	0		
1997	135	0	0		
1998	106	0	0		
1999	0	0	0		

Exports	Carvings	Carvings (kg)	Teeth	Tusks	Tusks (kg)	Ivory Scraps (kg)
1990	9,442,401	2,378	0	1	38	400
1991	1,003,351	30	0	0	0	0
1992	469	95	0	566	0	0
1993	576	0	0	1	0	0
1994	308	0	0	0	0	0
1995	5	0	0	0	0	0
1996	1220	0	5	0	0	0
1997	41	220	0	0	0	0
1998	141	0	0	0	0	0
1999	0	0	0	4	0	0

From CITES annual reports compiled by Caitlin O'Connell-Rodwell and Rob Parry-Jones, "An Assessment of China's Management of Trade in Elephants and Elephant Products," *TRAFFIC International* (July 2002): 14.

countries. Five were reported to be seized in the country of destination.[173] In one particular instance, pre-Convention tusks were reported as coming from Kenya with a final export to Japan, but Japan did not report the importation of these tusks to CITES authorities.

Authorities use customs seizure data as a proxy measure to determine the extent of the illegal trade in elephants. Similar to traditional types of stolen goods data, they are incomplete and inaccurate. However, from available data, China is identified as a "significant consumer of illegal ivory."[174] From January 1998 until September 2001, a minimum of 30 to 45 long tons of ivory were seized en route to China. Additionally, 2,000 elephant skins, equal to approximately 20 animals destined for the TAM industry in China, were seized from Myanmar.

Table 5.7 Destinations and Movement of Pre-convention Ivory Carvings, China, 1992–1999

Year	Destination	Quantity
Exports of PreConvention Carvings *Elephas maximus*		
1992	Japan	11
1993	-	0
1994	Japan	85
1995	-	0
1996	-	0
1997	South Korea	2
1998	Japan	23
1999	-	0
Re-exports of PreConvention Ivory Carvings *Loxodonta africana*		
1992	Hong Kong	423
1993	-	0
1994	-	0
1995	-	0
1996	Japan	1,206
1997	Japan	2
1998	Japan	17
1999	-	0

See Caitlin O'Connell-Rodwell and Rob Parry-Jones, "An Assessment of China's Management of Trade in Elephants and Elephant Products," *TRAFFIC International* (July 2002): 1–55.

In 2001, 10 long tons of skins, representing 260 animals were seized from a TAM company. An interview with a Chinese government official revealed that smuggling of ivory into China was not seen as a problem or a major concern. The discrepancies between perceptions among governmental officials and existing data are indicative of the need to centralize recordkeeping, reporting, and monitoring within China.[175]

From an intervention perspective, there exists a serious problem with TAMs. While they most certainly fit the CRAVED model, but it is extraordinarily difficult to determine that the products are, indeed, made from endangered species. Without scientific analysis, it will be impossible to discern if endangered species are a component ingredient. Officials are trained in the identification of various species in their natural state, but chemical analysis must be performed on powdered forms.

The carving industry is in decline, but main buyers have long been, and continue to be, Chinese nationals in larger cities like Shanghai, Guangzhou, and Beijing. China also has strong trade links with African nations, which may be facilitating the illegal ivory trade.[176] The vast majority of ivory seized is said to originate from African elephants. Additionally, diplomats of the government of the Democratic People's Republic of Korea have been involved in a number of large-scale ivory smuggling cases. There is little evidence that North Korea has a carving industry; rather, diplomats stop over in Beijing on their way home,[177] and ivory exchanges hands during these layovers.

While China has several legal instruments in place, enforcement is extremely weak. There has been no monitoring of ivory stocks since 1989, and there appears to be no required permit to sell ivory in spite of the hunting ban.[178] Currently, there is no way to determine if the ivory is pre- or post-Convention and no way to determine what happens to confiscated ivory. A relatively weak domestic demand for ivory exists in China, however, the country has very strong links with Africa. Nearly all seizures in China emanated from Africa through trade links and diplomatic missions taking place in over 35 countries, 30 of which are elephant range states.[179] Additionally, the expatriate Chinese community living in African nations appears to be active in the illegal trade in ivory. For example, 331 pounds (150 kg) of illegal ivory were seized in Belgium on its way from Africa to China in 2004. Fifteen members of the Chinese Medical Mission in Mali were involved.

Range countries in Africa are some of the most deprived in the world. The developing nations across Africa, except the sub-Saharan region, have the lowest Human Development Index in the world. Population projections estimate that Africa's population will reach 1.5 billion by 2031.[180] Currently, the vast majority of countries in Africa are primarily agrarian. Agriculture and farming provide two fundamental functions: food and income. Elephants relate to this in a number of ways. They represent a danger to crops, and therefore to food and money, but they are a source of revenue, as well. Ivory, meat, skin, and hair are all valuable commodities from the dead animal. Ivory is, however, the most valuable and demanded. Research shows that the demand for ivory is directly related to the decline in populations.

As a result, the plight of the African elephant became one of the first species to draw international attention. Conservationists around the world highlighted the need for protection, action, and, of course, funding. By 1989, the international community began drafting legislation to ban the importation of raw ivory. Even with legislation in place, demand for ivory remains constant. In 1997, TRAFFIC[181] reported that seven years after the international trade ban, the illegal trade in elephant ivory and other parts continued in the Far East. South Korea and Taiwan were then the prominent major illicit markets, but interestingly, the majority of illegal ivory emanated from Africa.

Approximately 70 percent of the African elephant's range is unprotected land, but lands where the largest elephant populations are located are in countries that actually offer legal safeguards. Levels of this protection vary, however, from country to country, largely because the animals in each country are faced with different threats. As an example, sport hunting is permitted in some range states but banned in others.

Populations have recovered dramatically in some range countries so that controlled culling and ivory stock sales have been permitted by CITES. Because of the increases in elephant populations in some of the southern nations, CITES relegated the African elephant in 1989 to Appendix II in Botswana, Namibia, South Africa, and Zimbabwe. CITES gave permission to hold sales of stockpiles of ivory in 1999 to Botswana, Namibia, and Zimbabwe.[182] A second sale was approved for Botswana, Namibia, and South Africa in 2002, but by the end of 2006, conditions set for the sale were not met, so the sale by CITES has not yet occurred.

The conservation community has openly criticized these one-off sales because of the fear that the legal sale of ivory stockpiles merely fuels the worldwide demand that stockpiles will not be able to satisfy. This would then set the vicious cycle in motion beginning with illegal killings, thus jeopardizing many years of successful conservation efforts. Research[183] on the effects of the post-ban period challenged some of the conventional wisdom. The CITES ban did indeed allow elephant populations to grow, but the increases were not consistent across all African elephant ranges. Rather, countries that continued to lose elephant populations post-ban were those that had unregulated ivory markets. Additionally, countries bordering those with unregulated markets also experienced losses due to poaching. The vast majority of population losses (75%) occurred in five countries.[184]

Conservation

African Elephant (Loxodonta africiana subsp.)

Conservation efforts are focused in two main areas: habitat management and law enforcement. Successful conservation is a double-edged sword. Because of the sheer size of the animal, increases in populations can put enormous pressure on the animal's habitat. A holistic approach, as with other species, offers the most promising outcomes. Securing habitat and maintaining the connectivity between fragmented parts is essential to the survival of the species. If the land is managed properly, reductions in human–elephant conflicts can be realized. Range countries must strengthen domestic legislation pertaining to elephant conservation, as well as increase their ability to adhere to international conventions. Related to the legal aspects, law enforcement practices must be improved and enhanced so that field patrolling and reducing illegal markets become the focus.

In 2000, the WWF implemented the African Elephant Programme. The aim of the program is addressing the threats to the species in targeted field projects.[185] The scope of the program was quite extensive and included training over 400 African professionals on population management, identification and establishment of protected areas, implementation of antipoaching patrols in protected areas, as well as the creation of monitoring systems like the Monitoring Illegal Killing of Elephants (MIKE) and the Elephant Trade Information System

(ETIS), creation of census procedures, and conducting studies on the illegal ivory trade in six African states.

The WWF reported[186] increases in populations in Kenya, Tanzania, and South Africa–all of which were supported by the agency. The program's goal is to ensure that elephant populations and habitats are stable or increasing in 20 landscapes. The program aims to accomplish much of the same outcomes as other conservation projects: develop useful laws and policies aimed at mandating the protection of the species, manage land areas as a way to allow habitat areas to reconnect, reduce poaching, reduce illicit market of elephant products, reduce human–animal conflict, and develop local communities. The fact that these landscapes do cross geopolitical boundaries confounds conservation efforts. Work by NGOs, government agencies, wildlife and park officials, the logging industry, and ecotourism must be a combined, effective and coordinated effort.[187]

Asian Elephant (Elephas maximus *subsp.*)

The year 2008 was an instrumental one in the fight against illegal logging. First, as a way forward in efforts to protect elephant landscapes (and those of other protected animals), the Indonesian government agreed to increase the size of Tesso Nilo National Park. Just 20 years previously, the forest covered approximately 500,000 hectares, but today less than 150,000 remain, of which only 38,576 hectares are protected areas. In 2008, the Indonesian government agreed to expand the protected area of Tesso Nilo to 100,000 hectares.[188] This, no doubt, will have tremendous impact on the preservation of elephants, and tigers, among other endangered or threatened species.

Second, the United States became the first nation worldwide to ban the importation and sale of illegally sourced wood and wood-products.[189] Illegal timber trafficking reduces wood prices by between 7 and 16 percent worldwide. The reduction in prices is estimated to cost the industry US$10 billion each year in addition to the US$5 billion lost by governments in revenue.[190]

Efforts such as these, coupled with improved domestic practices, will enhance efforts to save the species. Myanmar is home to the second largest population of Asian elephants in Asia.[191] Early 1980 population estimates ranged from 3,000 to 10,000, while in 1995, the populations were thought to have dwindled to 5,000–6,000. The country also is home to the largest domestic, privately owned, Asian elephant population (5,000–6,000) used in the logging industry. In 1995, the practice of capturing live elephants was banned totally, but it is thought to still continue.

Myanmar's efforts to protect the elephant can be traced back to 1879 when the government, under British rule, first regulated the capture of wild elephants. In 1902, the Burma Forest Act stipulated that preservation was the responsibility of the Forest Department. In 1994, the Forest Department implemented the Protection of Wild Life and Wild Plants and Conservation of Natural Areas

Law, which allows for fines up to 50,000 Burmese kyat (US$135) and/or up to seven years in prison for the capture of wild elephants. The law punishes the illegal possession, sale, or export of protected species and their parts, including ivory, but the law does not cover government-owned ivory.[192]

Monitoring Systems: MIKE and ETIS

In 1997, at the 10th CITES' Conference of Parties, elephant populations in Namibia, Zimbabwe, and Botswana were healthy enough to be downgraded to CITES Appendix II.[193] These countries sought and received permission for a one-off, experimental sale of stockpile ivory. Under certain conditions, 109,292 pounds (49,574 kg) of ivory was auctioned off to Japan in 1999.[194] The request for the experimental sales prompted a great debate during this Conference of Parties. One side believed that controlled sales were the only effective way to prevent the illegal trade in ivory, whereas the other took the view that controlled sales would actually increase demand, resulting in increased poaching. The consensus was that zero-tolerance was the only option.

During the 10th Conference of Parties, two monitoring systems were implemented in order to determine if elephant poaching and illegal trade were affected by the changes that CITES made by lifting some of their restrictions. The MIKE program was a site-based initiative that identified trends in illegal elephant killings in order to assess factors that precipitated the killings, as well as to determine if these factors were correlated to the changes within CITES.[195] As part of the initial implementation of MIKE, standardized data capturing systems were designed so data would be standardized at the various sites. MIKE areas are diverse in the level of concern shown to conservation efforts, levels of human activities, and the extent to which they suffer from civil unrest. These challenges are other measurable external factors that impact elephant populations and their monitoring. Other data collected include changes in elephant behavior, migration patterns, numbers of poaching camps, and changes in hunters' profiles. Information is collected via aerial and dung surveys, ground patrols, intelligence reports, patrol reports, and annual reports. At the time of this publication, MIKE data do not link an increase in poaching with the one-off sales of African ivory.[196]

The objective of the ETIS is to track current trends of illegal ivory trading through the use of law enforcement data on seizures.[197] ETIS aims to determine if and to what extent observed trends are a result of changes in listing of elephant populations in CITES Appendices, which will help in determining whether to resume the legal international sales in ivory. ETIS evolved from a TRAFFIC database, Bad Ivory Database System, which collated law enforcement records for ivory seizures or confiscation worldwide since 1989. Parties were mandated to report seizure information through the ETIS within 90 days of the actual seizure. ETIS recognizes the urgent need for regulation and enforcement. For example, China only officially reported two seizures of illegal ivory to CITES via ETIS between 1998 though the time of this publication. ETIS establishes co-ordination between relevant agencies in order to share information and activities pertaining to the illegal trade in elephants and their parts. ETIS also established a centralized Wildlife Crime Unit.[198]

ETIS defines and clarifies responsibilities for relevant government agencies in relation to the storage and disposal of stockpiled ivory and with regard to laws and regulations of sales.[199] ETIS recommends that each party adopt comprehensive internal legislation and regulation, as well as effective enforcement strategies. Activities outlined by ETIS include creation of registers and licenses for importers, manufacturers, wholesalers, and retailers that deal in raw or semi-worked ivory products. ETIS also wants parties to develop inspection procedures so that CITES Management Authorities can effectively monitor. ETIS also provides a training function for countries in order to help them implement their strategies for raising awareness about the trade, CITES regulations, and national legislation. It also calls for the reduction in the number of ports that can legally import and export wildlife. While ETIS is a step forward in efforts to protect elephants, it is very clear from research conducted by TRAFFIC in various countries that more illegal seizures are taking place than is being reported through either ETIS or the MIKE processes.[200]

6 ━━━

Marine Species

THE EARTH'S SURFACE is comprised of approximately 71 percent water, which is divided into five oceans: Pacific, Atlantic, Indian, Southern, and Arctic. Within these waters are innumerable species, some of which have yet to be discovered and some which are in need of international protection due to their threat of extinction. Conservationists and enforcement officials are faced with extraordinary challenges when dealing with marine life. Many species migrate through nearly all ocean waters, crossing numerous national and international boundaries. International treaties, such as CITES and the CMS, do offer protection for marine species; however, due to the nature of ocean-based species, these treaties are difficult to monitor and enforce. Of particular interest in this chapter are the case studies of endangered or vulnerable marine fishes and mammals. Specifically, this chapter will describe the situations of the great hammerhead shark (*Sphyrna mokarran*), the great white shark (*Carcharodon carcharias*), the whale shark (*Rhincodon typus*), and the beluga sturgeon (*Huso huso*). Each of these species are threatened with extinction due to the illegal activities on the part of humans. For each of the listed species, trade routes, reasons for threat, and proposed recovery programs will be discussed.

SHARKS

Sharks have been part of Earth's ecosystem for approximately 400 million years, which is roughly 100 million years before dinosaurs roamed the Earth. Sharks inhabit virtually every ocean and have extremely important roles in marine ecosystems. They are apex predators which means they are at the top of their food chain with no other higher predators except, for perhaps, the killer whale (*Orcinus orca*). Being apex predators, they help maintain the balance of ecosystems worldwide. If sharks continue to be overfished, healthy ocean biodiversity is at risk. Unfortunately, unless current practices are reversed, scientists are predicting that some shark species may become extinct before their vital role is truly understood and appreciated.[1]

Research on the exact nature and role of the shark is scarce. Marine scientists know, however, that the presence of sharks is critical to marine health.

The depletion of the species may alter the numbers of other species, which, in turn, has unpredictable consequences on the entire, delicate ecosystem. The balance of species, especially apex predators, affects not just the animals' food chains, but those of humans as well. For example, the decrease in sharks in the Caribbean resulted in the degradation of coral reefs. There were fewer sharks to eat carnivorous fish, so their numbers increased, which led to their increased capacity to attack herbivore fishes, which left none to clean the coral; therefore, algae invaded the coral, eventually killing it. As a result, humans were left with decreased fish stock capacity for sustenance fishing.

Aside from their value in the ecosystem, sharks play an important part in the lives of many people. Traditional fishermen in coastal communities in the Indian states of Andhra Pradesh and Tamil Nadu rely on shark for food, but they have reported significant declines in shark catches for a number of years.[2] Commercial vessels were the source of the serious decline, and finning was the driving force behind their work. In Kenya, roughly 6,500 artisanal fishermen account for 80 percent of the country's marine catches. Sharks are a valued source of meat, which is consumed locally. Fisherman and dealers in Kenya also report serious decline in the amount of their shark landings. They blame the commercial longliners and shrimp trawlers that bring in enormous numbers of shark as bycatches. Without alternative food sources, villages will simply starve. In Mexico, sharks provide nutrition to the poorest communities and, without them, many would suffer the effects of malnutrition or starvation.[3]

Furthermore, sharks still carry cultural significance. In Hawai'i culture, the shark (mano) is considered to be a guardian angel (aumakua) who guides paddlers back to shore in bad seas.[4] In Vietnam, the whale shark, also known as the lord shark, is given sacred burials upon its death.[5] In Fiji, high chiefs were thought to be direct descendents of shark gods (dakuwaqa).[6] In parts of Senegal, sharks are considered harmless to humans. If a shark does attack a human, it is considered to have been invaded by evil spirits as it would not have done so of its own volition.[7]

In 1974, Peter Benchley published a book titled *Jaws*—a story about a maniacal, man-eating, great white shark that methodically hunted humans. The story, which was later made into a blockbuster movie, permanently placed into the minds of an entire generation that sharks were to be feared and that if one dared to swim in the ocean, the swimmer was fair game to any shark that was lurking just beyond the sand bar. In reality, humans have a higher probability of being struck by lightning than being attacked by sharks. Attacks on humans are largely due to mistaken identity on the part of the shark. The shark simply wrongly interprets the human's presence as that of another marine species and attacks. In 2008, the International Shark Attack File reported that the number of shark attacks declined for the fifth year in a row. They investigated 118 alleged shark attacks on humans *worldwide* in 2008. Of these 118, it was determined that only 59 were confirmed as "unprovoked" attacks, which are defined as "incidents where an attack on a live human by a shark occurs in its natural habitat without human provocation of the shark."[8] Just think about how many thousands of miles of beaches are frequented by swimmers, windsurfers, skiers, and others who use the oceans throughout the world—59 is thus insignificant when compared to the number of people who use the oceans and seas as their playgrounds.

This rise in the fear of sharks spurred a rise in the mentality of "kill the shark before the shark kills us." While much has been done in the years since the movie release of *Jaws* to dismiss the many myths generated from the book and movies, there is still much to do. Trying to determine how many and which species of sharks are protected by the various international conventions is incredibly complicated. Perhaps, it is due to the nature of the animal itself being highly migratory in nature, but it most likely is due to the fact that efforts are regionalized. Tagging programs help scientists identify some sharks and therefore, help "count" them for conservation purposes; however, it begs the question—for every shark tagged, how many are left anonymous?

Unless specific varieties of sharks are tagged so that they can be monitored continually, researchers can never definitively know if they have routines for hunting, mating, or simply living. This lack of knowledge affects the ability to assess their routine activities, in order to begin collecting data for the construction of crime reduction tactics. Alternatively, fishermen worldwide may indeed have routines, which may serve well as a proxy for the routines of various shark species and which may well be worth exploring in order to monitor shark activities.

IUCN Status

The IUCN's Shark Specialist Group was developed in 1991 by the IUCN's Species Survival Commission in order to take leadership on the global growing concern about sharks.[9] Members include expert scientists, policy makers, and fishery management personnel. Their mission is to:

> promote the long-term conservation of the world's sharks and related species (the skates, rays, and chimaeras), effective management of their fisheries and habitats, and, where necessary, the recovery of their populations.[10]

The IUCN categorizes sharks into six manageable lists: pelagic,[11] migratory, deep sea, Mediterranean, northeast Atlantic, and Australasian. Statistics are reported for each of these categories, but what is not clear and consequently complicates the overall picture, is whether or not these categories are mutually exclusive. For example, we have no clear idea whether the great white sharks listed and counted in the migratory list are again counted in the pelagic list and, yet again, in the Australasian list. This type of shark appears in each of the other category types.

These methodological issues are of great concern in terms of research validity; however, a clarification could not be found, so the numbers as they are reported are reproduced here in order to give some indication of the scale of the conservation problem. It must be stressed that these "counting" issues raise serious problems for conservationists. In order for strategies to be deemed successful, accurate baseline accounts are needed of the state of the animals' condition in nature. The Shark Specialist Group is making great strides, but there is still much work to be done.

Table 6.1 shows the distribution of the Red List status of the various categories of the Shark Specialist Group's shark categories. One important thing to note is that many species lack sufficient data to make the necessary determination as to a species' status. No doubt, it will be many years before more definitive knowledge is advanced. Table 6.1 shows that the vast majority of those sharks studied are not considered endangered or critically endangered. Furthermore, the data provide a window of opportunity for conservationists to concentrate efforts on those species, as well as those considered near threatened or even those in the category of least concern.

This is not the only picture painted regarding sharks. To further complicate the issue, the Shark Specialist Group also produced another set of figures that states of all the shark species, on a global scale, there are 10 critically endangered, 9 endangered, 31 vulnerable, 62 near threatened, 84 least concern, and 115 data deficient (311 total). No matter what set of statistics is consulted, it becomes clear that between 20 and nearly 50 percent[12] of each category is vulnerable, endangered, or critically endangered. Again, this provides conservationists, fishing management authorities, and policy makers a prime opportunity to make change in order to save these extremely important fishes.

In spite of the fact that there are a number of shark species categorized as critically endangered, endangered, or vulnerable, there are only three shark species offered international protection. While there appears to be some misrepresentation in the literature, these species are listed by CITES in Appendix II: the basking shark (*Cetorhinus maxiumus*), the whale shark (*Rhinocodon typus*), and the great white shark *(Carcharodon carcharias).* Additionally, these same three sharks are listed for protection in the CMS.

While there are efforts underway to list more shark species, efforts are hampered by the politics that surround CITES, the CMS, and the special interests of their member parties. The plight of the shark perfectly illustrates the discord among scientists, conservationists, and the quasi-governmental agencies tasked with protecting species. Expert scientists compile the IUCN Red List, which identifies species under threat, through their research. Clearly, the Red List has listed the numerous shark species as needing protection to varying degrees; however, signatories of CITES and CMS have only agreed to list three! There is an obvious need to rectify politics with science for the sake of the animals. There is simply no acceptable logic for having so many animals listed scientifically as

Table 6.1 Global Red List Status of Condrichthyans[*], 2008

	Critically Endangered	Endangered	Vulnerable	Near Threatened	Least Concern	Data Deficient	Total
Pelagic	0	4	16	15	12	17	64
Migratory	8	4	26	22	7	13	80
Deep Sea	4	1	11	23	56	145	240
Mediterranean	5	4	7	12	3	4	35
Northeast Atlantic	4	6	20	21	34	31	116
Australasian	4	6	24	52	71	59	216

[*]Includes sharks, skates, rays, and chimaeras
Source: WildAid, *End of the Line?: Global Threats to Sharks*, (WildAid, 2007). Also available online at http://na.oceana.org/sites/default/files/o/fileadmin/oceana/uploads/Sharks/EndoftheLine_Spread_sm.pdf

critically endangered, endangered, or vulnerable and, yet, only three are afforded political and legal protection.

Characteristics, Uses, and Types

All sharks are built on a skeleton of cartilage. They have many senses: hearing, sight, touch, smell, taste, balance, and electrosense. The latter allows the animal to feel vibrations along a lateral line and pit organs. Sharks have no gills or scales; rather they have denticles that are tiny toothlike ridges that protect the skin. The shark's infamous teeth are attached to its jaw and are replaced continuously throughout its life.

Sharks have many uses. Their meat is consumed in nearly every country worldwide. Liver oil from the shark is used as a lubricant, in cosmetics, and in vitamin A. There are claims that shark cartilage has medicinal uses; although, those claims are unfounded. Sharkskin is used as leather; and jaws and teeth are oceanside tourist curios.

Great Hammerhead or Squat-headed Hammerhead Shark
(Sphyrna mokarran)

The great hammerhead shark is classified as endangered by IUCN, but it is *not* included in CITES nor is it included in the CMS.[13] The great hammerhead is a widely distributed tropical shark that is a costal-pelagic and semi-oceanic species largely restricted to continental shelves.[14] These sharks are also found in island terraces and in passes and lagoons of coral atolls, as well as over deep water near land.[15] Great hammerheads are found in depths of three feet to more than 262 feet (1 to 80m), as well as at the surface.[16]

The great hammerhead shark is recognized easily due to the unique hammer-shaped head and its first dorsal fin, which is very tall and curved. The shark's color ranges from dark olive green to gray on top and white below. The shark grows to between 18.3 feet (5.6 m) to 20 feet (16.1m). Most of those encountered are said to be between 10 and 14 feet (3 to 4.3 m). Females mature at a length of 8.2 to 9.8 ft (2.5 to 3m); males mature at a length of 7.7 to 8.8 ft (2.3 to 2.7 m).[17] Litter sizes range from 6 to 42 pups after an 11-month gestation. Their size at birth ranges between 19.6 to 27.5 inches (50 to 70 cm).

The range description of the great hammerhead shark is difficult, but the IUCN describes it as being widely throughout the tropical waters of the entire world from the latitudes of 40°N to 35°S. Some populations, due to their migratory nature, have been seen off the coast of Florida and in the South China Sea. Hammerheads are widespread in the southwest Indian Ocean. In South Africa, they are confined to the KawAulu-Natl coast. Breeding grounds also exist in the coastal mangrove estuarine area of southern Belize.[18] Countries where the hammerhead is present in their waters include Algeria, Anguilla and Barbuda, Aruba, Australia, Bahamas, Bangladesh, Belize, Brazil, British Indian Ocean Territory, Cambodia, Cape Verde, Cayman Islands, China, Costa Rica, Cuba, Djibouti, Dominica, Dominican Republic, Ecuador, Egypt, El Salvador, Eritrea, French Guiana, French Polynesia, Grenada, Guadeloupe, Guatemala, Guyana, Haiti, Honduras, Hong Kong, India, Indonesia, Iran, Iraq, Israel, Jamaica, Japan, Jordan, Kenya, Kuwait, Libyan Arab Jamahiriya, Macao, Madagascar, Malaysia, Martinique, Mauritius, Micronesia, Federated Sates of Montserrat, New Caledonia, Nicaragua, Oman, Pakistan, Palau, Panama, Philippines, Pitcairn, Puerto Rico, Qatar, Senegal, Seychelles, Somalia, South Africa, Spain, Sri Lanka, Sudan, Suriname, Taiwan, Province of China, Trinidad and Tobago, Tunisia, Turks and Caicos Islands, United Arabs Emirates, United Republic of Tanzania, United States, Venezuela, Vietnam, and Yemen.[19]

This lengthy list of countries illustrates the vast area these fish are capable of traveling. The enormous distance has implications for illegal trade, as well as conservation.

Great White Shark (Carcharodon carcharias)

The great white shark is perhaps the most well-known of all the shark species. It is this shark that Peter Benchley immortalized in *Jaws*. Of all the shark species, the least is known about this particular one. It was last assessed by IUCN in 2005 and is currently categorized as vulnerable and is included in CITES Appendix II.[20] It is also listed in the CMS Annex I and II.

Great white sharks are the largest apex fishes in the oceans. This shark has been recorded to reach lengths of up to 23.6 feet (7.2 m) long and 5,000 pounds (2,268kg) in weight.[21] It has a heavy, torpedo-shaped body with a conical-shaped snout and coal-black eyes. The great white gets its name from the color of its under-belly; however, tones vary from blue-gray to gray-brown on the upper part of the fish. Total gestation time is unknown, but is thought to be as long as one year. Pups are born live and range from 47 to 59 inches (120–150 cm). Females are thought to reproduce every two years.[22]

The great white sharks have one of the widest geographic ranges known among any of the marine species. They are found in cold water and tropical temperature waters 60°N latitude to 60°S latitude.[23] Their migration patterns are of great interest to scientists. For example, scientists tracked a female across the Indian Ocean from South Africa to Australia and back for over 12,427 miles (20,000 km) in just a nine-month period![24] The great white's range states include Albania, Algeria, Australia, Bahamas, Barbados, Bosnia and Herzegovina, Brazil, Chilé, Croatia, Cyprus, Egypt, France, Gibraltar, Greece, Israel, Italy, Japan, Kenya, Lebanon, Libyan Arab Jamahiriya, Madagascar, Mauritania, Mauritius, Montenegro, Morocco, Mozambique, Namibia, New Caledonia, New Zealand, Philippines, Seychelles, Slovenia, South Africa, Spain, Sri Lanka, Syrian Arab

Republic, Tunisia, Turkey, United Republic of Tanzania, United States, and Western Sahara.[25]

Whale Shark (Rhincodon typus)

The whale shark is the largest marine species known. At maturity, it can reach up to 29.5 feet (9 m) in length. The size of the whale shark at birth ranges between (22.8 and 25 inches) (58 and 64cm) respectively. Whale sharks are the most fertile of the shark species; one pregnant female had a litter of over 300 individuals.[26] The whale shark can grow up to 45.9 feet (14 m) in length. They have very long migration patterns—covering up to 14.9 miles (24 k) per day and over 8,000 miles (13,000 km) in a 37-month period.[27]

The color of the whale shark ranges from blue-gray to gray-brown with a "checkerboard" pattern of lines and spots on the dorsal (upper back) and side of the animal's body. The belly of the shark is white. It is a distinctive looking shark with its extremely wide mouth that acts like a huge filter. The whale shark has a markedly different diet than its shark cousins, consisting primarily of phytoplankton, macroalgae, plankton, krill and small nektonic life, such as small squid or vertebrates.[28]

The IUCN classifies the whale shark as vulnerable; it is listed in Appendix II of CITES and on the CMS.

Threats

Because sharks are apex predators, they have few natural enemies other than humans. While there are some reported uses for shark parts, such as cartilage for arthritis[29] and jaws and teeth for tourism trade—the main threat that sharks face is illegal, unreported, unregulated fishing, all for the practice of finning. They are either victims of bycatches or targeted specifically by fisherman for their fins due to the high demand in Asian markets for shark fin soup.

Finning, at its simplest, is an extremely cruel practice. Sharks are caught; fins are cut off and most times the sharks are thrown back in the water while still alive (see Figure 6.1). Many in this multibillion dollar industry *wrongly* believe that fins will grow back, but this is absolutely not true. Without fins, sharks cannot swim and therefore, they simply sink and drown. It is not only cruel, but it is wasteful to kill the shark merely for its fin when it can be dissected for meat and liver oil.

Shark by-products may be a challenge to assess using the CRAVED model. Primarily, sharks are taken for their fins, but other parts are sold in the tourist markets. Individual teeth would be easily concealable. Given the fact that in an average lifespan a shark will produce approximately 20,000 teeth, shark teeth are abundant and found in beach tourist shops around the world. Therefore, teeth are easily removable and available. However, because of their abundance, their value is relatively low. They are enjoyed for their novelty as jewelry or trinkets. Since they are readily for sale, their disposability is hardly an issue.

Figure 6.1 Cutting off the Caudal Fins of a Silky Shark (*Carcharhinus falcitormis*); Some with Cut-off Noses on Beach, Manta Ecuador, March 2007. (© Oceana/LX)

The circumstance around a shark's jaw is different. It is possible to identify a jaw to a specific species, as with teeth, but their CRAVED elements pose unique issues. Due to their size, illegal traffickers of these endangered species are very innovative in how they move their products from range through to consumer. Concealability becomes problematic, but not impossible in terms of transportation. It can take a different form in terms of trying to conceal the exact species from which the jaw was taken. DNA tests would be helpful in these circumstances. As with shark teeth, there are varying degrees of value and enjoyment, and as overfishing takes place, the availability of shark jaws will continue to increase.

Fins are of a completely different concern. The value of shark fins is correlated with the social importance of the soup in Far Eastern cultures. Fins will be cut from live sharks so long as there is a healthy demand for the soup's ingredient. One fin is relatively concealable, but the enormous volumes of fins that are taken are conspicuous in the drying phase and in the shipping phase. Fins are easily removable as part of the landing process; they are simply cut off on the boat or deck. Moving the fins from landing area to that for drying purposes is perhaps more complicated. Their value and desirability are unmistaken. Because of their high demand, a strong market exists so, therefore, their disposability is guaranteed.

Shark Fin Soup

Shark fin soup or *yu chi* is also known as fish wing soup in China and has long been a delicacy of the elite classes of Asian cultures. In China, it has been served since 960–1279 CE and was included in formal banquets through the Ming dynasty from 1368 to 1644.[30] Today, the boom in the Chinese economy has brought the dish of the rich and powerful to the tables of the masses. Banquet tables of new brides and businessmen throughout Asia are dotted with bowls of shark fin soup. This alone is giving rise to the slaughter of tens of thousands of sharks annually. In today's Chinese society to not serve shark fin soup is to risk losing face. The dish signifies affluence, position, and prestige and is a deeply rooted part of the culture.

Shark fin soup is favored for its thick, slippery texture that is provided for by the cartilage within the fin itself. The large dorsal fin is the preferred and the most expensive, followed by the tail, and lastly, the pectoral or side fins, which results in the cheapest soup. Harvesting the fins is a multistage process. The skin, cartilage, and attached meat are removed, whereas the fine fibers or needles are left. The fins are then blanched in hot water and the remaining skin scraped off. Fins are subsequently placed in ice water to remove cartilage. Next, the fins are left to dry on racks in the sun and are then transferred to cool in a drying room in order to prevent softening (see Figure 6.2). The fins go to refrigeration and finally

Figure 6.2 Shark Fins Drying on Rooftop in Callao, Peru, April 2007. (© Oceana/LX)

bleaching to make them white at which times, they are cooked one final time to remove any fishy smell.

The fins actually add no flavor to the soup; rather, they provide the thickness. More importantly, the fins add an ingredient that cannot be seen nor measured—shark fin soup is thought to bring vitality to those who eat it and is also believed to be an aphrodisiac. However, it also brings an unanticipated danger to those who consume it. In 2002, a study by WildAid showed that shark fin soup served in Thailand contained dangerously high levels of mercury.[31] One sample was said to have seven times the recommended mercury limits by the U.S. Food and Drug Administration.[32]

There has been no research to substantiate the cultural claims related to the soup. Nonetheless, the popularity of the soup continues to rise, thus increasing the demand, which in turn continues to threaten the shark. The soup's price depends on the amount of fin in the soup. Prices range from US$10 to US $100 per bowl; the longer and thicker the strands, the higher the price. Shark fin soup appears on various buffets for US$8.99. Japanese consumers enjoy shark fins in a variety of products: bread, sweet cookies, sushi, instant noodles, and cat food.[33]

There are some efforts underway to change attitudes about the soup. Changing cultural beliefs is not easy—sometimes, it is not possible, especially given the deeply rooted traditions in a culture as old as those who value the soup. Celebrities are offering their assistance to help campaign against eating shark fin soup. There have been mixed results. One Chinese basketball star, who now plays and resides in the United States, has sworn to never eat the soup again. However, his stature is gaining in popularity in the United States, but he is losing popularity in China.[34]

Illegal, Unreported, and Unregulated Fishing (IUU)

Fishing waters are regulated either by domestic or international laws. Operating outside legal parameters, obviously, makes the practices illegal and as with other illicit practices, illegal fishing is unreported and unregulated. Most sharks are taken incidental or accidental to fishing for other species. In the waters of Australia, it is estimated that tens of thousands of sharks are illegally removed every year through these practices.

In 1999, the UN Office of Food and Agriculture Organization (FAO) adopted the International Plan of Action for the Conservation and Management of Sharks (IPOA–Sharks), which outlines mechanisms aimed at conservation, management, and long-term sustainability of the species. The IPOA–Sharks identifies illegal, unreported, and unregulated (IUU) fishing as being at the center of the sharks' problem. Because fishing is done in national and international waters, monitoring and enforcing these activities is a monumental task that requires international cooperation and resources.

The IPOA–IUU defines illegal, unreported, and unregulated fishing and with their definitions, a number of scenarios[35] were developed to demonstrate how illegal shark fishing takes place. These scenarios are reproduced here as a way to give an accurate picture of how illegal fishing occurs today.

Scenario 1: A State has national regulations or conditions relating specifically to the taking of shark species. Those regulations are not adhered to by national vessels fishing either in national waters, or where the regulations apply to high seas operations, on the high seas (illegal fishing);

Scenario 2: A foreign-flagged vessel, authorized to fish in the waters of another State, fails to adhere to conditions relating to shark catch imposed by that State (illegal fishing);

Scenario 3: A foreign-flagged vessel fishes, without authorization, in the waters of another State and takes sharks either as a target species or as bycatch (illegal fishing);

Scenario 4: In a high seas area to which management measures for sharks established are by a regional fisheries management organization (RFMO), takes shark in direct contravention of those measures (illegal fishing);

Scenario 5: Where a vessel in any of the first four scenarios fails to report or misreports its catch of shark (unreported fishing);

Scenario 6: A vessel fails to report or misreports legal catch of shark in contravention of national laws and regulations or in contravention of the reporting requirements of an RFMO (unreported fishing);

Scenario 7: In a high seas area to which management measures for sharks specifically or for other species are established by an RFMO apply, a vessel, without a flag or flying the flag of a nonmember of that RFMO, takes shark in direct contravention of those shark specific measures or indirectly (as bycatch) in contravention of measures for other species (unregulated fishing); and

Scenario 8: A vessel fishes in an area where there are no applicable conservation or management measures, but where such activity is inconsistent with State responsibilities for conservation of living marine resources under international law (unregulated fishing).

These scenarios illustrate that it is extremely difficult to police open oceans. Moreover, garnering resources to actively police ports where fishermen bring their catch is nearly impossible. Perhaps, it is less difficult for commercial enterprises, but in places where private docks permit illegal enterprises to flourish similar to those found by Rob Stewart in Costa Rica, it will prove highly difficult.

Illegal fishing has the potential to wipe out species quickly. For example, the northern Australian waters are a hotspot for activities that have virtually eliminated silvertip whalers (*Carcharhinus albimarginatus)* and the scalloped hammerhead (*Sphyrna lewini*).[36] Illegal fishing is not isolated to Australian waters. In fact, practices in Moroccan waters by driftnet fleets are catching over 100,000 pelagic sharks each year, in spite of the target catch being swordfish. Because of the practice, the blue, short fin, mako, and thresher sharks are being pushed beyond their reproductive capacities and will no doubt face extinction in the coming years.[37]

There is a large bycatch practice in Taiwan, Japan, and Spain—largely due to the large and thriving demand for shark fins.[38] Over 518,086 tons (470,000 mt) of three species, the blue (*Prionace glauca*), the oceanic whitetip (*Carcharhinus longimanus*), and the silky shark (*Carcharhinus falciformis*) have been caught in a single year.[39] Once again, given the reproductive cycle of these creatures, these fishing practices are not sustainable. The latter two shark populations have declined by 99 and 90 percent, respectively, in the Gulf of Mexico since the onset of industrialized offshore tuna and billfish fishing.[40]

A substantial review of literature pertaining to shark takes was conducted and found that most IUU fishing of sharks is indeed illegal, which makes it also unreported. It is occurring on a global scale; however, there are hot spots: Central/South America, in the Western and Central Pacific Ocean, and in the northern waters of Australia.[41] Most illegal shark fishing is carried out in national waters by both foreign and domestic vessels. Oftentimes, neighboring countries carry out the illegal fishing in a particular country's domestic waters. Illegal foreign fishing centers on the retention of shark fins, which are caught through unauthorized access or breaches of access to domestic waters. In most instances, species from the catches are not reported. Of those that are reported, the most frequently encountered species taken are the hammerhead sharks and silky shark.

Longlining and gillnetting are the most frequently cited ways sharks are illegally fished.[42] A longline is a fishing line made of monofilament that ranges from one mile (1.6 km) to 62 miles (100 km) in length. This line is buoyed every hundred feet or so and a secondary line strung downward, which is baited with multiple hooks. These lines are left for up to 24 hours, and, afterwards fishermen retrieve their catch.[43] Gillnets, euphemistically known as "walls of death," are mesh panels of monofilament plastic. Gillnet fisheries deploy hundreds of yards and more of these nets at a time and leave them in the seas for days on end to catch numerous species at a time. They are extremely efficient in gathering turtles, dolphins, and other endangered and protected species. These nets are responsible for the vast majority of bycatch deaths in the fishing trade today.[44]

Research indicates that shark fins account for only about 7 percent of the volume of the shark trade, but amount to approximately 40 percent of the value.[45] Figure 6.3 shows shark fins from a single boat's catch. Obviously, this volume is only a small indication of the total volume taken each year. There are specific species fished simply for their meat to include the spiny dogfish (*Squalus acanthias*), the porbeagle (*Lamna nasus*), and the school shark (*Galeorhinnus galeus*). Sharks that have been identified to be at risk due to IUU fishing are requiem,

Figure 6.3 Dried Shark Fins Sorted by Type, Species, and Size, Callao, Peru, April 2007. (© Oceana/LX)

pelagic, gulper (*Centrophorus granulosus*), great white (*Carcharodon carcharias*), hammerheads (*Sphyrna* subsp.), carpet (Order: Orectolobiformes), basking (*Cetorhinus maxiumus*), grey nurse (*Carcharias taurus*), leopard (*Stegostoma fasciatum* or *Triakis semifasciata*), school (*Galeorhinnus galeus*), tope or soupfin (*Galeorhinus galeus*), and whale (*Rhinocodon typus*).[46]

Continuing Problems

IPOA–Sharks and international laws aim to ban the practice of discarding sharks once their fins are removed.[47] For obvious reasons, conservation aims to decrease the mortality rate among targeted species in order for the species to recover to recoverable and sustainable levels. Regardless of the international call to protect various shark species, global shark catches has been climbing for several years. The FAO[48] reported a peak in the number of global shark catches in 2003 at a record 970,034 tons (880,000 mt), which was a 17 percent increase from the decade earlier; 826,733 tons (750,000 mt) in 2006 and 859,803 tons (780,000 mt) in 2007. From 1990 to 2004, the top 20 major shark-catching countries has relatively stable membership.[49] Between 1990 and 2004, Indonesia and India were first and second, respectively in the number of sharks caught. In 2004, Indonesia caught 134,482 tons (122,000 mt) of sharks, accounting for 15 percent of global shark catches. India was a distant second—catching 67,241 tons (61,000 mt), which was approximately 7.6 percent of the total recorded global catch. There was some flux between rankings of the other countries during the time period. For example, between 1990 and 2004, Peru was responsible for 1.3 percent of the global shark catches, but dropped from the list in 2004. In 2004, two newcomers appeared: The Islamic Republic of Iran and Yemen. The Islamic Republic of Iran caught 19,841 tons (18,000 mt), 2.3 percent of global catches and Yemen caught 14,330 tons (13,000 mt), 1.6 percent of the total global catches.[50] It is important to keep in mind that these numbers are *recorded* catches. IUU catches, of course, are not counted or tabulated in these figures. Table 6.2 ranks the *average* catch of key shark-catching countries between 2000 and 2007.

The countries with the largest catches are not always those with the largest exports. Taiwan and Spain led the world in exports in 2004 with 17,999 tons (16,329 mt) and 12,894 tons (11,670 mt) respectively. Combined, these countries accounted for 31 percent of the world's shark exports.[51]

Researchers and investigators must come to terms with the discrepancies in the data. For example, why would the top two catching countries not be in the top exporting lists? Only four of the top catching countries in 2004 are top exporters, Taiwan, Spain, Japan, and the United Kingdom. It must be noted here that Costa Rica is included in the top ten exporting countries. Costa Rica is home to a large population of hammerhead sharks, which are considered endangered, but not currently protected by any international convention. There is widespread agreement that they are severely overfished at unsustainable levels. If Costa Rica continues to export at its current rates, these animals will no doubt escalate along the endangered continuum.

Each nation-state is expected to draft its own IPOA–Shark; however, some nation-states are more actively writing their plan than others. Only 13 countries have National Plan of Action–Sharks (NPOA–Sharks) written and in varying stages of implementation: Japan (2009), Argentina (2009), Uruguay (2008), New Zealand (2008), Canada (2007), Seychelles (2007), Malaysia (2006), Ecuador (2005), Australia (2004), Mexico (2004), Taiwan (2004) United Kingdom (2001), and the United States (2001).[52] In 2006, the following countries reported that they did not have a plan: India, Spain, Argentina, Pakistan, France, Brazil, Nigeria, and Portugal. Indonesia was said to have a draft NPOA–Shark document in 2004, but it remains unclear as to whether the government has actually finalized this plan or if the plan has ever been enacted.[53]

In addition to the various action plans, other ways to help regulate fishing behavior are being developed. For example, vessel-monitoring systems help to

Table 6.2 Average Catch of Key Shark Catching Countries, 2000–2007

Rank	Country/Territory	Average Catch US tons (metric tons)
1	Indonesia	121,836 (110,528)
2	India	77,997 (70,758)
3	Spain	63,587 (57,685)
4	Taiwan	53,454 (48,493)
5	Mexico	38,068 (34,535)
6	Pakistan	37,776 (34,270)
7	Argentina	37,081 (33,639)
8	USA	32,969 (29,909)
9	Japan	28,523 (25,930)
10	Malaysia	27,007 (24,500)
11	Thailand	26,627 (24,156)
12	France	24,612 (22,328)
13	Sri Lanka	24,283 (22,029)
14	Brazil	22,595 (20,498)
15	New Zealand	20,128 (18,260)
16	Portugal	16,686 (15,137)
17	UK	15,764 (14,301)

Adapted from Mary Lack and Glenn Sant. "Trends in Global Shark Catch and Recent Developments in Management" (*TRAFFIC International*, 2009).

monitor the catches landed by various vessels in a given RFMO.[54] The technology allows RFMO authorities on shore to receive up-to-date information on catches and the location of a particular vessel. Vehicle-monitoring systems were first used by the RFMO Convention for the Conservation of Antarctic Marine Living Resources (CCAMLR) to monitor the IUU of the Patagonian toothfish, which is also known as the Chilean Sea bass (*Dissostichus eleginoides*).[55] The technology can compare data of actual landings with those pertaining to the location of the catches, thus challenging or confirming claims about the legality of the catch. The vehicle-monitoring systems also help with the count of the marine life, thus helping to monitor quotas set by the various RFMOs.

Enforcement and monitoring are problematic. There are no state-sanctioned police on the high seas. A few environmental NGOs like Greenpeace and the Sea Shepherd Conservation Society (see Boxes 6.1 and 6.2) actively look for poachers and IUU activities. However, RFMOs have no police force to help them intercept violators, but regulatory mechanisms have been offered as a way forward. For example, Blacklists have been put forth as a way to stop fishing vessels caught in IUU practices. Once caught in these activities, a vessel would be prohibited from entering the port of a party state. The Blacklist method relies on comprehensive and up-to-date lists that must be disseminated in a timely manner in order to be effective.[56]

Box 6.1 Greenpeace and Whaling

Greenpeace is an international organization committed to the nonviolent protection of the world's environment. Started in 1971 with a small group of activists and an old fishing boat, advocates set forth on a journey to save the globe from irreparable environmental damage. Forty years later, the organization continues to expose global environmental abuses by interfering with the offensive practices or by simply witnessing the abuse and reporting it to the public. Greenpeace has its roots in the protesting of nuclear testing near a tiny island, Amchitka, off the west coast of Alaska. Today, it has expanded its overall work to include campaigns aimed at stopping global warming, saving the oceans, whales, and seafood; protecting forests, stopping nuclear power, eliminating toxic chemicals, and promoting sustainable agriculture.

Their efforts to save the whales are markedly different from the approach taken by the Sea Shepherd Conservation Society (see Box 6.2). Greenpeace seeks governmental policy changes that encourage compliance with the 1986 moratorium on commercial whaling. Their actions include placing their vessels in between whaling ships and their prey. Greenpeace also works to end overfishing, bycatch killings, bottom trawling, and pirate fishing, along with their efforts to stop ocean pollution.

(For additional information, see www.greenpeace.org/usa/campaigns/oceans).

Box 6.2 The Sea Shepherd Conservation Society

The Sea Shepherd Conservation Society was established by Captain Paul Watson in 1977 with the aim of protecting ocean habitat and the killing of marine wildlife. The activities of the Sea Shepherd is much more action-oriented and confrontational than the activities of Greenpeace. In 1978, the first voyage of the vessel, *Sea Shepherd*, was to protect the baby harp seals from slaughter. The next voyage saw the intentional sinking of the pirate whaler, *Sierra*, in Portugal.

The Sea Shepherd Conservation Society's history is rife with stories of successful ship interventions, many to the point of the offending ship being sunk. Captain Watson has been arrested a number of times due to his very aggressive tactics. Indeed, his approach has caused much controversy with his relationship with Greenpeace, of which he was considered a founding father. However, Greenpeace has worked diligently to distance their work from his.

Interestingly, Captain Watson has been invited by several governments to either patrol their oceans against illegal fishing or to negotiate with offending fishermen. Requests like these are highlighted in the film, *Sharkwater*, where he and his crew patrolled the waters of Costa Rica and the Galapagos Islands—a UNESCO World Heritage site and marine reserve where fishing is banned. They have also been present in Taiji, Japan where the slaughter of dolphins has come to the public view after being the topic of the Academy Award winning documentary, *The Cove*.

(For more information see: www.seashepherd.org).

GREAT STURGEON (*Huso huso*)

The great sturgeon (also known as the beluga, European, and Russian sturgeon) is the largest sturgeon in the world and is also the largest freshwater fish in Europe. It also holds another distinction as it is critically endangered and included in Appendix II of CITES and of the CMS. Global fisheries report that there has been a 93 percent decline in catch from 1992 to 2007 from a high of 573 tons (520 mt) to 36 tons (33 mt), respectively.[57] The numbers of this great fish are decreasing dramatically due to extreme overfishing for roe, in addition to the loss of spawning grounds from dam sites. Catch data and the recorded number of spawning individuals indicate that this species of fish will soon be the newest member of the globally extinct of wild populations. Survival is solely dependent on stocking and fisheries management, in conjunction with efforts to fight illegal fishing and reduce the trade in illegal caviar.

Characteristics

The beluga is an ancient and enormous fish, reaching up to 16.4 feet (5 m) in length and weighing up to 4,568 pounds (2,072 kg).[58] The length and weight vary greatly depending on the environmental conditions within which the fish lives.[59]

The body is long and slightly flat with a snout slightly-turned upward and a crescent-shaped mouth located underneath the nose. There are small, fleshy, whiskerlike sensory organs in front of its mouth. Running the length of the body are five rows of bony plates called scutes. The color of the beluga sturgeon ranges from dark gray to green with a whitish underbelly.

The beluga sturgeon matures later than other sturgeon, reaching maturity after 12 years. In the Caspian Sea, the female beluga sturgeon become sexually active between ages four and eight, while males reach that point between four and seven.[60] Females, however, do not spawn until they reach sexual maturity, which is between ages 6 and 25 years, with an average of 18 years. Beluga sturgeon do not spawn every year and the females will reabsorb their eggs if the conditions are less than optimal for breeding. An individual beluga sturgeon can spawn up to nine times in a lifetime.[61]

This species is one of the longest living fishes. Some are reported to have lived for over 100 years[62] and while the fish once died primarily of natural causes, this is no longer the case. Beluga caviar is a hot product and whenever there is a hot product, there is high demand, and subsequently, a killing field. This species of sturgeon has been decimated in recent years to the point that many of the fish never reach maturity.

Habitat and Range States

The beluga sturgeon has been found in the basins of the Caspian, Black, Azov, and Adriatic seas. Its native, wild habitat is limited only to the Black Sea in the Danube River and the Caspian Sea in the Ural River. The fish is stocked in the Azov Sea and Volga River. Native countries include Azerbaijan, Bulgaria, Georgia, Iran, Islamic Republic of Iran, Kazakhstan, Moldova, Romania, Russian Federation, Serbia, and Turkey. It is regionally extinct in Austria, Croatia, Hungary, and Slovakia and vagrant in Turkmenistan and Ukraine.[63]

Beluga sturgeon migrate in large numbers[64] from the sea to freshwater in order to spawn. This migration is known as an anadromous migration. They spawn every three to four years from April to June; however, this species of sturgeon has a complicated pattern of spawning. There is one peak migration in late winter and spring and one in late summer and autumn.[65] In the spring, the fish migrate from the sea to the rivers, but in the autumn, the fish remain in the rivers until the following spring. They spawn in large numbers in relatively shallow waters and do not provide care to the eggs laid.

Threats

The high demand for beluga caviar has basically given the species a death sentence. This demand has set in motion the process of illegal, unreported, and unregulated fishing, which caused the overfishing of the species, and which, in turn, has left the species at unsustainable levels. Overfishing, poaching, overharvesting, and bycatch are the major threats to the beluga sturgeon. Additionally, the destruction of spawning grounds has compounded the problem. The Volgograd dam was built in 1955 and decreased available spawning ground by 88 to100 percent in the Volga River and areas in the Terek and Sulak rivers from about 132 hectares and 202 hectares, respectively.[66] The Don River dam, about 37 miles (60 km) southeast from Tula and southeast of Moscow, eliminated 68,000 hectares of spawning ground. Additionally, this dam affected flow regulation in the Kuban River, which led to the loss of a further 140,000 hectares of spawning ground.[67]

IUCN assessments show that the number of beluga sturgeon entering the Volga River each year dropped from 26,000 between 1961 and 1965 to 2,800 between 1998 and 2002, a decrease of 89 percent.[68] Of the beluga sturgeon in the Volga River, nearly 100 percent are thought to be hatchery-reared, as are about 91 percent of those from the Caspian Sea. Official catch statistics seem to support the declining numbers; where there once was abundance, there is now virtually nothing. The agreed beluga sturgeon catch quota for the entire Caspian Sea was 110 tons (99.8 mt), but in 2007 and 2008, that quota was not met. During the latest trawl surveys, the number of individuals per year did not exceed 31 annually.[69]

It should be noted here that farmed or hatchery-reared sturgeon present the same problems as the Chinese tiger farms. Caviar becomes legally available from the farmed fishes. This availability keeps demand very high, so wild fish are put at further risk of harm. Customers have no way to know, for certain, that the caviar they are consuming originates from farmed sturgeon or the wild, critically endangered variety.

Between 1979 and1981 in the Sea of Azov, it was estimated that about 551,000 beluga sturgeon from stocked species existed. Those numbers dropped significantly between 1988 and 1993 to 25,000 and thereafter, the fish were only caught sporadically.[70] In 1986, commercial fishing was banned, and the major threat to the beluga sturgeon remained bycatch fishing.

Catches of sturgeon in the Danube River have also continued to decline. In the mid-1970s, the annual catch was approximately 25 US tons (23 mt), but by the mid- to late 1980s, the area had witnessed a 67 percent decline to 8.3 tons (7.5 mt).[71] In 2006, catching beluga in the Danube River was banned.

CONSERVATION

Given the current state of affairs, the international concern for shark has been rising over the past several years, but there is far more that needs to be done. There are a number of international agencies working to protect and conserve shark populations. CITES, FAO, and the UN General Assembly all have called for monitoring shark numbers. FAO has particularly acknowledged that inaccurate data about shark catch and landings is impairing conservation efforts. Most of the shark populations worldwide remain unmanaged.

The level of concern for various sharks is not adequately reflected in the actual written international conventions and agreements. In 1991, CITES responded to international concern by adding the CITES Shark Working Group to the CITES Animals Committee. The research of the Shark Working Group aims to highlight the need to increase the protection for the shark and related species. Despite their work, no shark is listed in Appendix I of CITES and only three are listed in Appendix II. Of the hundreds of shark species, this simply does not seem sufficient, especially given that 20 percent of the 547 species of sharks[72] on the Red List are considered threatened with extinction!

The development of the IPOA–Sharks reflects the international concern regarding the condition sharks are facing, but the plan is voluntary and, therefore, problematic. States and RFMOs are not required to implement the plan, so at best, efforts are sketchy and sporadic. Calls for international regulation and intervention have largely been ignored.

The primary international laws that provide protection for sharks are the UN Convention on the Law of the Sea (UNCLOS) and the UN Fish Stocks Agreement. Additionally, there are internationally agreed-upon standards and protocols such as the *Code of Conduct for Responsible Fisheries*[73] and IPO–Sharks. National legislation also shapes policy and conservation efforts. Finally, conventions that allow for the implementation of RFMOs decree varying degrees of conservation management responsibilities.

UNCLOS requires member nation-states to conserve living resources on the high seas and maintain/restore populations of harvested species to sustainable levels.[74] UN Fish Stocks Agreement aims to ensure the long-term conservation and sustainability of straddling[75] and highly migratory fish[76] and pertains directly to oceanic shark species such as the whale, basking, requiem, and hammerheads. This agreement requires that its signatories, through their RFMOs:

- apply precautionary approaches to management of targeted and nontargeted species of sharks;
- implement management strategies that seek to maintain or restore populations of these species at levels consistent with previously agreed precautionary levels;
- implement enhanced monitoring of targeted and nontargeted stocks of concern to determine effectiveness of conservation and management of measures; and
- development of data collection and research programs that assess impact of fishing on nontargeted species.[77]

One of the main issues with finning is the wasteful discard of the rest of the animal. Related to this practice is the *Code of Conduct for Responsible Fisheries*, which stipulates guidelines for the minimization of waste and discards. The IPOA–Sharks relies on national compliance for success. Specifically, NPOAs are necessary for the conservation and preservation of shark populations. Within individual nation-states, the nutritional and socioeconomic contribution of sharks should be explained to those regions that exploit the species through finning practices.[78]

The *Code of Conduct for Responsible Fisheries* also calls for party states to carry out regular assessments of shark stocks, to work with and, in collaboration with other states, to develop plans that allow for data sharing efforts to account for highly migratory species and stocks on the high seas. According to the FAO, international laws pertaining to harvested species and to the management of them by individual nation-states and RFMO apply. The rationale for this is simple: sharks are taken as targeted species or retained through bycatches. International laws impose responsibility on nation-states to manage their shark populations to sustainable levels.

Regional Fisheries Management Organizations (RFMOs)

There are three types of regional fishery bodies: (1) RFMOs, (2) advisory bodies, and (3) scientific bodies. RFMOs are created by international agreements and play an important part in the management and conservation of marine species. RFMOs are comprised of a number of representatives from different fishing nations within a given area. The RFMO is responsible for setting fishing quotas for those stocks under their direct management. They are also in charge of enforcing their quotas and for ensuring that illegal and unreported fishing is stopped.[79]

UNCLOS and the UN Agreement on Straddling Fish Stocks and Highly Migratory Fish Stocks clearly state that managing fish of the high seas is of critical importance[80] and RFMOs are tasked with this crucial role. Table 6.3 lists the main RFMOs by region and their main area of focus. The FAO regional fisheries management organizations, in addition to a number of other scientific agencies, help design conservation programs that enhance RFMO's activities.[81] Unless and until these organizations work in unison toward conservation, the sustainability of fish/marine stocks remain in jeopardy of becoming extinct. Additional contributing, negative factors include weak enforcement of illegal, unreported, and unregulated fishing.

There are many implementation problems with RFMOs. Primarily, the problem lies with adherence to regulations. Nations can opt in or out at any given time and fishermen can fly flags of convenience on their ships in order to avoid the rules. The basic problem is the illegal, unreported, and unregulated fishing of fish and marine life in waters that are supposed to be protected through various international fishing regulations.

Shark Finning Bans

There are three main aims to the outright ban of finning:[82] (1) sustainable management of sharks, (2) minimization of waste, and (3) improvement of species through specific identification and data collection. Because of various cultural practices and subsequent market demands, it is questionable whether an outright ban will come into practice anytime soon, but there is no doubt that if practices are modified, species will be saved.

Table 6.3 Regional Fishing Management Organizations

Atlantic Ocean

Northwest Atlantic Fisheries Organization (NAFO)

North East Atlantic Fisheries Commision (NEAFC)

North Atlantic Salmon Conservation Organization (NASCO)

International Commission for the Conservation of Atlantic Tuna (ICCAT)

Fisheries Committee for the Eastern Central Atlantic (CECAF)

South East Atlantic Fisheries Organization (SEAFO)

Inter-American Tropical Tuna Commission (IATTC)

Commission for the Conservation of Southern Bluefin Tuna (CCSBT)

Pacific

Western and Central Pacific Fisheries Commission (WCPFC)

North Pacific Anadromous Fish Commission (NPAFC)

Antarctic Ocean

Commission for Conservation of Antarctic Marine Living Resources (CCAMLR)

Indian Ocean

Indian Ocean Tuna Commission (IOTC)

Southern Indian Ocean Fisheries Agreement (SIOFA)

Mediterranean Ocean

General Fisheries Council for the Mediterranean (GFCM)

International Baltic Sea Fisheries Commission (IBSFC) (ended 1/1/07)

Miscellaneous

International Dolphin Conservation Programme (IDCP)

Western and Central Pacific Fisheries Commission (WCPFC)

South Tasman Rise Agreement (STRA)

The ban puts into place several requirements that add capacity burdens to vessel captains. For example, if a finning ban were in place, fishermen would be forced to land the shark whole; therefore, the captain must have sufficient refrigeration and hold capacity to store the carcasses until he/she reaches shore. There are options[83] other than landing the entire shark intact. A second option is for sharks to be landed as headed and gutted with skins, fins, claspers, and dorsal spins attached. A third option is the same as the second, but with the fins removed and kept as sets. Procedures should also be written so that sets are required to be matched to their shark. The fourth option is for sharks to be landed as headed, gutted, and skinned, with fins removed and retained apart from the trunk; however, fin sets must be matched to the shark trunk from which they came. The fifth and final option is for sharks to be landed, headed, gutted, and skinned with fins removed. Fins that are removed must be weighed and must represent a specified proportion of the trunk weight.

These options range from the most to least effective option for having the largest impact on conservation and sustainability. The first option will offer the largest contribution to shark conservation, species identification, and enforcement. It is also considered the least feasible, since gutting and gilling is necessary to preserve the quality of the meat. The least preferable of the options, the fifth option, provides avenues through which fishermen can cheat the system. Shark identification and matching fins can be extremely difficult. Of course, as with any regulation, success is dependent upon enforcement and compliance.

Shark Tourism

Global shark conservation groups have been calling for innovative ways to conserve the species. Marine-based tourism programs, especially for developing nations, have the potential to bring significant amounts of revenue to typically frail economies. Figure 6.4 shows a scuba diver diving with a whale shark on Toril Beach in Okinawa, Japan.

Figure 6.4 Scuba Diving with Whale Shark, Okinawa, Japan, September 2009. (Clay and Yvonne Ruffner)

In the Philippines, shark fishermen in the Donsol region are now retrained as tour guides for whale shark watch tours. Over 7,000 tourists visited Donsol's sharks in 2005, which is up from the 867 who came in 2002. This has created over 300 jobs and contributed US$620,000 to the Filipino economy since the business started.[84]

Another example is that of the Maldives, an island nation[85] located in the Indian Ocean. Tourism and fishing are the primary industries there. Shark dives have been introduced and are now big business, bringing in US$2.3 million per year to the country; this is more than 100 times the export value of shark meat from fishing. In 1993, a single reef shark's renewable value was US$35,000 from diving, whereas that same shark was worth US$32 to a local fisherman.[86] However, it must be noted that in a country where the average annual income in 2008 was less than US$4,500, catching sharks is an extremely lucrative business. If the diving tourism industry does not ensure that money is managed well, fishermen may have no alternative but to return to the practice of finning sharks.

In Belize, divers worldwide go to Placenia to see whale sharks in Gladden Spit Marine Reserve.[87] The number of whale sharks there has increased from one in 1997 to 22 in 2004. There is a six-week peak tourism period each year worth US$3.7 million to the town. A live whale shark's estimated worth is US$35,000 per year and if it lives to its normal life span of 60 years, each whale shark is worth over US$2 million if visitors continue to visit the reserve.[88]

Great Sturgeon

Despite efforts worldwide, sturgeon populations have not recovered. The outlook for the beluga sturgeon is not hopeful. Conservation efforts continue and are largely focused on repopulating stocks in the fishes' natural habitats. According to the IUCN,[89] some natural reproduction is occurring, but not in sufficient quantities. The fight to fully protect the species continues, as no range state offers full protection in place for the fish. Fishing licenses are required in most countries, but enforcement is lacking. CITES has encouraged range states to provide protection in spawning and feeding grounds, but again this is not consistent nor is it required. Azerbaijan, as of 2009, is the only range state to have submitted a zero quota for caviar exports to CITES.[90]

The Big Leaf Mahogany

THE BIG LEAF MAHOGANY (*Swietenia macrophylla*)

DETERMINING THE REASONS why plants become endangered or extinct is far more difficult than for terrestrial or marine animals. Weather conditions, insects, and other natural interferences decimate species of plants. However, there is one particular plant, the big leaf Brazilian mahogany[1] (*Swietenia macrophylla*) that provides a good case study because data have been collected and analyzed about this majestic tropical tree for many years. There are three subspecies in this family: (1) the big leaf Brazilian mahogany (*Swietenia macrophylla*), (2) the Caribbean mahogany (*Swietenia mahagoni*), and (3) the Honduras mahogany (*Swietenia humilis*). All three have protected status with the IUCN and CITES. The big leaf was upgraded from CITES Appendix III to Appendix II in 2002 because of the incredibly high demand for mahogany timber products. It is important to note that mahogany grown outside the neotropics[2] is not covered under the protection of CITES.

Because tree inventories are difficult to conduct, the exact number of living mahoganies is not known. It is estimated, however, that back inventories are lacking for most of the species' range. Some tree stands exist in parts of Brazil and Bolivia. Although researchers have surveyed mahogany populations in Bolivia, the country has no commercially viable mahogany trees with a diameter greater than 24 inches (60 cm) at breast height spanning nearly 80 percent of the tree's range.[3] Overharvesting, depletion, and exploitation of the Amazon rain forest has put this tree in serious jeopardy. Peru's range shrunk by 50 percent, and researchers estimated that the range will shrink an additional 20 percent by 2014.[4] Approximately 15 percent of the big leaf mahogany's historic range in Bolivia and Peru is protected; however, this designation has little impact or importance for illegal loggers. Approximately 14 percent of Peru's protected areas are believed to be illegally logged.

Last assessed in 1998, the IUCN is calling for a much-needed update on the big leaf mahogany so that new population estimates can be made. Based on the 1998 assessment data, the big leaf is considered vulnerable on the Red List. The dilemma caused by the overharvesting not only jeopardizes the tree itself, but it also endangers an entire ecosystem, including communities of indigenous people. Social problems may result if the trees become extinct because local communities are reliant on the timber to provide wood for shelter, food from its fruit, and profits from its trade, thus providing an important case study showing that the extinction or threatened extinction of a species can affect the survival of others.

Characteristics

The big leaf mahogany is a species of tree that rises far above the forest canopy. It is very slow-growing, reaching maturity at approximately 100 years. At full maturity, the big leaf mahogany can reach 148 to 197 feet (45 to 60 m), which helps to protect smaller trees by providing them much needed shelter under its massive canopy.[5] The average trunk diameter at maturity is about 31.5 inches (80 cm). The tree gets its name from its large leaves that can grow up to nearly 18 inches (45 cm) in length. It has an even number of leaflets that run up on each side of the central midrils. The mahogany produces small white flowers and large fruit, whose color ranges from light gray to brown. The fruit grows to almost 16 inches (40 cm) and contains up to 71 winged seeds that range from 2.7 to 5 inches (7 to 12 cm) in length. The tree bark itself has a sweet odor and a dark brown, fleshy texture.[6]

Hardwood from the big leaf mahogany is very sought after by consumers worldwide. The wood is renowned for its deep rich color and grain, along with its durability. Mahogany has been used for centuries to make fine furniture and musical instruments. It is the leading commercial timber traded in Latin America. The demand for the timber has increased over the past several decades because two other members of the genus, Caribbean mahogany and Honduras mahogany, have become commercially extinct due to overharvesting and exploitation.[7] Experts are worried that the overreliance on the big leaf mahogany will further jeopardize its viability. They are estimating that unless current practices are modified, the tree will become extinct within the next decade.

Habitat and Range States

The big leaf mahogany prefers rich, deep, and well-drained soil. It grows in elevations from sea level up to 4,593 feet (1,400 m). It can survive in a wide range of environments—whether the forests are wet or dry. These trees thrive in areas with an average precipitation of 39 to nearly 100 inches (1 and 2.5 m) and with an average temperature between 74 to 83 degrees Fahrenheit (23 to 28 degrees Celsius).[8]

The big leaf mahogany lives in tropical climates. It is found throughout the forests of South and Central America, specifically in Belize, Bolivia, Brazil, Columbia, Costa Rica, Dominica, Ecuador, El Salvador, French Guiana, Guatemala, Guyana, Honduras, Mexico, Nicaragua, Panama, Peru, and Venezuela.[9] A sustainable tree inventory is lacking throughout most of its range states, but the largest number of trees exist in Brazil, Bolivia, and Peru.

The Amazon basin is about the size of Europe. It is home to the world's largest river,[10] the Amazon. The Amazon rain forest is largely situated in Brazil, but
it actually spans several other countries: Bolivia, Peru, Ecuador, Colombia, Venezuela, Guyana, Suriname, and French Guiana. The Amazon is home to savannas, flooded forests, and a rich variety of wildlife, including 1,000 plant
species, over 1 million insect species, 3,000 fish species, 1,250 bird species,
and 420 mammals.[11] The Amazon rain forest contains approximately 10 percent
of the globe's biodiversity and a change in its composition has a tremendous
impact on the world's atmosphere and biodiversity.[12]

Threats

There are two threats to this species: forest conversion and illegal logging. Sister
trees of the big leaf mahogany have already been so overharvested that they are
considered commercially extinct.[13] Furthermore, the WWF–Global confirms that
the forests are being decimated at unsustainable rates due to illegal logging and
the lack of implementation of international trade requirements.[14] (For Greenpeace's role, see Box 7.1.) More than 120,000 cubed meters (m^3) of big leaf
mahogany are exported from Latin America each year from unmanaged forests
(see Table 7.1). Due to the lack of incentives to employ more sustainable management practices, the big leaf mahogany is at serious risk of becoming commercially extinct unless trends are reversed. CITES gave protection to the three types
of mahoganies, but in the cases of the Caribbean and Honduras mahogany, the
listings came far too late. CITES protection includes the following by-products
from the trees: logs, sawn wood, veneer sheets, and plywood. The status of commercial extinction brings with it economic devastation to local people and communities. Allowing a species to reach this point undermines all conservation
efforts to designate and maintain sustainable forests.[15]

Box 7.1 Greenpeace and Forests

Greenpeace also has a presence in the Amazon. For ten years, their work has brought the
destruction of the rainforests and its consequences to the attention of the media. Their
work in the Amazon and other large forest ranges is on the practices of illegal logging,
consequences of global warming, strengthening communities, and the efforts against the
construction of soya and palm oil plantations. Species protection stems out of their work
to save the forests.

　　As part of their widespread, global lobbying efforts, Greenpeace works with corporations to increase their reliance on recycled fiber, the use of woods from sustainable and
certified forests, and to prevent the clearing of endangered forests.

　　(For more information see: www.greenpeace.org/usa/campaigns/forests).

Table 7.1 Annual Volume of Legal Big Leaf Mahogany Exported (timber m^3), 1996–2002* as Recorded in CITES Trade Statistics

Export Country	1996	1997	1998	1999	2000	2001	2002	Mean m^3
Brazil	101,473	94,744	43,438	54,961	39,857	40,413	41,183	59,430
Peru	4,448	10,893	20,720	51,487	33,048	41,400	50,429	30,346
Bolivia	25,989	27,963	20,159	8,520	10,549	7,613	4,596	15,056
Nicaragua	17,106	19,029	5,773	5,165	3,863	5,991	7,278	9,172
Guatemala	2,100	1,687	1,098	406	2,716	3,135	2,483	1,946
Belize	1,931	233	125	2,326	2,030	709	1,173	1,218
Mexico	2,266	497	271	168	—	2,473	589	895
Honduras	—	885	880	1,324	666	556	—	616

*International Tropical Timber Organization, *Making the Mahogany Trade Work: Report of the Workshop on Capacity-building for the Implementation of the CITES Appendix-II Listing of Mahogany*, (INRENA, 2004): 18.

Because these large trees play such an important role in the overall ecosystem, concern is not just about the loss of sustainable tree growth. These forests are home to innumerable species, many of which are endangered and critically endangered. For example, the giant otter (*Pteronura brasiliensis*) lives in the same habitat as the big leaf mahogany. Without the mahogany, the survivability of many other endangered species would be in doubt.

Forest Conversion

Forest conversion occurs when the needs of the community are pushed against the needs of the ecosystem. Through the conversion process, forests are turned into land for animal grazing or planting crops. Forest conversion is not reversible. Obviously, growing communities have an economic interest in transforming land for agricultural purposes; however, traditional indigenous communities who voluntarily live in the forest are losing their much-needed resources. Trying to balance the needs of indigenous communities, local nontraditional communities, and the ecosystem is an arduous, if not impossible, task.

Forest conversion and farming in surrounding communities includes "slash and burn" agricultural practices. It is common for farmers to set fire to forested areas with the aim of creating additional farmland. Not only is forestland lost for crops, but collateral damage of full-scale forest fires occurs as a result of the slash and burn technology and the loss of other flora and fauna. Alternatives are being introduced, but the practice is historic and change will not occur quickly.

The problems related to deforestation are not new. The Brazilian rain forest has been under threat for many decades. WWF–Brazil implemented "Lungs of the World" in 1998 to address the problem of deforestation due to illegal logging and land/community development. By 2003, an area about the size of Switzerland was lost to cattle ranching and agriculture in Brazil. Most of the land being destroyed was conservation land; therefore specific action needed to be taken. "Lungs of the World" focused on developing better relations with government units in order to consolidate conservation areas and to promote sustainable use of natural resources.[16]

Other agricultural practices impact the sustainability of the forests. As an example, the cultivation of soy, one of the major crops in these areas, is extremely hard on the rain forests. Efforts are underway between forest managers, conservationists, and the soy industry to reduce the damage created by soy farming. Soy negatively impacts the big leaf mahogany and other forest species in two ways: eroding land and conversion of the actual rain forest necessary for the crop.[17] Soy is a crop that is extremely erodible. It is planted in wide rows, takes large plots of land, and needs a considerable amount of time for its canopy to grow to such a degree when the soil can be protected. Until that happens, nutrient rich soil is destroyed through constant exposure to the elements—sun and rain. In order for the crops to be planted, forests have to be eliminated. Again, the process of forest conversion is irreversible; once the crops are planted, tree species have absolutely no chance of repopulating the area. The consequences of the decision to plant soy are often ignored when placed in the context of the amount of profit to be made from soy farming.[18] In years to come, it is hoped that the soy industry develops more sound and responsible production methods so that other species are not at risk due to their practices.

Forest management has traditionally included forest concessions. These concessions are contracts or licenses given to firms and/or individuals permitting them to harvest and to commercially market timber from a specifically-defined area in the forest.[19] Concessions are usually constrained by time and specific species, as well as by tree size. Problems surrounding forest concessions include forgery of permits, taking protected trees, and taking trees that are below specific breast heights and diameter.

The practice of selective logging (taking only high value trees) is also detrimental to the species.[20] Selective logging removes seed-producing trees, which in return, reduces the probability of reseeding. Also, when the tree canopy is tampered with, natural and necessary light is altered, thus reducing the survivability of the species.

International conservation agencies like the Sierra Club are helping to spread the message about the negative consequences that result from eliminating forests.[21] Harmful carbon dioxide cannot be filtered without trees and forests; therefore, the greenhouse gas effects strengthen, resulting in an increase in global warming. Scientists estimate the need to reduce carbon dioxide by one-quarter in order to stabilize the atmosphere. Roughly 30 percent of global warming can be caused by deforestation, so it makes sense to preserve forests worldwide.[22]

Illegal Logging

Illegal logging includes the harvesting, transporting, processing, and buying or selling of timber in violation of national laws.[23] It is an extremely lucrative business that is literally putting the Amazon and other forests at risk of destruction. About 73 percent of the timber production in Indonesia is said to be from illegal logging.[24] Twenty-five percent of Russian timber exports is also thought to be the result of illegal logging.[25] In Gabon, about 70 percent of harvested timber is illegal.[26] Countries in the Amazon Basin, the Baltic States, the Congo Basin, East Africa, Indonesia, and Russia are thought to lose €10 to €15 billion (US$14–21billion) annually because of the illicit timber trade.[27] The European Union estimates their loss at about €3 billion (US$4 billion) due to its active, illegal timber trade practices with these countries.[28]

Most of the mahogany range states have national legislation in place that criminalizes certain logging practices and supports sustainable forestry. These same countries are parties of CITES and other international timber trade agreements, which provide international safeguards. The amount of money that is being pumped into the illegal trade makes it difficult to disrupt the market. For example, in 1996, Asian companies invested US$500 million into the Brazilian timber industry.[29] Trees were being harvested illegally at record pace. Illegal logging thrives throughout the region and occurs in a number of venues: inside forest concessions, inside protected national parks, and on the reserves of indigenous communities. The WWF calls illegal logging a "well-documented scourge globally[30]" and is a prolific problem in Latin America. Research conducted in the 1990s found that approximately 80 percent of all logging done in the Amazon is illegal.[31]

Illegal logging encompasses much more than simply cutting down trees without permission. Practices include forged permits, cutting any commercially available trees regardless of their protected status, cutting more than official quotas allow, harvesting trees outside the concession area, and stealing timber resources from protected lands and those of indigenous communities.[32] Some forest areas are sold as concession areas for far below market values, thus undermining the potential for valuable tax benefits to local and national governments. As a result, illegal logging also includes tax evasion, corruption, and interfering with access rights.

Illegal timber products present a unique problem for crime reduction. The CRAVED model helps to determine the risk of a specific good. Within CRAVED, illegally sawn lumber is not readily concealable unless it is accompanied by obviously forged documents that claim its legality. Removing timber from forests around the world takes large operations, heavy equipment, and roads. While it is not easy, it is possible and viable on very large scales. Clearly, the wood is extremely valuable and its high demand indicates its enjoyment. Because of the beauty of the wood, the demand supports a structure for the sale of the timber. This completes the CRAVED model because a structure exists that allows for its disposal.

The control of logging practices deep within the forest is extremely difficult. The legality or illicit harvesting of timber is markedly different than the same action with most animals. Timber harvesting requires large and heavy equipment, teams of people, and roads. As with the research conducted on Siberian tigers, studies show that logging is linked to the existence of roads. Roads provide access to natural resources, which increases the illegal taking of natural resources. An interview with José Luis Camino, chief of Instituto Nacional de Recursos Naturales (INRENA), revealed that "the [Peruvian government] does not have the capacity to control the forests. Last year alone, 4,200 permissions were granted for the extraction of wood from local forests . . . The corruption in the INRENA is worse than . . . any other situation in the country at the moment."[33]

Incongruent views exist between the CITES Management and Scientific Authorities.[34] In 2007, INRENA, Peru's CITES Management Authority, established export quotas, but did not take into consideration the recommendations put forth by the Scientific Authority. In 2007, the Scientific Authority recommended that export volume greater than 1,200 mahogany trees should not be permitted, but the Management Authority approved export quotas of 1,600. Additionally, the Scientific Authority recommended a size restriction for legal harvests, but INRENA ignored that restriction as well.[35] A lack of consensus seems to exist as to what the necessary requirements should be. Export quotas are still based on volumes unapproved or verified, thus showing the continued distrust between the two governing authorities.

A call has been made to CITES and its party members for an immediate moratorium on logging and exports from Peru until sufficient evidence has been produced that an administrative ability to stop and sustain illegal practices is in effect.[36] Unfortunately, CITES cannot force a country into compliance, so it is incumbent upon each individual country to persuade Peru to comply. In order for conservation to succeed, a better relationship between the two authorities must be developed.

Taking timber has a negative effect on forest management. The impact of heavy machinery erodes soil, which diminishes soil nutrients. Additionally, when soil is badly disturbed, it takes many years to regenerate to the level necessary to sustain substantial tree growth. In the time it takes for that regeneration, the land can be taken over by farmers for crops or cattle, and the destructive cycle continues to manifest itself. In the mid-1990s, researchers examined the recovery of areas cleared of their timber.[37] The land within the Tapajós National Forest (Brazilian Amazon) that was studied has been logged since 1979. Logging practices there stimulated growth, but only for very limited time periods of approximately three years. After longer periods of time, forests experienced growth rates similar to those parts of the forest not logged.

Nearly 90 percent of Columbia is covered by forest; however, about 300,000 hectares of their forest is lost to both legal and illegal forest clearing.[38] Wood products stemming from these illegal activities are being smuggled into Peru and Brazil where tree populations are suffering. Results of these activities have far-reaching effects. Income from the timber trade will fall due to unsustainable practices and forest species fragmentation will occur, thus jeopardizing the existence of forest species.

A critical piece in the reduction of any illegal market is the publication of the negative consequences of participation in the supply/demand cycle. In other words, those who are creating the demand for the product must be educated as to what actually occurs after the resources are removed from their natural habitat. The primary importers of mahogany are the United States, Dominican Republic, and the United Kingdom. In 1990s, UK consumers began to systematically boycott timber and, as a result, the import volume decreased substantially (see Table 7.2). Unfortunately, the United States has made up for the loss of the UK's trade. The United States imports 93 percent of Peru's mahogany, most of which is illegally harvested. Furthermore, the U.S. timber industry estimates that annual losses of about US$1 billion occur because cheaper imports of other countries undercut prices.[39] Other importing countries include Dominican Republic, Germany, The Netherlands, Spain, Finland, South Africa, Saudi Arabia, and the various range states.[40] Because of its high level of consumption,

Table 7.2 Annual Imports of Mahogany Timber (m³), 1996–2002* as Recorded in CITES Trade Statistics

Country of Import	1996	1997	1998	1999	2000	2001	2002	Mean
USA	54,455	73,846	74,485	89,161	70,601	85,615	68,632	73,828
Dominican Republic	10,214	10,643	5,163	17,771	14,165	9,911	16,610	12,068
UK	16,832	1,739	4,167	5,664	2,741	2,922	1,136	5,029
Canada	10	28	102	278	344	–	21,224	3,141
Spain	791	825	2,392	2,147	775	766	710	1,201
Netherlands	880	537	1,685	2,797	1,139	601	730	1,196
Mexico	778	107	201	140	553	2,461	475	674
Ireland	2,303	1,146	310	145	84	17	18	575
Denmark	1,558	557	68	412	299	611	273	540
Germany	–	254	857	522	289	500	347	396

*International Tropical Timber Organization, *Making the Mahogany Trade Work: Report of the Workshop on Capacity-building for the Implementation of the CITES Appendix-II Listing of Mahogany*, (INRENA, 2004): 19.

the United States has a major conservation role to play in saving these trees from extinction.

The National Association of Amazon Indians (AIDESEP[41]) of Peru and the Rainforest Foundation of Norway found that Peru's mahogany exports threaten the survival of indigenous tribes, especially in Madre de Dios, Ucayoli, and Loreto regions of Peru, in violation of international law.[42] Violence has broken out between loggers and various indigenous people. International law protects communities living in voluntary isolation, in order to protect their way of life and access to valued resources. AIDESP uncovered illegalities, such an issuance of exports licenses for timber, in violation of CITES guidelines. In 72 percent of logging areas visited by Peruvian officials, it was found that export quotas for 2005 and 2006 were based on false and/or misleading data provided by timber companies.[43]

Many consumers are ignorant of the complicated consequences of these illegal practices; others simply do not care. With regard to illegal logging activities, it is imperative to provide information to consumers about responsible purchasing, as well as information about sources of the products. Many companies are labeling their wood-based products to indicate that they were made from "sustainable forests." When buying wood products, questions to ask include: What exact species of tree yielded the timber product? From where was the timber harvested? Was it from a certified forest? Was it a generated from a forest run by trustworthy managers who take the responsibility of stewardship seriously? Were laws violated in the obtaining of the timber? A myriad of questions surround this issue, but the key point is that consumers need to ask them before purchasing.

Conservation

The IUCN currently classifies the big leaf mahogany as vulnerable, but they acknowledge that the data pertaining to the species needs updating.[44] CITES includes each of the three species of mahogany in Appendix II, which dictates that importers and exporters must demonstrate clearly that the harvest of the tree has not negatively impacted its sustainability, in addition to the provision of proof of legal harvest. This is known as a nondetrimental finding, which is a requirement for export/import. Some countries are implementing voluntary export quotas and cutting restrictions, such as minimum cutting diameters as part of their efforts to build and maintain sustainable forests.[45] It is somewhat encouraging that countries are putting these types of measures in place, but they alone will have little positive impact due to the enormity of the problem and the vast area covered by the range of the mahogany.

WWF is a key organization in the conservation efforts to save the big leaf mahogany. The importance and presence of the international offices of WWF, as well as their national offices, cannot be emphasized enough. WWF initially entered the Amazon rain forest in 1967.[46] Originally, WWF's activity in the area was simply that of field research. In the late 1970s, a long-term study on deforestation and fragmentation began in the Brazilian Amazon. Studies continue today throughout the Amazon rain forests.

The WWF's initiative, the Global Trade & Forest Network (GFTN), works to design, promote, and implement successful forest stewardship.[47] Specifically, WWF—GFTN has brought together over 300 companies and agencies worldwide to create a network of professionals committed to harvesting and trading timber legally and sustainably. This network is working to implement a forest certification system whereby timber, pulp, and other forest products are inspected and tracked at all stages of the production process. By instituting a system such as this, harvests are better controlled in order to ensure environmentally sound practices. GFTN also strives to improve forest management, concessions, and trade practices with the purpose of reducing inefficiencies and illegal practices. The overall goal of GFTN and their partner organizations is to eliminate illegal logging and to transform the worldwide timber trade in such a way as to save threatened forests.[48]

Currently there are 286 companies with roughly 2.4 million people working for the common goal. They represent an industry with combined annual sales globally of US$68 billion. Those within the network manage over 202 million hectares of certified forests and are in the process of certifying an additional 7.2 million hectares. They account for roughly 16 percent of the volume of global trade. GFTN's activities help support 42,749 local families.[49]

From Around the World

Because this mahogany species is located throughout parts of Central and South America and is largely imported by the United States, some specific efforts within these regions will be discussed. The symbiotic nature of the import/export relationship makes it is critical that they work together to find solutions to illegal logging, deforestation, and the exploitation of local communities and natural resources.

United States

The United States has legislation that assists in the fight against illegal logging. The Lacey Act, in addition to the ESA, was amended in 2008 with the aim of strengthening efforts to combat this trade. The Lacey Act prohibits all trade in plants and plant products that are illegally obtained within the United States and from countries exporting products into the United States.[50] The Act also requires importers to declare the harvest country, species' scientific name, measurements, quality, and value. Finally, the Act stipulates penalties for corporations and individuals who violate its tenets, which includes forgery of documents. Penalties can include fines up to US$500,000 for corporations, US $250,000 for individuals, or twice the profits whichever is highest. Additional punishment can include five years in prison and seizure of all goods. In determining penalties, the nature and severity of the crime is considered, along with the amount of due care exhibited.[51]

The Lacey Act requires documentation related to theft of plants/logs, taking from officially protected areas, taking from other officially designated areas other than protected areas, taking without authorization, failure to pay appropriate taxes, fees, and royalties, and violations of international agreements like CITES.

Activists have called for an outright refusal of shipments that fail to provide nondetrimental findings or show proper CITES permits. However, the United States has not responded to calls for tougher shipment inspections of mahogany in order to comply with CITES.[52]

Peru

Peru also was the target for increased pressure to address the illegal trade of mahogany stemming from its forests. In 2010, CITES gave Peru a directive to address the illegal timber trade within a six-month period.[53] Within this time frame Peru was to have enacted legislation that regulated the mahogany trade, implemented a computerized tracking system for the timber, and harmonized various harvest and export quota systems operating in the country. CITES explained to the Peruvian authorities that a failure to comply would result in a worldwide ban on exports of Peruvian mahogany. Estimates show a substantial decrease in Peruvian exports, but experts from WWF believe this is due to the plundered forests, rather than changes in forest management practices.[54]

Working with the WWF, Peru has established Alto Purús National Park, which sits alongside the border of Brazil in the southwestern ecoregion of the Amazon moist forest.[55] The park has approximately 49,710 mi^2 (80,000 km^2) of protected forests within both Peru and Brazil. The area encompasses an amazing array of biodiversity; it contains lowland tropical moist forests, flooded savannas, and is home to the last remaining large populations of big leaf mahoganies and over 80 terrestrial animals, 157 reptiles/amphibians, 100 fish, and a "remarkable level of bird and butterfly endemism.[56]" It is also home to numerous endangered species like the scarlet macaw (*Ara macao*), jaguar (*Panthera onca*), and the black spider monkey (*Ateles paniscus*). The forest has had little human disruption since the rubber industry first entered the forests in the late 1800s to early 1900s.

It is highly desirable to include communities living in voluntary isolation in the management of natural resources. Because of their isolated existence, these people are incredibly vulnerable to diseases brought in by those plundering the resources of their home. In order to help protect these communities, WWF helped to create within Alto Purús National Park a 16,927 mi^2 (27,242 km^2)

communal reserve that supports nine indigenous groups. WWF is also working with an additional 20 indigenous communities in Peru's Condorcanqui Province near the Ecuadorian border.[57] The purpose of WWF's presence is to help these communities build sustainable land-use techniques and to increase their ability to manage their natural resources. Specifically, the main objectives include (1) strengthening their socio-organizational capacities, (2) land use, and (3) improvement of the ability of individual families to produce their own income.[58] Additionally, WWF works to assist these communities in building conflict resolution skills pertaining to natural resource use, to help with their current timber harvesting, to incorporate market structures within the communities, and to help build their capacity to strengthen their production systems.[59]

Brazil

The Amazon Region Protected Areas (ARPA) is an expansive area, roughly twice the size of the United Kingdom that provides protection for 12 percent of the Brazilian Amazon.[60] To ensure that funding continues to reach the program, WWF set up a trust fund so efforts can continue and to help alleviate Brazil's financial burden. The goal is to create and maintain a well-managed conservation project for years to come. In 2003, ARPA outlined its main goals: (1) to establish approximately 109,267 mi^2 (283,000 km^2) of new conservation areas, (2) to introduce effective forest management systems in 48,263 mi^2 (125,000 km^2) of existing parks that have been neglected, (3) to create 34,303 mi^2 (89,000 km^2) of sustainable use reserves for local/forest communities so that they are empowered with a sense of benefit from effective stewardship of their valuable resources, and (4) to create a trust fund so that these reserves and park systems can operate in perpetuity. The target amount to accomplish these goals is US $20 million. In 2004, through a large donation from WWF–Brazil and the Ford Foundation, permanent capital was invested, thus providing long-term financial stability to the initiative. Other contributors include the World Bank, the Brazilian Biodiversity Fund, among others.[61]

As a result of ARPA's efforts, Tumucumaque Mountains National Park[62] was created, covering 14,980 mi^2 (38,800 km^2). Roughly the size of Switzerland, it is the world's largest tropical forest national park and the second largest overall national park in Brazil. By July 2006, about 21 million hectares were part of the protected areas within the Amazon. The size of the protected area has more than doubled since the beginning of the program.

The Amazon Keystone Initiative (AKI) is a project partially funded by Italy and Brazil.[63] AKI helps to implement front line conservation in the Acre and Purús conservation blocks and in Iténez Mamoré. AKI builds upon ARPA's work to improve and secure managerial and financial long-term practices and viability. The most recent estimates indicate that US$81 million has been raised, but the overall projected need for sustainable work is estimated at US$395 million.[64]

Efforts are underway in already established protected areas; however, AKI also aims to increase these areas by an additional 10 million hectares, as well as to improve managerial practices in 20 million hectares of protected areas.

Columbia

Columbia recognizes the importance of their forest natural resources. In an attempt to preserve their incredibly rich biodiversity, work has been underway for many years to improve the integrity of the forest ecosystem and to minimize the loss of damage because of deforestation and forest fragmentation. With help from WWF–UK and WWF-Columbia, the country has worked to institute policy changes that strengthen local conservation in conjunction with local community groups, nongovernmental agencies, public agencies, and relevant agencies at local, regional, national, and international levels.[65] The focus was concentrated in the Northern Andes, Choco-Darien, and Orinoco areas of Columbia.

French Guiana, Guyana, and Suriname

The Guiana Forests and Environmental Conservation Project (GFECP) rests within theses three countries.[66] The purpose of GFECP is the conservation of the region's forest ecosystem, primarily those in the Guianas. Within this area, there are over 154,441 mi^2 (400,000 km^2) of undisturbed rain forest that need the protection of conservationists. The biodiversity of these forests and those of adjacent countries is so unique that WWF estimates that approximately 40 percent of the world's flowering plants are native to and only found in this area. The threats in this area are much the same as in other forests and include mining, logging (legal and illegal), and plans for a hydropower plant, which will require the flooding of entire sectors of forests. Efforts to address these threats encompass the mobilization of conservation action, the protection of key sites containing high concentrations of valued flora and fauna, including those endangered, and finally, laying the foundation for a sustained conservation movement in the region.[67]

New Forestry Management Tools

The way forward to achieve sustainable forests is through new, modern management tools and practices. Without them, existing practices will continue to permit thefts from indigenous communities and other protected areas, as well as ignore the proliferation of illegal logging. Improved and modernized management practices allow for enhanced technical quality of existing forest operations, reduced costs, and improved relationships between the timber industry, forest managers, and consumers, who can provide more information about forest concession practices.

Toolkits have been developed to assist forest managers in their work of achieving sustainable forests. These toolkits offer systematic procedures pertaining to tracing activities from harvest to consumption. This tracking system helps identify and prove that timber and timber products are harvested legally and sustainably.[68] Modular Implementation and Verification Toolkits provided forest managers with a set of industry standards and certification, in order to help shape their practices.[69] Each module covers and offers an array of practical applications for real problems encountered while managing forest resources. Five main categories are included in the toolkits: (1) legal, (2) technical, (3) environmental, (4) social, and (5) chain of custody. Within the legal component, three main areas are covered: (1) resource rights, (2) legal aspects of operating legally, and (3) control of unauthorized activities. The technical component includes management planning, silviculture and sustained yield, plantation design, economic viability, forest operations and operational planning, monitoring, training and capacity building, forest protection, and chemical and biological control.[70] There are four main topics within the environmental component that include (1) waste management, (2) assessment of environmental resources and impacts, (3) conservation and environmental recourse impacts, and (4) conservation and environment protection. The social component of the toolkit covers health and safety, workers' rights, stakeholder analysis and social impact appraisal, rights and needs of forest users, and employment and local development. The final component deals exclusively with issues pertaining to chain of custody.

Sets of timber harvesting guidelines have been written to help mitigate unsustainable logging practices worldwide. These guidelines cover tree felling, yarding,[71] and hauling. Known as "reduced-impact logging," these practices are written to assist forest managers and logging companies in the minimization of harm to the environment. Reduced-impact logging practices are not new and the extent to which they reduce bad practices and profit are dependent on site conditions. Reduced-impact logging is planned, strategic, and carefully controlled by trained workers. The goal is timber-harvesting practices that minimize detrimental effects of tree harvesting.[72] A research study, comparing conventional logging to reduced-impact logging for effectiveness and financial viability, found that reduced-impact logging practices do not seem to help with sustainable timber yields or with sustainable forest management.[73]

WWF–Peru is working toward the implementation of modern, responsible, and efficient forest management practices, which include and focus on forest certification. Through a program called CEDEFOR (Certification and Development of the Forest Sector), WWF–Peru, with assistance from USAid, offers technical and monetary assistance to government, local communities, and private entities that contribute to the national economic growth, and forest conservation.[74] According to various authorities associated with CEDEFOR, "illegal problems remain the major obstacle to the proper functioning of the forest sector."[75] The overall aim of CEDEFOR is to certify a minimum of 565,000 hectares of Peruvian rain forest.

CONCLUSION

Agriculture is built upon routine activities; planting, rotating, and harvesting crops are all done at specific times of the year. If the care of crops is predictable, so, too, are the illegal farmers' activities. While it is extremely difficult to know exactly where in the illegal clearings of the forest and other activities are taking place from ground level vantage point, routine aerial patrols can easily uncover where clearings are located.

National parks and reserves provide a safe haven for a complicated ecosystem that contains some of the most endangered species on the globe. Additionally, these areas contribute to reducing carbon levels in the atmosphere. Furthermore, the parameters of these lands help local/forest communities establish their land rights and provide to them a sense of ownership of their valued resources. By doing this, conflicts between groups diminish.

Five areas of concern must be addressed before illegal logging is curtailed. First, forest policy and legal frameworks are incoherent, unrealistic, and unenforceable. Governments are unwilling to crackdown on illegal practices and institutional support is lacking. Second, institutional and political weaknesses, corruption, and lack of agency coordination destine efforts up for failure. Third, better data must be collated regarding the condition of current forest conditions, tree populations, production and movement of timber, and the volume of wood that actually crosses country borders. These are mere a sampling of the information needed; there are many more subjects that need to be identified and developed. The fourth area that needs redress is the corruption that surrounds the illegal timber trade. Corruption is associated with weak mechanisms of control, lack of transparency in policy making and implementation, and the marginalization of indigenous people, among others. Finally, the circumstances of market conditions pertaining to the illegal trade in timber must be explored and addressed.[76]

Efforts to save the big leaf mahogany are complicated, like other species, by their remote existence and the ability to illegally transport products across national lines. Corruption and weak border controls are major contributing factors to the continued illicit trade. Each country has its own unique approach to the problem, but until countries in the Amazon Basin agree to standardized timber practices, the survivability of the tree will remain in doubt. Further, the demand side of the equation must be addressed. As long as countries like the United States are willing to ignore the illicit origins of their goods, forests will continue to be decimated.

8

Avian Species

AS WITH MARINE SPECIES, bird species are difficult to track and count. Many breeds are migratory and yet some linger near where they live and breed. The importance of birds, cannot be understated. Plant seeds are part of their diet; through their expulsion, they help propagate new plants throughout their range. Birds most certainly contribute to the delicate structure of the ecosystem and, without their presence, higher-level species will feel the negative effects of their absence. A substantial number of bird species are at risk of or are vulnerable to extinction. Of course, far too many have already "gone the way of the Dodo."

Birds are among the most least researched of all endangered species. A dearth of literature pertaining to these creatures is slowly reversing with the extremely interesting research about the illegal trade of parrots in Mexico and Bolivia from Rutgers University[1] (see Boxes 8.1 and 8.2). These studies are informing us not only about the state of the parrot trade in these two countries, but perhaps more importantly, they provide a solid foundation for future conservation and crime reduction research.

Two bird species whose lives are jeopardized by human behavior are presented in this chapter: the Hyacinth Macaw (*Anodorhynchus hyacinthinus*) and the Red Kite (*Milvus milvus*).

HYACINTH MACAW (*Anodorhynchus hyacinthinus*)

Macaws are members of the parrot family. The hyacinth macaw (IUCN status 2008, endangered) is one of four known as blue macaws, which include Lear's (*Anodorhynchus leari*, IUCN status 2009, endangered), Spix's (*Cyanopsitta spixii*, IUCN status 2010, critically endangered), and Glaucous (*Anodorhynchus glaucus*, IUCN status 2010, critically endangered).

There are currently 22 species of macaws assessed by the IUCN (see Table 8.1). The following is a brief synopsis of the condition of the blue macaws. The Lear's Macaw population has been uncertain; surveys are being conducted to determine the proportion of mature to young individuals.[2] The Spix's Macaw has a grim future; several captive populations exist, but no individuals have been seen in the wild since 2000. The IUCN has not yet classified this species as

Box 8.1 Parrot Poaching in Mexico

The CRAVED model was first introduced to help identify those products most at risk of being stolen or "hot products." Stolen goods markets help to keep theft levels high and poaching helps to keep the illegal trafficking of wild flora and fauna at seriously high levels. Characteristics of the types of goods illegally traded influence the probability that those goods will be stolen or poached. Pires and Clarke (Rutgers University) applied CRAVED to the illegal poaching of parrots in Mexico.

They found that parrot poaching in Mexico was an opportunistic crime in which local villagers used poaching to supplement incomes. This finding countered conventional wisdom that most poaching, and hence, the subsequent selling of the catch, is done by highly professional poachers and traffickers.

The research also found CRAVED to be an extremely valuable tool when identifying species most at risk of being poached and sold into extinction. Particularly, the availability of a specific type of parrot made it easier for poachers to take them. Scarcity appeared to deter some of the local villagers from taking the birds. Additionally, poachers seemed to take the more valuable and disposable parrots less frequently.

Criminologists are entering unchartered waters when studying the crime of poaching and trafficking endangered species. In such a short amount of time, great strides are being made, but there are problems to overcome.

Source: Stephen F. Pires and Ronald V. Clarke, "Are Parrots CRAVED?: An Analysis of Parrot Poaching in Mexico," *Journal of Research in Crime and Delinquency*, published online March 15, 2011, DOI: 10.1177/0022427810397950.

extinct in the wild because surveys are still being conducted.[3] The Glaucous Macaw's population was last recorded in the 1960s.[4] The IUCN estimates that any surviving populations are thought to be extremely small. Furthermore, the IUCN does not believe that the bird's natural range has been adequately assessed.[5]

In 1988, the Hyacinth Macaw was listed as threatened by the IUCN; in 1994, it was listed as vulnerable. The last assessment of Hyacinth Macaws was in 2008 and, at that point, the bird was listed as endangered. The population account, coupled with historical declines in populations and the threat of illegal trafficking, supports the endangered listing.[6] According to the Hyacinth Macaw Project, there are about 6,500 wild Hyacinth Macaws with roughly 5,000 of those living in the Pantanal.[7]

Characteristics

The Hyacinth Macaw is the largest of all the macaws. It is 3 feet (1 m) in length from beak to the very tail, has a wingspan of 5 feet (1.5 m), and weighs over four pounds (1.8 kg).[8] It has vibrant, almost electrifying plumage of cobalt blue with yellow rings around its eyes. This macaw's beak is very strong. The bird has a

Box 8.2 Parrot Poaching in Bolivia

Professor Ronald V. Clarke, Rutgers University, is forging forward the understanding of crimes against nature, as well as developing a new perspective for researching them. He and his doctoral students have begun exploring these crimes from a crime reduction perspective thus allowing opportunities for interventions. Using geographic information systems, situational crime prevention, and optimal foraging theory, a study of poaching parrots in Bolivia investigated why certain species of parrots appeared in markets while others did not.

The starting point was to determine if poaching parrots in Bolivia was opportunistic in nature. Clarke and Pires hypothesized that if poaching was opportunistic, it would be expected to see indigenous species being illegally sold in local markets. Another hypothesis to be tested was that more exotic varieties of parrots would never reach local markets, but rather, would be sold elsewhere. In order to test these hypotheses, Clarke and Pires used specific techniques, which included geographic information systems data on the parrots' range and the distribution of human populations. Optimal foraging theory typically deals with exploring how animals find food, but Clarke and Pires apply it to their research to explore how poachers find their prey. They also introduce the concept of "itinerant and sequential fences" who also forage for animals to sell.

Findings confirmed the original hypotheses, but more importantly, the authors present an important methodological way forward in the way trafficking crimes are researched.

Source: Stephen Pires and Ron Clarke, "Sequential Foraging, Itinerant Fences, and Parrot Poaching in Bolivia," *British Journal of Criminology* 51, no. 2 (2011): 314.

Table 8.1 Macaws Listed by the IUCN

Common Name	Scientific Name	Status
Glaucous Macaw	*Anodorhynchus glaucus*	Critically Endangered
Hyacinth Macaw	*Anodorhynchus hyacinthinus*	Endangered
Lear's Macaw	*Anodorhynchus leari*	Endangered
Great Green Macaw (also Buffon's Macaw)	*Ara ambiguus*	Endangered
Blue & Yellow Macaw	*Ara ararauna*	Least Concern
Dominican Green & Yellow Macaw	*Ara atwoodi*	Extinct
Red & Green Macaw (also Green-winged Macaw)	*Ara chloropterus*	Least Concern
Jamaican Green & Yellow Macaw	*Ara erythrocephala*	Extinct
Blue-throated Macaw	*Ara glaucogularis*	Critically Endangered

(*Continued*)

Table 8.1 (Continued)

Common Name	Scientific Name	Status
Jamaican Red Macaw	*Ara gossei*	Extinct
Lesser Antillean Macaw	*Ara guadeloupensis*	Extinct
Scarlet Macaw	*Ara macao*	Least Concern
Military Macaw	*Ara militaris*	Vulnerable
Red-fronted Macaw	*Ara rubrogenys*	Endangered
Chestnut-fronted Macaw (also Severe Macaw)	*Ara severus*	Least Concern
Cuban Macaw	*Ara tricolor*	Extinct
Spix's Macaw	*Cyanopsitta spixii*	Critically Endangered
Red-shouldered Macaw (also Noble Macaw)	*Diopsittaca nobilis*	Least Concern
Red-bellied Macaw	*Orthopsittaca manilata*	Least Concern
Yellow-collared Macaw	*Primolius auricollis*	Least Concern
Blue-headed Macaw (also Coulon's Macaw)	*Primolius couloni*	Vulnerable
Blue-winged Macaw (also Illiger's Macaw)	*Primolius maracana*	Near Threatened

scaly tongue that has a bone in it so as to better remove the insides of fruit and nuts; they eat the acuri nut, but only after it is expelled from cows. This reliance on such a specific nut for sustenance limits their range. Their talons are able to grip strongly. These birds are very intelligent and are valued for their ability to mimic human speech. They are able to communicate through various sounds in order to communicate with others in their flock and to mark their territory. The Hyacinth Macaws, like many other species of birds, mate for life, share each other's food, and groom each other. The female is responsible for incubating the eggs while the male hunts for food.[9]

They nest in the cavity of high trees and on cliff faces from July through December. In the Pantanal, 90 percent of nests reside in manduvi trees. The birds use existing holes, which they will fill with sawdust. Normally, the female lays two eggs, but it is common for only one of the eggs to survive. It is estimated that only 15 to 30 percent of all adults attempt breeding each year. The 100 mated pairs at breeding age may only produce seven to 25 young each year.[10]

Habitat and Range

The Hyacinth Macaw lives in three distinct areas in South America: (1) east Amazonia and east central Brazil, (2) Brazil and Pantanal region, and

(3) southwestern Brazil into Bolivia and Paraguay. Their habitat is varied and includes savanna grasslands, dry thorn forests, palm stands, and swamplands specifically in the Pantanal. The estimated size of the entire range is 208,109 mile^2 (539,000 km^2).[11]

The Pantanal is the world's largest wetland and it has the largest collection of fauna in the Americas. It is 10 times larger than the Florida Everglades and is the size of Belgium, Switzerland, Portugal, and the Netherlands combined.[12] The Pantanal is 81,081 mi^2 (210,00 km^2) and stretches into Brazil, Paraguay, and Bolivia. The region is mostly flat—rich in rivers, lagoons, and lowland forests. When the annual floods come, the Pantanal is roughly 80 percent covered in water.[13]

The Pantanal is also a UNESCO biosphere reserve, as well as one of WWF's Global 200 Ecoregions.[14] However, this region is at risk due to human settlements, unsustainable farming, illegal mining, hydroelectric power plants, and unregulated tourism.

Threats

The two primary threats facing this bird species include deforestation and illegal trading. Deforestation causes the loss of their very specialized diet, the loss of appropriate nesting grounds, and the reduction of genetic viability as a result of the loss of species. These lovely birds are incredibly desired for their beauty and companionship. Because this species is protected via several international treaties, it is illegal to purchase the bird in its entirety or its parts, specifically the feathers. Historically, local and indigenous populations kill the bird in order to harvest its beautifully colored feathers for headdresses and for souvenirs. Because of deforestation and the illegal trade, populations have decreased significantly with only 2,500 to 3,000 in the wild at the end of the 1980s.

In the past two decades, populations of these birds were decimated due to the brisk pace at which poachers were removing them from their natural habitat.[15] In the 1980s, roughly 10,000 Hyacinth Macaws were poached for sale on the black market, largely in Brazil, but some were a result of local hunters killing the bird for its feathers.[16] While some populations have slowly increased, poaching, unfortunately has not.

A study[17] of the parrot trade in Los Pozos, Bolivia demonstrated that even though the Bolivian government banned the export of live birds in 1985, the parrot population, including the Hyacinth Macaw, still continued to decline. Los Pozos, at the time, was one of four main trading places for the parrot trade. Interviews with individuals, including poachers, indicated that poachers would sell to retailers. Between July 2004 and December 2007, a total of 27,535 parrots from 36 species were recorded as being sold at market. The most frequently sold was the Monk Parakeet (6,934), the Yellow-chevroned Parakeet (6,693), Turquoise-fronted Parrot (4,417), and only 11 Hyacinth Macaws, which were sold for markets outside Bolivia, mostly for those in Peru, Chilé, and Brazil.[18]

The most disturbing example of trafficking in endangered species is that of Tony Silva.[19] At one time, he was a famous bird conservationist, but greed turned him into a noted smuggler. Silva was the curator of the rare bird sanctuary in the Canary Islands, off the Spanish coast. He would smuggle birds in two ways: (1) he would tranquilize the birds and stuff them into small plastic tubes and put them into hollowed car doors; and (2) he would put them in false-bottomed suitcases under clothing. Most of the birds were dead on arrival.[20]

In 1994, a grand jury in Illinois indicted Silva of smuggling endangered species. Eventually found guilty, he was sentenced to seven years in prison for participating in a US$1.4 million smuggling ring. There were 37 others who were also convicted, including his mother. His organization was thought to cause the death of five to ten percent of the worldwide population of Hyacinth Macaws.[21] Unfortunately, the conviction of Tony Silva has not deterred other poachers.

A more recent case took place in Brazil where Brazilian federal police uncovered the largest operation of smuggling endangered species in the country's history.[22] Operation San Francisco was an eight-month investigation into illegal trafficking of endangered species. The investigation resulted in charges being levied against the leader of a group who worked with current and former police and environmental officers from the state of Paraná to traffic endangered species. Thirty-two others were also charged in the operation. The group was considered to be a complex organization that trafficked birds to and from Brazil into other nations; however, eggs were also targeted. The illegal operations included two money-laundering fronts, a factory, and a retail shop that enabled them to "clean" the illicit products.[23] One online auction had a Hyacinth Macaw sell for US$82,000.

Charges stemming from Operation San Francisco included illegal trafficking in protected Brazilian species, trafficking in exotic species without authorization, conspiracy, receiving stolen property, forgery of public documents, money laundering, and operating a financial institution without a license. The types of charges are indicative of the seriousness with which Brazil is taking this case. More often than not, countries have extremely light charges and sentences. The 10,000 seized animals were returned to their range state, some having to be re-imported into Brazil.[24]

Criminologist Ronald V. Clarke developed the CRAVED model in order to explain why thieves steal particular products (for a discussion of "hot products," see Box 5.1) and helps to explain this species' vulnerability. The Hyacinth Macaw is so large that concealing the entire bird is not easily done; however, it does not stop poachers from trying. Their feathers, on the other hand, are extremely easy to hide. Whether or not it is the entire bird or its feathers, this species is incredibly valuable and enjoyable by its consumers. Because these birds nest extremely high in manduvi trees, the availability and removability become relevant barriers. Poachers are very resourceful and take great strides to overcome the obstacles to capture the Hyacinth Macaw. Once the birds are taken, the entire bird, its feathers or its eggs are incredibly easy to sell; in other words, they are disposable.

Conservation

One woman, Neiva Guedes, is responsible for the vast majority of conservation efforts of Hyacinth Macaws in Brazil. In 1990, the biologist started the Hyacinth Macaw Project with the help of WWF–Brazil and other agencies.[25] The aim of the project is to simply save this species in the Pantanal region of Brazil, in the state of Mato Grosso du Sul. When the first project began, there were only about 1,500 wild hyacinth macaws living in the Pantanal region. With conservation efforts, the numbers have steadily increased.[26]

The team works with local ranchers and farmers to set up nesting grounds and to help protect against poaching. Those working on the project also repaired existing nests created by the birds, as well as building nests for them high above in the trees. Because there are so many different varieties of bird species in the Pantanal, competition exists for nesting space. Project team members construct nests for the Hyacinth Macaws, taking great care to ensure authenticity. In a disappointing turn, it was found that these macaws were not using them, but that other birds were.[27]

Additionally, the project team focused on successful incubation of eggs. Project members take the macaw's eggs when under threat and place them in a mechanical incubator.[28] The original egg is replaced with a chicken's egg. When the hatchling is strong enough, it is returned to the mother's nest. These egg protection efforts have resulted in the successful growth to maturity of a number of Hyacinth Macaws. Without doubt, the work of Neiva Guedes and the Hyacinth Macaw Project team support the sustainable development of the species.

Genetic variability provides sustainability for any species and the Hyacinth Macaw is no exception. Because of the low numbers of birds in existence, inbreeding is another possible threat to the long-term survivability of this species. A study was conducted in 2008 with the purpose of discovering the level of genetic variability among three nesting groups in Brazil.[29] The study found that the macaws in two separate locations in the Pantanal possess relatively low genetic variability, but they are genetically distinct from their counterparts in the state of Piauí, Brazil.[30]

Researchers analyzed five recovered Hyacinth Macaws. Findings suggest that the Pantanal is not the source of the illegally traded birds. This type of knowledge is extremely important for conservation efforts like the market reduction approach as this approach requires specific information about each species. Knowing that these seized birds were not from the Pantanal leads authorities to seek out data to confirm their origin. Once it becomes known, authorities have a unique opportunity to build intervention strategies within the areas where poachers are taking the targeted species. These types of data are the E.R.A.S.O.R. (for more details on E.R.A.S.O.R., see Chapter 1) which is part of the market reduction approach model. Conservation requires an evaluation of genetic variation[31] and it is also instrumental to crime reduction efforts.

RED KITE (*Milvus milvus*)

The Red Kite has disappeared from much of its historic range. Today, the IUCN categorizes it as near threatened because the species has undergone a moderate, yet rapid population decrease.[32] This is largely due to poisoning from pesticides, human persecution, and changes in land use. While there are rapid declines in numbers in southern Europe, some populations in northern countries are witnessing increases. It has had a tumultuous history in terms of census counts. The IUCN in 1988 classified the species as threatened, but in the 1994 and 2000 assessments, their status was changed to lower risk/least concern. In 2004, it was considered to be of least concern; however in the last two censuses, 2005 and 2008, the bird was classified as near threatened.[33]

Characteristics

The Red Kite has been described as, "the most beautiful bird of prey in Britain."[34] Its plumage includes the colors of black, chestnut, gray, and reddish-brown. The under wings are pure white with patches and black wing tips. It is about 24 inches (61 cm) long with a wingspan of 67 inches (170 cm).

The Red Kite is a scavenger bird, feeding on a variety of dead animals, as well as on garbage. The species is capable of killing its own prey, which consists of small mammals. Its primary diet consists of dead animals.[35]

The birds are monogamous and tend to mate for life. Their nests are messy and largely built on existing crows' nests using man-made items like plastics, paper, and cloth. The Red Kite has been known to steal clothing left hanging to dry on backyard clotheslines for their nests! The birds tend to lay between one and four eggs in April. The females incubate the eggs while the males serve as protectors of the nest. Hatchlings leave the nest around the seven-week mark, but they rely on their parents for food and protection for up to another month.[36]

These patterns typify the nature of the routine activity theory. The birds mate and nest at predictable times of the year. As long as poachers are aware of the location of nesting grounds, eggs are at risk of being taken. Due to the small size of the eggs, they are concealable. The Red Kite nests in areas that are readily accessible, thus making them removable. When poachers understand patterns of breeding, they know when eggs become available. With a vibrant collectors' market, eggs can be easily sold through illegal markets for large profits. The characteristics and natural patterns of the Red Kite fit the CRAVED model and, therefore, help to keep the species at risk.

Habitat and Range

The Red Kite has an extensive range, including the western Palearctic, which includes Europe; Africa, north of the Tropic of Cancer; the northern part of the

Arabian Peninsula; and Asia, north of the Himalayas. The birds are highly adaptable and can thrive in a number of different landscapes, but the species does require an open landscape so they can forage for food. However, about 95 percent (19,000–23,000) of the global breeding ground is situated in Europe.[37] Furthermore, the vast majority of the European population resides in Germany. Another 890 pairs live and breed in Spain and Portugal, east to the Ukraine, and north to Sweden, Latvia, and the United Kingdom.

Populations throughout their breeding grounds suffered in the late 1990s and early 2000s as the entire population experienced about a 20 percent drop during that time period.[38] Specifically, the East German population decreased 25 to 30 percent from 1991 to 1997, but numbers have remained stable since that time. France does not have an official population monitoring system, but it is estimated that numbers fell by about 80 percent. Other regions experienced similar declines ranging between 46 and 50 percent.[39] Numbers of breeding pairs were decimated to just 10 in the Balearic Islands, which are situated near the Iberian Peninsula. The population in the United Kingdom recovered from virtual extinction in the 1900s to extreme lows in 2008 (1,350 breeding pairs) to over 10,000 at last census count. The Red Kites are regionally extinct in Cape Verde, a string of islands in the Atlantic Ocean, off the coast of northern Africa near Mauritania and Senegal. They are absent in 17 countries worldwide.[40]

Threats

In the Middle Ages, the bird was an extremely valued part of the community. They cleaned the streets from a variety of debris. So valued, the bird was protected by a British Royal Decree, which applied the death penalty to anyone who killed a Red Kite.[41] By the sixteenth century, the bird was loathed and a bounty was placed on its head. This bird has truly fallen from grace—from royal protection to vermin.

Gamekeepers and farmers began blaming the Red Kite for killing game and livestock and, as a result, farmers have killed as many of the "menaces" as possible.[42] Because the bird carries a large bill and strong talons, it was extremely easy and convenient to blame the bird whenever something on the farm was killed. It is estimated that in the early twentieth century when Red Kite populations were at critically low numbers, gamekeepers and farmers killed about 80 simply with poisoned bait.[43]

Illegal poisoning, along with the existence of poison bait for other animals and egg collection, are the two most serious threats to the Red Kite.[44] Rat poison is particularly dangerous because if a rat ingests the anticoagulant, and then the bird eats the dead rat, the bird will die secondarily from the poison. It is estimated that about half of all poisonings of Red Kites is through deliberate abuse of agricultural chemicals. Aside from the threat from poisoning, taxidermists and eggs taken merely accelerated their decline in numbers. Lead poisoning also is a contributing factor to deaths. Animals that are killed by gunshot are eaten by the birds and, because of their size and consumption amounts, are poisoned by the lead in the shots.[45]

Conservation

The United Kingdom has taken the lead on efforts to conserve the species, despite the fact that nearly two-thirds of the world's Red Kite population resides in Germany.[46] As a result of the various threats, the birds became extinct in England in 1871 and 1879 in Scotland. The species was offered protection in 1903 because only a few pairs remained in the most remote parts of both countries. Because of the critical population census, scientists and conservationists became very concerned about the genetic viability of the species. DNA analysis confirmed their fears as the entire Welsh population of Red Kites stemmed from a single female bird!

In the 1950s, poisoning continued, but food sources became scarce due to the outbreak of myxomatosis[47] in rabbits. The number of pairs did not begin to increase until the 1960s. Breeding became problematic due to the lack of genetic diversity in existing populations. The Royal Society for the Protection of Birds (RSPB) began work under English Nature and Scottish National Heritage. RSPB lobbied to get the bird protected under the UK's Wildlife and Countryside Act of 1981, and they are now fully protected by (Schedule 1) of the Act. After the listing, it became a crime in England to take, injure, or kill a Red Kite, including its nest and eggs. Additionally, it criminalized the intentional, reckless disturbing of the nest during breeding season. If convicted, the offender can be incarcerated up to six months and fined up to £5,000 (US$7,971).[48]

The Red Kite has been the focus of conservation projects worldwide for over 100 years. In 1903, the first Red Kite committee was formed of concerned individuals whose first program entailed nest protection efforts. The RSPB became involved in 1905 and, in spite of their efforts through to the 1950s, about one-quarter of all nests were destroyed each year. In the next decade, better nest protection strategies were introduced, so destruction appeared to be less of a problem than in previous years.[49] In the 1980s, the Red Kite was one of three globally threatened species, which necessitated the United Kingdom to act. English Nature and Scottish Natural Heritage decided to reintroduce the bird in its various habitats; however, IUCN criteria had to be met before reintroduction was to proceed. These included:

- Evidence that the species was naturally occurring in the area where introduction was to take place;
- Conservationists had to have a clear idea as to why the species vanished and what part human interaction played. If humans were the reason for the disappearance, conservationists had to discern if the species was unable to naturally recolonize;
- Conservationists had to demonstrate that the factors that contributed to the species' disappearance were corrected;

- The genetic viability of the birds to be introduced had to be similar to those that previously inhabited the area; and
- It had to be established that no detrimental effects would be felt on the populations from which the birds were being taken.[50]

Conservationists released a total of 93 birds from Sweden and Spain. They were successfully released between 1989 and 1993 in Scotland and 1994 in England. In 1992, England and Scotland lay witness to breeding at both of the reintroduction sites. Two years after that, Red Kites reared in the wild produced hatchlings. This marked the end of the first stage of conservation and the beginning of the next stage.[51]

The goal of the second stage was to produce five, self-sustaining breeding populations in the United Kingdom by the year 2000 and to ensure these breeding populations were self-sustaining.[52] This goal was met as populations in the United Kingdom have indeed increased, albeit in small numbers. For example in 1996, the 19 birds from Germany were released in central Scotland. They nested in 1998 and two pair produced five fledglings. The small numbers produced in each nesting make the task of increasing populations a slow process. The British Broadcasting Corporation (BBC) reported in 2010 that the first 30 of 90 birds were released in Grizedale Forest in the Lake District of England.[53] This was considered yet another "conservation coup" and over the next three years, the remaining 60 would be released.

Continued conservation efforts center around monitoring population trends, in addition to managing the reintroduced populations.[54] Conservationists continue to urge increased severity for legal remedies against those who threaten the species. They also call for increased public awareness campaigns about the need to protect the Red Kite. Conservationists press for increased areas of suitable habitat and further studies to examine how successful, continued efforts are faring. Finally, they are lobbying the European Union against certain lax policies.[55]

Despite all the efforts and successful techniques in place, the Red Kite still faces difficulty. All birds born through the reintroduction programs are all tagged for monitoring. In 2007, the BBC reported that police were investigating the poisonings of Red Kites.[56] Wildlife police in central Scotland said that the postmortem of the dead birds revealed extremely high levels of poison and that the levels were not accidental. Those most recent deaths were among other Red Kite poisonings. The wildlife officer had harsh words to say to whomever committed the crime; he described them as "deplorable, irresponsible, criminal, and shameful."[57] Earlier that year, another poisoning death was uncovered in central Scotland. Wildlife officers commented that there were hotspots of killings "that blight our civilisation and our reputation worldwide."[58] Statements like these indicate the seriousness of conservation efforts on behalf of the Red Kite.

In 2010, another Red Kite was found shot to death in the Cumbrian Forest in England.[59] The bird was one of those reintroduced; the male was one of 30 released in Grizedale Forest. The shooting was no accident; the bird had been shot four times in the chest. Police are still investigating the case.

PART III

A Way Forward

The Way Toward Survival

THE WAY FORWARD in the protection of wild flora and fauna that are at risk of extinction is the use of innovative crime reduction approaches. The illicit trade in endangered species is a superb opportunity for a unique partnership between conservation and criminology. A small, but growing group of researchers in criminology are forging these types of relationships, despite two main challenges. First, crime reduction models and techniques require different data from what currently exists. Second, when existing data are used, getting conservationists and ecopolicy makers to take notice of the new approaches may take considerable time.

CRIME REDUCTION USING THE MARKET REDUCTION APPROACH

The success of the market reduction approach is dependent on sound data and precise implementation. The model is reliant on the analyses of a variety of data in order to understand how flora and fauna are hunted, killed, processed, and shipped to consumers. The market reduction approach aims to develop a clear understanding of how illicit markets operate so partner agencies can work together to reduce those markets. This market reduction will then reduce illegal poaching and trafficking. In order to achieve this, several types of data must first be collected and analyzed.

Partnerships are integral to the market reduction approach. The reliance on partnerships fits well within in the community-policing paradigm, whereby the police identify a problem and then seek to establish relevant partnerships, which may be species-dependent. Therefore, when applying the market reduction approach to specific endangered flora or fauna, it is important to identify which potential partnerships are most germane to solving the problem.

The market reduction approach is a structured one that can be applied to any illegal market. The basic framework provides for a series of steps: collecting various types of data that help frame the nature of the problem, using data to strategize with relevant partners as to which illegal market to tackle, designing intervention tactics for the specific market and species under review, implementing the interventions, marketing results of intervention tactics, along with the negative consequences of markets; monitoring results, making changes in tactics when necessary; and consolidating efforts. These steps are continually assessed and modified in order to maximize results.

Traditional Crime Data Analysis

The market reduction approach incorporates traditional police crime data to help shape the understanding of illegal markets. Police data are extremely rich with information that can be mined for specific purposes. With regard to traditional stolen goods markets, analyses of the types and quantities of stolen property illustrate the types of goods that are in high demand. Additionally, data about offenders (nodes of activities, pathways to/from those nodes, and association with other criminals related to theft and fencing goods) are also critical in developing an overall picture of how stolen goods are moved from the point of theft to the consumer.

In terms of nontraditional stolen goods markets, such as those in endangered species, local, national, and international police agencies have an important role in deciphering the illegal activity of killing and selling wild endangered flora and fauna. The dynamics of the crime are much the same as with traditional stolen goods markets. The property simply takes a different form, and the disposal locations can cross various international borders.

Property Data

Items seized by police provide an excellent indication of what consumers are collecting and for what they are willing to pay. By their nature, CRAVED products are most likely hot products. Traditional crime interventions focus on the offender—working to determine *who* committed the crime. However, the market reduction approach focuses efforts on determining *what types of property* are most at risk of being stolen whether through shop theft, burglary, or robbery.

Therefore, analyzing property is a key component in tackling illegal markets, including those focusing on protected plants and animals. The aim of the property analysis is to uncover what the "hot products" are so that policy makers and practitioners can begin to prioritize intervention activities. A study pertaining to traditional stolen goods markets in the United Kingdom examined the types of property that were most stolen.[1] The most frequently stolen goods were clothing items. Electronic goods that included video and DVD players followed. Food items (coffee, meats, and cheeses) were also the frequent target of thieves. Finally household appliances, compact discs and their players, and power tools rounded out the hottest products in the study area. Once it was known what was stolen, an analysis was performed as to how these goods made it into the hands of consumers after the theft. Combined—hot products and market types—permitted law enforcement and their partners valuable information so that they could begin designing intervention strategies.

In terms of endangered species, partners have to determine if tigers or elephants are targeted and if they are, they must discover what by-products are exchanging hands. Various species have different parts that fit within the CRAVED paradigm. As an example, tigers are susceptible to killing due to the high demand for their teeth, claws, tails, penises, and skin. The desire to have items made from ivory make elephants vulnerable. Unworked ivory is perhaps difficult to dispose more so than worked pieces, which, depending on size, can be easily moved throughout various points of transportation. Bushmeat, depending on the size of the pieces, can be dried for easier transportation. In its raw form, disposing of it can be more difficult. Knowing details about what items are harvested can help inform interventions.

Market Analysis

It is helpful to know the identity of past and current poachers, as this information will become important in the next stage of data collection. Information on property helps to discern the network of offenders. Once patterns of property are identified, the next step is to explore the ways that property exchanges hands. Interviews with past and current poachers reveal those exchange relationships— in other words, the markets. Knowing how the markets operate helps to inform intervention policies. Disrupting a market whereby goods are sold through friends requires different tactics than one where goods are sold through commercial outlets. Other patterns are revealed through these interviews.

In traditional stolen goods markets, it is evident that thieves do not steal simply for pleasure or steal items for personal use; rather, handlers play a pivotal role in the stolen goods market by giving thieves lists of things to steal because buyers were already in place. Research also showed that reducing the time of possession of stolen goods also reduces the handlers' probability of being detected by authorities.[2] Disposing stolen goods quickly helps to keep the crime relatively invisible. In this scenario, there is no time for authorities to merely react; by implementing the market reduction approach, authorities are able to proactively and strategically pursue offenders. Other traditional crime data includes analyses of map locations from where the property is stolen compared to locations of known theft-related offenders, including handlers, and finally to locations of disposal sites.

Mapping and Geospatial Analysis

Crime mapping is a critical tool imbedded in the market reduction approach because it strengthens spatial understandings about crime and crime problems. Crime maps can be used in a number of ways: to predict where the next hot spot may occur, to inform and guide tactical operations, and to help understand where the most vulnerable places are located. Conservation mapping identifies ranges where species live in which landscapes are fractured or destroyed, thus affecting the survivability of the species. Crime mapping contributes additional information, such as proximity of poachers to kill zones/areas, animals to communities, and kill zones/areas to sales outlets. The relevance of knowing about proximity is revealed in the "journey to crime" literature. While very specialized criminals may travel large distances in order to commit their crimes, it is far more typical for criminals to commit crime close to where they live, work, and play. In other words, crimes are committed as criminals go about their routine activities and when opportunities arise. Research must be undertaken, similar to that emanating from Rutgers University,[3] to determine how far poachers and fences go in order to kill and sell endangered species.

The IUCN has added mapping capabilities to their publicly available data. These maps are a valuable addition for the purpose of the assessment of threatened species. Spatial data exist for 20,000 Red List species, including amphibians, mammals, birds, and reef-building corals. These maps do have limited criminological use. The data are arranged in order to yield information about presence, origin, and seasonality.[4] The data cannot discern what villages are near the species' presence, where poachers and handlers are located, or where transshipments are processed. This spatial database was simply not constructed with crime prevention in mind. Both the market reduction approach and situational crime prevention demand specificity. Without knowing the intricacies of the nature of the crime under consideration, effective intervention mechanisms will no doubt fail when implemented. The risk of designing interventions based on generalities is a belief that interventions are useless.

There exists an excellent opportunity for crime analysts to work with conservationists. Conservationists have necessary global positioning system (GPS) data points that outline range or landscape boundaries, upon which crime analysts can build a database with relevant crime-related variables, such as coordinates where animals are killed, known residences of poachers, locations of villages near or in the conservation areas, access roads/pathways, distances between villages and kill areas, locations of handlers, shopping areas, areas of rebel conflict, among others. Working in tandem, policy makers and tacticians from partner agencies will have more complete information about the nature of how species are hunted and sold, which, in turn, can help educate conservation responses.

E.R.A.S.O.R.

This component of the market reduction approach picks up where traditional data analysis does not go. To understand **E**xtra **R**outine **A**nd **S**ystematic **O**pportunistic **R**esearch (E.R.A.S.O.R.), it is best to think of what social scientists or journalists do—they ask questions in order to garner information to better understand situations, not to prosecute offenders. Social science research can contribute to the holistic approach of preventing or reducing the illegal trade by interviewing a variety of groups and individuals. A neutral interviewer can be invaluable because an imminent threat of arrest or prosecution is absent. Information obtained from structured interviews with the following:

- Current/former poachers can provide an explanation or description on how and why they decide on which species to hunt/harvest/kill, areas where they hunt, methods of disposing the flora/fauna, length of time it takes to dispose of their catch, money made from illegal activities, things that deter their illegal activities, among other topics.
- Handlers operate in secrecy and under the veil of anonymity. It is important to know whether they task the poachers to hunt/kill/harvest specific varieties of flora and fauna, are willing to buy anything, specialize in one type of species, use the same transshipment locations each time they need to move illicit products to another handler, have regular poachers with whom they work, run a legitimate business alongside their trafficking activities, keep the by-products for long periods of time or if they immediately sell it to someone else.
- Legitimate hunters could also be useful sources of information about how and where animals are tracked and hunted.
- Local residents are excellent sources of information about illegal markets. They generally know who participates in the illegal trade and, therefore, may know how goods are disposed. They might also know what shopkeepers may sell illicit goods. They can provide a source of protection through patrols or work with ecotourism.
- Shop owners have participated in selling stolen goods in addition to their legitimate businesses. It is important to know if they do the same with endangered species.
- Relevant partners include conservation officers, government officials; local, regional, and national police; customs and border officers, CITES representatives, schools, farmers, and plantation owners.
- Journalists are becoming extremely interested in the endangered species trade. They are often given access to situations where others are excluded. Details that journalists uncover about the mechanisms of the illegal trade could be used to supplement other materials to better appreciate the complexity of the problem.

E.R.A.S.O.R. data, along with traditional data, will identify what type of market exists, which, in turn, will inform partners when prioritizing what type of illegal endangered species market is to be targeted. There most probably will be several ways to buy and/or to sell endangered goods. Some markets are easier to disrupt than others, so it may be prudent to initially choose the market for which there may be the most success. This is important for a number of reasons. It provides the community quick evidence that something is actually being done to combat the problem, thus increasing the legitimacy of the approach in the community. It also boosts enthusiasm among team members to know that they can influence the illegal operations. Decisions as to which market to disrupt first may be influenced by available financial resources, human resources, and the level of threat that the species is facing.

Once the priorities are set, partners can design tactical planning and implementation can begin. Crackdown operations are dependent on resources available to the team and the type of market to be disrupted. Priorities are also influenced by which partners are involved in the decision making. Law enforcement may not be the best way to reduce an illegal endangered species market. It may well be a community group or conservation groups. Whatever crackdowns are used, results must be shared with local and regional communities. Marketing successes help to highlight the problem and also send the important message that officials are taking the problem seriously. Marketing is not just reserved for success stories. The market reduction approach seeks to inform the public about the negative consequences of buying and selling endangered species. This can be done through local media, schools, and neighborhood meetings.

Data collection and analyses continue through crackdown and marketing activities. If a specific crackdown technique is used, but proves ineffective, partners immediately can decide on a different course of action as opposed to waiting several weeks or months. The cycle of the market reduction approach is perpetual, as it constantly builds on successes, collects data, and troubleshoots the problem. It is important to note here that crackdowns can have both short- and long-term effects. The market reduction approach sees crackdowns of either type as useful. The primary purpose is to disrupt the illegal markets, which makes dealing in the illegal goods much more risky and difficult. Crackdowns that have short-term effects help officials maintain pressure on the participants in the illicit markets.

Once priorities have been set, interventions are planned using the 25 techniques of situational crime prevention.[5] The mechanisms and corresponding techniques are designed with the aim of making the commission of a particular crime more difficult. The mechanisms (increase the effort, increase the risk, decrease the rewards, reduce provocations, and remove excuses) provide for a variety of techniques that may help to impact the offender's desire to commit a crime. Not all of the techniques will be suitable for every crime type or situation; therefore, a complete analysis of pertinent data is necessary in order to utilize the most relevant mechanism and techniques.

Situational Crime Prevention—Endangered Species

Reducing the illegal trade in endangered flora and fauna requires its own matrix of situational crime prevention mechanisms (see Table 9.1). The market reduction approach is a holistic strategy that can help officials reduce virtually any

Table 9.1 Twenty-five Techniques of Situational Crime Prevention—Endangered Species

Increase the Effort	Increase the Risks	Decrease the Rewards	Reduce Provocations	Remove Excuses
Target Harden • Radio collars with GPS ability on highly demanded species • Spray smart water on legally sawn lumber—monitor at checkpoints	*Extend Guardianship* • Antipoaching patrols • Community/village patrols • Placement and use of rangers	*Conceal Targets* • Not possible to remove animals/plants from their natural habitat (most ranges are concealed due to natural surroundings)	*Reduce Frustrations and Stress* • Governments work to reduce or eliminate conflict with rebels • Work to protect villages/communities from animal encroachment	*Set Rules* • Manufacturers cannot use endangered species in their products • Chefs are forbidden to use shark fins and other endangered species' meat and/or by-products in their dishes
Control Access to Facilities • Not feasible for large nature reserves or oceans	*Assist Natural Surveillance* • Partner with conservation agency to mount hidden cameras to monitor activity around known habitats • CCTV in village/cities near outlets for illegal goods	*Remove Targets* • Not possible given natural range habitats	*Avoid Disputes* • Build fences around villages to avoid animal encroachment • Mediate with rebel groups to allow access to various species	*Post Instructions* • "No hunting" signs • "This shop does not sell endangered species products" sign • "Poachers will be prosecuted" signs
Screen Exits • Searches at various ports • Check customs documents	*Reduce Anonymity* • Arrest and prosecute those who poach endangered species	*Identify Property* • Animal branding • Spray smart water on legally harvested timber	*Reduce Emotional Arousal*	*Alert Conscience* • "Buying Products Made from Endangered Species Supports Killing" signs at tourist shops

(Continued)

Table 9.1 (Continued)

Increase the Effort	Increase the Risks	Decrease the Rewards	Reduce Provocations	Remove Excuses
• Check shipping manifests • Check for CITES documents	• Publicize the identities of those arrested/convicted for poaching • Arrest and prosecute those who purchase goods made of endangered species • Publicize the identities of those arrested/convicted for purchasing goods made of endangered species • Publicize restaurants that cook with endangered species			• Marketing campaign discouraging the consumption of shark fin soup • Marketing campaign explaining the link between buying endangered species products and the increased risk of extinction • Marketing alternatives to TAMs
Deflect Offenders • Develop alternative ways for locals to earn money • Develop ecotourism venues • Employ former poachers in alternative industries	*Utilize Place Managers* • CCTV in nature reserves • Reward vigilance	*Disrupt Markets* • Implement the market reduction approach • Monitor pawn shops • Controls on classified ads • License street vendors • Employ media campaigns • Develop partnerships between police, conservation agencies, and local residents	*Neutralize Peer Pressure* • Recruit elders to use alternatives to TAMs • Recruit elders to use alternatives in headdress or ceremonial garb	*Assist Compliance* • Monitor shipments of mahogany from point of origin through final destination • Examine customs documents • Examine CITES documents

Control Tools/Weapons	Strengthen Formal Surveillance	Deny Benefits	Discourage Imitation	Control Drugs and Alcohol
	• Use forensics to verify species of illegally traded products • Cameras at points in national reserves where people and endangered species live/grow	• Mark demanded animals so their fur is undesirable to poachers • Use science to develop nonharmful ways to alter nature	• Close farms that breed endangered species (e.g., tiger farms, sturgeon farms)	• Monitor drug routes • Explore links between drug trafficking and endangered species trafficking

market that involves illegally traded illicit goods, like endangered species by-products. Disrupting illegal markets is one of the situational crime prevention techniques to reduce rewards. There are other situational crime prevention techniques that are plausible for tackling this particular crime. The following is an overview of the specific techniques that will influence wildlife trafficking.

Increase the Effort

The techniques included in this situational crime prevention mechanism are target harden, control access to facilities, screen exits, deflect offenders, and control tools/weapons. Target hardening is the protection of vulnerable areas and things. In relation to endangered species, this becomes a challenge simply due to the nature of the circumstance and crime. That said, there are some basic techniques that could be employed, such as affixing radio/GPS devices and/or collars in order to track flora and fauna most at risk of poaching. Once the devices are attached, monitoring must take place to determine the location of species in addition to patterns of behavior. If individual animals are killed, researchers and officials will be able to identify the exact location, which could aid in the development of responses. Ideally, if poachers see the technology in use, they may decide not to commit the crime.

Controlling access to facilities (access to animals) is another technique to increase the effort it takes on the part of an offender to accomplish a crime. It would be extremely difficult and unwise to build enclosures around the range state of a species. It would be impossible within the oceans. Ranges are already incredibly fractured. To prohibit the free movement of potential offenders would also prohibit the free movement of animals. It is simply not feasible to restrict access, nor is it feasible to screen exits, which is another tactic under the same category. What might be more reasonable is to prohibit road building in or around range areas.

Screening exits are also impossible in terms of nature reserves or national parks. However, screening becomes important in the endangered species trade at various ports of entry and exit. Officials must be diligent in their screening of customs and CITES documentation, as well as shipping manifests. Inspections of these important documents can uncover inaccuracies and fraud.

Deflecting offenders in the endangered species trade is somewhat different than with traditional crimes. Rather than dispersing crowds at pubs or separating facilities, deflecting offenders in the illicit trade of protected flora and fauna lies within the development of alternative ways for locals and poachers to earn money. A successful example of this is ecotourism. In most operations, former poachers are hired, thus providing them an alternative income stream. Various species are being targeted for the tourist industry. Scuba divers are afforded the opportunity to dive with various sharks and whales; hikers can enter the heart of various forests and reserves to observe natural flora and fauna. The income generated from these endeavors is far greater and more steady than poaching.

Increase the Risks

Techniques included within this mechanism are extended guardianship, assistance with natural surveillance, reduction of anonymity, utilization of place managers, and the strengthening of formal surveillance. External guardianship is already in place in some areas with the use of antipoaching patrols and the increased use of rangers who attempt to stop poaching and other related activities, such as the illegal charcoal trade. Some communities have adopted neighborhood patrols to thwart illegal hunting and killing. For example, women in India have started to become particularly active in protecting tigers that reside around their villages. Activities such as these play a critical role as part of market reduction approach partnerships.

Another useful tactic that could complement the efforts of the market reduction approach to reduce illegal endangered species markets is that of assisting natural surveillance. Conservation agencies are a critical partner when trying to implement this tactic. Oftentimes agencies mount hidden cameras within specific ranges in order to monitor animal behavior. The cameras could be used to film poaching activities, which would, in turn, help police develop and understand how and where poachers approach the flora and/or fauna. Further, if the technology is available and if the data support their use, cameras could be placed in various places within villages and towns where poachers go to sell their goods. These types of activities also represent the technique of utilizing place managers.

In order to inform people of the seriousness of poaching and trading protected species, it is important to reduce the anonymity associated with the crime. Arresting offenders and publishing their names in local, regional, national, and international venues is one way to strip them of their anonymity. It is equally important to publicize the identities of those who buy the illegally obtained endangered species. Further, restaurants that cook with endangered species must be made known to the public. By doing so, it provides conservationists and activists time to prepare protests or other types of campaigns to bring negative attention to their practices.

Using forensic science to positively identify the types of species being traded is a valuable tool in strengthening formal surveillance. Placing cameras near those locations where animals and humans interact will also help to protect endangered species, as well as humans. Monitoring these activities is also a technique included as a way to strengthen formal surveillance.

Decrease the Rewards

Within this category are the following techniques: concealment of targets, removal of targets, identification of property, disruption of markets, and denial of benefits. The market reduction approach can develop tactics that would help to reduce rewards gained by offenders. The identification of property (in this case, endangered species) is an important aspect of reducing rewards. With conservation agencies, officials could design a way to mark those animals most in demand so as to identify the range from which they were removed and as a way to ruin the look of the coveted by-product. Ink tags are used to protect high-value clothing so that when improperly removed, the ink destroys the garment. Obviously, ink tags will not work on animals, so criminologists and conservationists must turn to science in order to design a way to make the skin or ivory less appealing. A far-fetched example is to genetically alter the DNA of the elephant so it produces neon-green tusks. Science has already produced a neon-green pig and a glow in the dark cat—evidence that with science anything is possible.

Of course, tactics like this raise ethical issues of altering nature. Without a doubt, this type of action would cause alarm among several interest groups. Today, there are no definitive answers on how or if nature could or should be altered, but it does open a discussion on what extremes can and should be taken to in order to save species from extinction. Altering nature with science can have unanticipated consequences. For example, there may be consumers who would highly desire neon-green elephant tusks! Modifying nature may cause more problems than expected, so for obvious reasons, careful considerations must be given to any solution offered.

Creation of ecotourism was previously introduced as a way to deflect benefits. However, the introduction of ecotourism can also provide alternative rewards to communities that are home to some of the most endangered species in the world. Poachers, who previously made their living from illegal activities, can be retrained to participate in ecotourism activities, thus providing them legal sources of income.

Reduce Provocations

Reducing provocations can be accomplished through the following techniques: reduction of frustrations and stress, avoidance of disputes, reduction of emotional arousal, neutralization of peer pressure, and discouragement of imitation.

Many endangered species are located within areas of conflict, deprivation, and other sources of frustration. Governments must work to reduce relevant frustrations by acknowledging the source of them. This is related to the next technique—avoiding disputes. Disputes exist in and around natural areas where wild flora and fauna live and they must be reduced. These disputes take the form of human–animal conflicts, but they also manifest themselves in the form of civil unrest and war. In areas where human–animal conflicts occur, fences have been built around human settlements so animals can be deterred from entering. Civil unrest and war are outside the scope of the market reduction approach, but it is critical that governments realize what negative effect these conflicts have on endangered species. The gorillas in Virunga National Park are placed at even greater risk due to the presence of rebel soldiers who sell access to the animals or who are believed to have played a part in recent mass killings.

Neutralizing peer pressure is instrumental to changing attitudes and values. For example, TAMs are a driving force for a fair amount of plant and animal destruction. Engaging with elders in the community to seek alternatives to these medicines would be a way forward. Similarly, if elders are seen to wear head-dresses and costumes that are made from alternative materials, the likelihood increases that younger generations will follow suit.

Many believe that farming various endangered species will simply solve the problem; however, imitations must be discouraged whenever possible. Those who demand various aspects of an endangered plant or animal can simply satisfy their demand by purchasing items that are derived from farmed animals. The Chinese have insisted that tiger farms are the way to satisfy the demand for tiger parts. Historically, there has been no way to distinguish between parts that come from wild tigers or from farmed ones. However, in recent years, technology has been developed that may help distinguish between wild and farmed livestock. Radio frequency identification (RFID) chip technology has been used in food in order to allow for the tracking of food through its entire supply chain.[6] Not only does the technology allow consumers to calculate caloric intake or cooking time, it allows the movement of livestock to be traced from its point of origin through to its final destination. The chipping allows for greater stock control, which can increase consumer confidence, as well as reduce overall costs. The technology is being used in Thailand, Spain, Canada, and Japan.[7]

Until such time as the technology is perfected or used routinely, farmed products could be construed as being imitations and legal alternatives. Allowing farmed products to enter the market only fuels further demand, which puts wild tigers at further risk of killing, and, thus, extinction. Farmed wild flora and fauna should be discouraged and preferably eliminated.

Remove Excuses

The final mechanism within the matrix pertains to removing excuses. To achieve this goal, the following techniques are put forward: setting of rules, posting of instructions, alerting of conscience, assisting in compliance, and controlling drugs and alcohol. One of the first steps in removing excuses is to set the rules. The message must be circulated that partaking in any part of the illicit market of endangered species is to damage the human condition. For example, those industries that include endangered species by-products must be schooled about the problem in which they are participating. Additionally, "naming and shaming" these industries may help to raise the issue with consumers. Along these lines, posting instructions about permissible behavior will help highlight what activities are prohibited.

Marketing is an integral part of the market reduction approach and envelops several situational crime prevention tactics like posting instructions and alerting the human conscience. Marketing the ill fate of wild flora and fauna helps to educate the community of the negative consequences to the ecosystem. It also helps to inform the public about alternatives to using TAMs. It discourages rule breaking and, with proper messages, can encourage compliance. Marketing takes on the role of education in communities where endangered species and human coexist. Understanding the important role wild flora and fauna play is the first step in conservation.

Furthermore, it is important to assist with compliance. Customs agents must investigate shipments coming from range states worldwide. In addition to monitoring observance of domestic laws, it is critical for officials to scrutinize CITES documents. Governments must also look for patterns in shipping manifests to see if countries are serving as illegal, secondary entry points. If a pattern emerges, the CITES Secretariat could consider applying sanctions against offending nations.

Claims are surfacing that those who illegally trade endangered species are acting in concert with those who also trade in illegal drugs and weapons or that traffickers in endangered flora and fauna are using their counterparts' trade routes. Research must be undertaken to confirm or refute these claims.

CHALLENGES TO THE WAY FORWARD

The market reduction approach is an extremely innovative crime reduction tool that can inform the conservation community of ways to assist in the protection of endangered species. The challenge is how to make crime reduction approaches known to the traditional conservation society. Conservation criminology techniques can provide a systematic way of constructing conservation schemes, species-by-species.

At this point in time, there exist no systematic ways of collecting necessary data in order to construct crime reduction programs. Using descriptive data is a good starting point, but there are still problems with the manner in which the data are derived. For example, the IUCN Red List data are insufficient for crime reduction reasons, due to the manner in which they are categorized. While it may be useful for conservationists and biologists to know the number of endangered species in a given category, crime reduction approaches require more detailed information. For example, knowing that Madagascar has 63 threatened, (including critically endangered and endangered) mammals is not particularly useful for crime reduction purposes! Specific and detailed information about what types and numbers of mammals is needed in order for strategies to be designed and become potentially useful.

Research would also benefit from structured methods of data collection and analyses so that global comparisons could be made. No such organized and systematic approach exists. If it did, the benefit would be tremendous, as existing literature sponsored by the same funding agency has produced conflicting results.[8] This only muddles the existing literature and confuses those wanting to create useful and successful programs.

Work that came out of Rutgers University on the plight of parrots in Mexico and Bolivia, as well as elephant poaching in Africa, has provided a much-needed framework for exploring trafficking in endangered species from a crime reduction viewpoint. The Rutgers' research projects address the challenges that exist and offer alternative methods for researching the issues. Geographic mapping is used in ways that inform crime reduction—not conservation—therefore demonstrating that criminology does add a unique perspective to existing conservation frameworks.[9]

Conservation mapping clearly outlines ranges and areas of deforestation, but it does not situate these ranges in relation to illegal markets or outlets. Conservationists who study and work with tigers and elephants clearly identify ranges and fragmentation; however, they can do little else with the type of data collected. Crime reduction maps should show specific flora/fauna ranges in relation to the proximity of illegal and/or legal markets, legal and/or legal trade outlets, poachers, locations of kills/harvests, roads, and traffickers and their routine activities. Existing research on markets is, again, only half complete. Much more data are needed about the nature of the global illegal trade in endangered wild flora and fauna. Studies illustrate where endangered species products appear in local trading markets, but they lack the ability to describe the intricate nature of the actual *market*—how the goods are moved from the range through to consumers' hands. As with traditional stolen goods markets, research is incomplete and very cursory.[10]

CONCLUSION

The cases presented here represent the tens of thousands of species that are endangered and in need of protection. Conservationists have worked tirelessly to preserve the natural habitat in which these wild flora and fauna live. Their ultimate aim is to ensure the survivability of these precious natural resources. The illegal activities of humans are the main cause of the demise of these species. Now is the time for the science of criminology to enter conservation activities.

The market reduction approach is an innovative crime reduction strategy that can assist in the disruption of illegal markets trading in endangered species. It is only one of a suite of new approaches that can be applied to environmentally-based crimes. In order for it to be truly successful, data must be analyzed in order to fully understand the nature of the problem, and policing officials must engage in partnership with a variety of agencies that also work to reduce the illegal killing and selling of wild protected plants and animals. Unless the *crimes* are addressed, the activities will continue to flourish, thus putting endangered species at further risk.

The way forward is to forge relationships between relevant government agencies and NGOs. Each has specific perspectives and unique contributions that together can reduce the trafficking in endangered species. Governments have the responsibility to make and enforce conservation-friendly laws and regulations. NGOs offer expertise and access to communities that suffer from illegal activities. Together, they can develop sound and effective policies and strategies that can truly make a difference. Criminologists can help inform policy by introducing concepts like situational crime prevention and the market reduction approach to government and NGOs. All combined efforts can lead to a true reduction of these insidious crimes.

Notes

Preface

1. See Daniel Gilling, *Crime Prevention: Theory, Policy and Politics* (London: Routledge, 1997).

2. The IUCN includes species that are critically endangered, endangered, and vulnerable under the umbrella term, "threatened."

Chapter 1

1. The terms "endangered species," "endangered flora and/or fauna," and "protected species" are used interchangeably throughout the text.

2. Environment Florida, "Why We Need a Strong Endangered Species Act," accessed May 24, 2011, http://www.environmentflorida.org/preservation/endangered-species/why-we-need-a-strong-endangered-species-act.

3. Beccaria's essay *On Crimes and Punishment* (1764) is one of the first complete critical reviews of the criminal justice system and its purpose. In it, Beccaria calls for sweeping reforms. Cesare Beccaria, *On Crimes and Punishment*, trans. Stephen Gould (New York: Gould & Van Winkle, 1809).

4. See Mara E. Zimmerman, "The Black Market for Wildlife: Combating Transnational Organized Crime in Illegal Wildlife Trade,"*Vanderbilt Journal of Transnational Law* 36 (2003): 1657–1689.

5. Dee Cook, Martin Roberts, and Jason Lowther, *The International Wildlife Trade and Organised Crime: A Review of the Evidence and the Role of the UK* (Wolverhampton, UK: WWF–UK, 2002).

6. J. Rubin and S. Stucky, "Fighting Black Markets and Oily Water: The Department of Justice's National Initiatives to Combat Transnational Environmental Crime," *Sustainable Development Law and Policy* 21 (2004): 21–26.

7. Cook et al., 2002.

8. Liana Sun Wyler and Pervaze A. Sheikh, *CRS Report for Congress: International Illegal Trade in Wildlife: Threats and U.S. Policy*. (Washington, D.C.: Congressional Research Service, August 2008).

9. See Randi E. Alacón, "The Convention on the International Trade of Endangered Species: The Difficulty in Enforcing CITES and the United States Solution to Hindering the Trade in Endangered Species," *New York International Law Review* 14, no. 2 (2001): 105–108.

10. The name "World Conservation Union" was used interchangeably with IUCN beginning in 1990; however, it is no longer commonly used this way today.

11. Simply known as the Red List.

12. Jacqueline Schneider, "Reducing the Illicit Trade in Endangered Wildlife: The Market Reduction Approach," *Journal of Contemporary Criminal Justice* 24 (2008): 274.

13. Ibid.

14. Cook et al., 2002.

15. Ibid.

16. Paul Wiles and Andrew Costello. "The 'Road to Nowhere': The Evidence for Travelling Criminals," *Home Office Research Study No. 207* (Home Office: London, 2000).

17. This is adapted from the original model by Mike Sutton, Jacqueline Schneider, and Sarah Hetherington, "Tackling Theft with the Market Reduction Approach," *Crime Reduction Series, Paper 8.* (London: Research, Development, and Statistics Directorate, Home Office, 2001.)

18. Mike Sutton, "Supply by Theft: Does the Market for Second-hand Goods Play a Role in Keeping Crime Figures High?," *British Journal of Criminology* 38, no. 3 (1995).

19. Ibid.

20. See "Convention on International Trade in Endangered Species of Wild Fauna and Flora," http://cites.org/eng/disc/text.shtml.

21. See "International Union for Conservation of Nature," http://www.iucn.org/what/.

22. See "The IUCN Red List of Threatened Species, Data Organization," accessed June 3, 2009, http://www.iucnredlist.org/technical-documents/data-organization #documentation.

23. See Interpol, "Wildlife Crime," accessed April 30, 2010, www.interpol.int/Public/EnvironmentalCrime/Wildlife/Default.asp.

24. Ibid.

Chapter 2

1. It should be noted that this is a common problem with the policing of traditional crimes, even in the wealthiest countries. Police forces within the same state or country do not collect or analyze data in similar or systematic ways; therefore, different jurisdictions oftentimes define specific crimes differently. Furthermore, police forces are notorious for having incomplete data.

2. See Jacqueline L. Schneider, "The Link Between Shoplifting and Burglary: The Booster Burglar," *British Journal of Criminology* 45, no. 3 (2005), doi:10.1093/bjc/azh101, hard copy pages: 395–401 and Jacqueline L. Schneider, "Stolen Goods Markets:

Methods of Disposal," *British Journal of Criminology* 45, no. 2 (2005), doi:10.1093/bjc/azh100, hard copy pages: 129–140.

3. CITES, *A Guide to Using the CITES Trade Database, version 7*. United Nations Environment Programme, World Conservation Monitoring Centre, accessed December 22, 2010, http://www.unep-wcmc.org/citestrade/docs/CITESTradeDatabaseGuide_v7.pdf.

4. Ibid., 4.

5. Ibid., 10.

6. Ibid., 11.

7. Convention on International Trade in Endangered Species of Wild Fauna and Flora, "CITES Trade Data Dashboards," accessed December 20, 2010, www.http://cites-dashboards.unep-wcmc.org/about.

8. IUCN Red List of Threatened Species, "Red List Overview," accessed November 22, 2010, www.iucnRedList.org/about/red-list-overview.

9. Ibid.

10. IUCN Red List of Threatened Species, "Data Organization," accessed November 23, 2010, www.iucnredlist.org/technical-documents/data-organization#documentation.

11. Ibid.

12. IUCN Red List of Threatened Species, "IUCN Red List Categories and Criteria: Version 3.1," IUCN Species Survival Commission: Gland, Switzerland and Cambridge, UK. (2001): 5.

13. Ibid.

14. Ibid., 16–23.

15. IUCN Red List of Threatened Species, "Summary Statistics," accessed June 15–20, 2009, December 12–15 2009, http://www.iucnredlist.org/about/summary-statistics.

16. See Jacqueline L. Schneider, "Reducing the Illicit Trade in Endangered Species," *Journal of Contemporary Criminal Justice* 24, no. 3 (2008).

17. Japanese Auto Pages, "Ports," accessed November 23, 2010, http://www.japanautopages.com/useful_resources/ports.php.

Chapter 3

1. J. Marcus Rowcliffe, et al., "Do Wildlife Laws Work? Species Protection and the Application of a Prey Choice Model to Poaching Decisions," *Proceedings: Biological Sciences* 271, no. 1557 (December 2004): 2631–2636.

2. See Jacqueline L. Schneider, "Reducing the Illicit Trade in Endangered Wildlife: The Market Reduction Approach," *Journal of Contemporary Criminal Justice* 24, no. 3 (2008): 274–295. See also Linda Fasulo, *An Insider's Guide to the UN* (New Haven, CT: Yale University Press, 2004) and Roger S. Clarke, *The United Nations Crime Prevention and Criminal Justice Program: Formulation of Standards and Efforts at Their Implementation* (Philadelphia: University of Pennsylvania Press, 1994) for a detailed description of the workings of the United Nations, the UN Crime Commissions, and the UN Crime Congresses.

3. Elizabeth R. DeSombre, *Global Environmental Institutions* (Abingdon, Oxon, UK: Routledge Press, 2006): 4.

4. The IUCN was formerly known as the World Conservation Union. That name is no longer used.

5. The United States voiced its opposition to the program, in addition to 18 other countries abstaining from the vote.

6. Yvonne Fiadjoe, "Cites in Africa: An Examination of Domestic Implementation and Compliance," *Sustainable Development Law & Policy* 4 (2004).

7. See Ginnette Hemley, ed., *International Wildlife Trade: A CITES Sourcebook* (Washington, D. C.: WWF/Island Press, 1994).

8. CITES, "National Reports, Reporting Under the Convention," accessed August 3, 2009, http://www.cites.org/eng/resources/reports.shtml.

9. See DeSombre, 2006.

10. U.S. Government Accountability Office, "Protected Species: International Convention and U.S. Laws Protect Wildlife Differently. Report to the Chairman, Committee on Resources, House of Representatives," accessed August 8, 2010, http://www.gao.gov/new.items/d04964.pdf.

11. Elizabeth M. McOmber, "Note: Problems in Enforcement of the Connection on International Trade: Endangered Species," *Brooklyn Journal of International Law* 27 (2002): 673.

12. NOAA Fisheries, Office of Protected Resources, "Marine Mammal Protection Act (MMPA) of 1972," accessed November 2, 2010, http://www.nmfs.noaa.gov/pr/laws/mmpa/.

13. "Take" is defined to include hunt, harass, capture, or kill.

14. "Endangered Species Act of 1973: As Amended by the 108th Congress," Department of the Interior, U.S. Fish & Wildlife Service, accessed June 24, 2010. http://www.fws.gov/endangered/esa-library/pdf/ESAall.pdf.

15. Ibid.

16. McOmber, 2002.

17. NOAA Fisheries, Office of Protected Resources, "Marine Mammal Protection Act (MMPA) of 1972," accessed November 2, 2010, http://www.nmfs.noaa.gov/pr/laws/mmpa/.

18. Ibid.

19. Fishermen's Protective Act (Pelly Amendment) 22 U.S.C. §§ 1971–1979, August 27, 1954, as amended 1968, 1972, 1976–1981, 1984, 1986–1988, 1990, 1992, and 1995.

20. European Commission Environment, "Wildlife Trade Legislation," accessed August 20, 2010, http://ec.europa.eu/environment/cites/legis_wildlife_en.htm.

21. Joint Nature Conservation Committee, "The Wildlife and Countryside Act 1981," accessed August 23, 2010, http://jncc.defra.gov.uk/page-1377.

22. Under UK law, an arrestable offense is one that is punishable by five years of imprisonment or more upon first conviction.

23. *China's Biodiversity: A Country Study*, Beijing: China Environmental Science Press, 1998. Also available online at http://bpsp-neca.brim.ac.cn/books/cntrysdy_cn/index.html.

24. Lawrence Watters and Wang Xi, "The Protection of Wildlife and Endangered Species in China," *Georgetown International Environmental Law Review* 14, no. 2 (2002): 489–525.

25. Ibid.

26. Watters and Xi, 2002, do an excellent job providing a time line of legal advancements protecting endangered species in China.

27. Ibid.

28. Fiadjoe, 2004.

29. Ibid.

30. Several pieces of legislation have either failed or stalled in Parliament, for example: Bill C-65, Canadian Species Protection Act; Bill C-33, Species at Risk Act.

31. "Canada's Species At Risk Act," David Suzuki Foundation, accessed December 29, 2010, http://www.davidsuzuki.org/issues/wildlife-habitat/science/endangered-species-legislation/canadas-species-at-risk-act/.

32. Committee on the Status of Endangered Wildlife in Canada (COSEWIC).

33. "Canada's Species At Risk Act," David Suzuki Foundation, accessed December 29, 2010, http://www.davidsuzuki.org/issues/wildlife-habitat/science/endangered-species-legislation/canadas-species-at-risk-act/.

34. Also known as the Bonn Convention.

35. Convention on Migratory Species, "Convention on Conservation of Migratory Species," accessed May 9, 2010, http://www.cms.int/about/index.htm.

36. INTERPOL, "About INTERPOL," accessed June 20, 2010. http://www.interpol.int/public/icpo/default.asp.

37. Ibid.

38. INTERPOL, "Wildlife Crime," accessed June 20, 2010. http://www.interpol.int/Public/EnvironmentalCrime/Wildlife/Default.asp.

39. Ibid.

40. Phoenix Fund. "Support for the Antipoaching Activities," accessed January 15, 2011, http://www.phoenix.vl.ru/suport.htm.

41. Transparency International, *The Global Corruption Report, 2009: Corruption and the Private Sector*, (Cambridge University Press, Cambridge, UK, 2009). Also available online at http://www.cgu.gov.br/conferenciabrocde/arquivos/English-Global-Corruption-Report-2009.pdf.

42. Vincent Gudmia-Mfonfu, "High Level Fight Against Corruption in the Wildlife Sector in Cameroon," *Wildlife Justice*, no. 6 (2009): 3.

43. Ibid.

44. Olive Nahkuna Mfonfu, "Is Corruption Hampering Conservation Efforts?," *Wildlife Justice* no. 005 (2007): 3.

45. U.S. Department of Homeland Security, Customs, and Border Protection, accessed November 21, 2009, http://www.cbp.gov/xp/cgov/toolbox/ports/.

46. Ibid.

47. Ibid.

48. Also known as Scotland Yard.

49. Metropolitan Police, Operation Charm, "Fact Sheet," accessed November 21, 2010, http://www.operationcharm.org/documents/factsheet_english.pdf.

50. Species at Risk Public Registry, "Species at Risk Act, Compliance and Enforcement," accessed November 21, 2010, pp. 32–35, http://www.sararegistry.gc.ca/virtual_sara/files/reports/ar_SARA_AnnualReport_0209_e.pdf.

51. Canada Border Service Agency, accessed November 21, 2010, http://cbsa-asfc.gc.ca/menu-eng.html.

52. Defra, *Wildlife Crime: A Guide to the Use of Forensic and Specialist Techniques in the Investigation of Wildlife Crime*, (London: HMSO, 2009).

53. Ibid.

54. TRAFFIC, "Police in Viet Nam Uncover Wildlife Bone Trade Network," accessed January 18, 2011, http://www.traffic.org/home/2010/9/20/police-in-viet-nam-uncover-wildlife-bone-trade-network.html.

55. TRAFFIC, "Seized Notebooks Give Unique Insight Into Scale of Illicit Pangolin Trade," accessed January 18, 2011, http://www.traffic.org/home/2010/10/28/seized-notebooks-give-unique-insight-into-scale-of-illicit-p.html. October 28, 2010.

56. TRAFFIC, "Chinese Citizens Risk Imprisonment for Ivory Smuggling," accessed January 18, 2011, http://www.traffic.org/home/2010/9/13/chinese-citizens-risk-imprisonment-for-ivory-smuggling.html.

57. TRAFFIC, "Beluga Caviar Seized in Transit," accessed January 18, 2011, http://www.traffic.org/home/2010/12/3/beluga-caviar-seized-in-transit.html.

58. TRAFFIC, "Man Arrested Over Tiger Poisoning Incident," accessed January 18, 2011, http://www.traffic.org/home/2010/6/22/man-arrested-over-tiger-poisoning-incident.html.

59. TRAFFIC, "Monkey Smuggler Arrested in Mexico," accessed January 18, 2011, http://www.traffic.org/home/2010/7/20/monkey-smuggler-arrested-in-mexico.html.

60. TRAFFIC, "Thai Customs Seize Four Suitcase Filled With Ivory," accessed January 18, 2011, http://www.traffic.org/home/2010/9/27/thai-customs-seize-four-suitcases-filled-with-ivory.html.

61. Bryant Christy, "The Serpent King," *Foreign Policy* accessed January 4, 2011, http://www.foreignpolicy.com/articles/2010/12/28/the_serpent_king.

62. Ibid., 1.

Chapter 4

1. The Home Office is the British government's department for immigration and passports, drugs policy, crime, counterterrorism, and police. See www.homeoffice.gov.uk.

2. Home Office, Research Development Statistics, "Organised Crime," accessed March 9, 2009, http://rds.homeoffice.gov.uk/rds/orgcrime1.html.

3. United Nations, "United Nations Convention against Transnational Organized Crime," last modified November 10, 2010, http://www.unodc.org/unodc/en/treaties/CTOC/index.html or http://www.un-documents.net/uncatoc.htm.

4. U.S. Federal Bureau of Investigations, "Organized Crime," accessed April 10, 2009, http://www.fbi.gov/about-us/investigate/organizedcrime/organized_crime.

5. G.L. Warchol, L. Zupan, and W. Clack, "Transnational Criminality: An Analysis of the Illegal Wildlife Market in Southern Africa," *International Criminal Justice Review* 13, no. 1 (2003): 1.

6. L.S. Wyler and A. Sheikh, 2008 and Jonathon Kazmar, "The International Illegal Plant and Wildlife Trade: Biological Suicide," *U.C. Davis Journal of International Law and Policy* 6, no. 105 (February 2009).

7. Jonathon Kazmar, "The International Illegal Plant and Wildlife Trade: Biological Suicide," *University of California Davis Journal of International Law and Policy* 6, no. 105 (2009).

8. Warchol, Zupan, and Clack, 2003 and Zimmerman, 2003.

9. Jay Albanese, "OC: A Perspective from South Africa," in *OC World Perspectives*, ed. Jay Albanese, Dilip Das, and Arvina Verma (New York: Prentice Hall), 438–459.

10. Kazmar (2000), and Cook, Roberts, and Lowther, 2002.

11. Wyler and Sheikh, 2008.

12. Kazmar, 2000.

13. Wyler and Sheikh, 2008.

14. Renctas, *1st National Report on the Traffic of Wild Animals* (Brasilia, Brazil: Rentcas, 2001).

15. U.S. Department of Justice, "Operation Jungle Trade," accessed January 2, 2010, http://www.justice.gov/enrd/3339.htm.

16. Zimmerman, 2003.

17. R.S. Anderson, "Investigation, Prosecution, and Sentencing of International Wildlife Trafficking Offenses in the U.S. Federal System," *National Environmental Enforcement Journal* 12: 14 June (1997).

18. See Adrian Levy and Cathy Scott-Clark, "Poaching for Bin Laden," accessed November 1, 2010, http://www.guardian.co.uk/world/2007/may/05/terrorism.animalwelfare.

19. See Wyler and Pervaze, 2008.

20. Ibid.

21. Ibid.

22. Associated Press, "Airport Inspection Reveals Smuggled Songbirds," last modified May 9, 2009, http://www.msnbc.msn.com/id/30598542/ns/travel-news/t/airport -inspection-reveals-smuggled-songbirds/.

23. *The Telegraph* (New Zealand), "Reptile Collector Who Smuggled Geckos in his Underwear Jailed in New Zealand," accessed June 19, 2010, http://www.telegraph.co.uk/ news/worldnews/australiaandthepacific/newzealand/7080799/Reptile-collector-who -smuggled-geckos-in-his-underwear-jailed-in-New-Zealand.html.

24. Reuters, "Thai Customs Seize Hundreds of Smuggled Turtles: Live Turtles and Other Rare Reptiles were Stuffed into Four Suitcases and Smuggled into Bangkok's Suva-mabhumi Airport," accessed July 1, 2011, http://www.guardian.co.uk/environment/2011/ jun/02/thai-customs-turtles-suitcase-smuggled.

25. Wyler and Pervaze, 2008.

26. Ibid.

27. See University of Canberra Media Centre, "Blackmarket Wildlife Sold Online: UC Researchers," accessed December 1, 2010, http://www.canberra.edu.au/media -centre/2008/december-2008/19_wildlife.

28. It must be kept in mind that various studies differ in their conclusions about the extent to which organized crime is present in general, and also about which species organized crime is trafficking.

29. Warchol, Zupan, and Clack, 2003.

30. Ibid.

31. Ibid.

32. Includes the Central Intelligence Agency, Federal Bureau of Investigation, U.S. Customs and Borders, U. S. Secret Service, Financial Crimes Enforcement Network, National Drug Intelligence Center; Departments of State, Treasury, Justice, and Transportation; Office of National Drug Control Policy, and National Security Council.

33. U.S. Government, *International Crime Threat Assessment*, accessed May 29, 2010, http://www.fas.org/irp/threat/pub45270index.html.

34. Ibid.

35. See Ellen K. Pikitch et al., "Status, Trends, and Management of Sturgeon and Paddlefish Fisheries," *Fish and Fisheries 6* (2005): 233–265.

36. See Maryann Bird, "Black Gold Comeback," *Time* 159, March 18, 2002, www
.time.com/time/magazine/europe/0,9263,901020318,00.html, accessed November 2, 2009.

37. A. Knapp, C. Kitschke, and S. von Meibom, "Proceedings of the International
Sturgeon Enforcement Workshop to Combat Illegal Trade in Caviar," accessed January 18,
2010, www.traffic.org/species-reports/traffic_species_fish14.pdf.

38. International Crime Threat Assessment, (n.d.).

39. Patrick Cockburn, "Black Gold, Black Death," *The Independent*, May 25, 2000,
accessed February 3, 2009, http://www.independent.co.uk/news/world/europe/black-gold
-black-death-716387.html.

40. Ronald V. Clarke, "Hot Products: Understanding, Anticipating, and Reducing
Demand for Stolen Goods," *Police Research Series* Paper 112 (1999).

41. TRAFFIC, "Black Gold: The Caviar Trade in Western Europe. *TRAFFIC Fact
Sheet*," accessed March 13, 2010, www.traffic.org/species-reports/caviar-factsheet
-english-2.pdf.

42. See Pikitch et al., 2005.

43. IRNA, "German Authorities Clamp Down on Caspian Sea Caviar Smuggling,"
accessed December 21, 2010, http://www.mathaba.net/news/?x=613665?flattr.

44. Anthony Barnett, "London Raids Expose Mafia Caviar Racket," accessed
November 2, 2009, http://www.guardian.co.uk/uk/2003/Nov/09/ukcrime.london.

45. Barnett, 2003.

46. Dmitry Korobeinikov, "Astrakhan Police Destroy 300 kg of Contraband Black
Caviar," accessed December 1, 2010, http://en.rian.ru/crime/20090803/155714409.html.

47. See Knapp et al., 2006.

48. Ibid.

49. See S. Vorobjiov, "Main Problems and Challenges in Combating Illegal Trade in
Caviar–Expectations and Needs of Range States: Russian Federation," in Knapp et al., 2006,
p. 70, accessed October 16, 2010, http://www.cites.org/common/com/SC/54/E54i-06.pdf.

50. John M. Sellar, "Anti-smuggling, Fraud, and Organized Crime," CITES Secretariat in Knapp et al., 2006, accessed November 14, 2010, http://www.policechiefmagazine
.org/magazine/index.cfm?fuseaction=display_arch&article_id=1203&issue_id=62007.

51. It must be noted here that during the research for this book, no other source
indicated or alluded to terrorist groups being involved in the illicit trade of endangered
species.

52. Susie Watts, *Shark Finning: Unrecorded Wastage on a Global Scale* (San Francisco, CA.: WildAid, 2003), 21.

53. Susie Watts and Victor Wu, *At Rock Bottom: The Declining Sharks of the
Eastern Tropical Pacific* (San Francisco, CA: WildAid, 2003).

54. Executive producers of this film are Brian Stewart, Sandra Campbell, and Alex-
andra Stewart. It was produced and directed by Rob Stewart.

55. Captain Watson was also a founding member of Greenpeace.

Chapter 5

1. See IUCN Red List of Threatened Species, "Mammals Key Findings," accessed
May 9, 2010, www.iucnredlist.org/mammals/key_findings.

2. IUCN Red List of Threatened Species, "Geographic Patterns," accessed May 9,
2010, http://www.iucnredlist.org/initiatives/mammals/analysis/geographic-patterns.

3. Ibid.

4. Information compiled from a number of sources including WWF, Animal Corner, the Smithsonian, and Arkive.

5. See E. Sanderson, J. Forrest, C. Loucks, J. Ginsberg, E. Dinerstein, J. Seiden-sticker, P. Leimgruber, M. Songer, A. Heydlauff, T. O'Brien, G. Bryja, S. Klenzendorf, and E. Wikramanayake, *Setting Priorities for the Conservation and Recovery of Wild Tigers: 2005–2015. The Technical Assessment.* (Washington, D.C.: WCS, WWF, Smith-sonian, and NFWF-STF, 2006). This study is also referred to as *The Tiger Study.*

6. Andrew Buncombe, "Hunter Who Turned to Conservation: The Remarkable Leg-acy of Tiger Jim," *The Independent on Sunday*, November 1, 2007, accessed September 8, 2010, http://www.independent.co.uk/environment/nature/hunter-who-turned-to -conservation-the-remarkable-legacy-of-tiger-jim-398493.html. Also see Andrew Bun-combe, "The Face of a Doomed Species: Tigers Driven to Edge of Extinction by Poachers and Loss of Habitat,"*The Independent*, Wednesday, October 31, 2007, accessed Septem-ber 8, 2010, http://www.independent.co.uk/environment/nature/the-face-of-a-doomed -species-398373.html.

7. Ibid.

8. See *The Tiger Study*, 2006.

9. The Terari Arc is an immense area containing approximately 49,000k^2 stretching across Nepal's Bagmati River in the east to India's Yamuna River in the west.

10. See Chris R. Shepherd and Nolan Magnus, *Nowhere to Hide: The Trade in Sumatran Tiger* (Southeast Asia: TRAFFIC, 2004).

11. See WWF, *Conserving Tigers in the Wild: A WWF Framework Strategy for Action 2002–2010* (Gland, Switzerland: WWF: International, Species Programme, 2002).

12. Buncombe, October 31 and November 1, 2007.

13. Julia Ng and Nemora, *Tiger Trade Revisited in Sumatra, Indonesia* (Petaling Jaya, Malaysia: TRAFFIC Southeast Asia, 2007). Also available online www.traffic.org/ species-reports/traffic_species_mammals37.pdf. Kristen Nowell and Xu Ling. *Taming the Tiger Trade: China's Markets for Wild and Captive Tiger Products Since the 1993 Domestic Trade Ban* (East Asia: TRAFFIC, 2007). Also available online at http://www .worldwildlife.org/species/finder/tigers/WWFBinaryitem15400.pdf. Also see Shepherd and Magnus, 2004.

14. Shepherd and Magnus, 2004; Ng and Nemora, 2007.

15. Ibid. Medan is the capital of North Sumatra and is the third largest city in Indonesia.

16. Shepherd and Magnus, 2004.

17. Ibid.

18. Ibid.

19. Ng and Nemora, 2007.

20. Ibid.

21. Ibid.

22. Ibid.

23. Ibid.

24. Ibid.

25. Ibid.

26. This information is summarized from Ng and Nemora, 2007.

27. One case was not brought to trial because the accused escaped.

28. The value is based on 2001 exchange rates.

29. These values are based on 2006 exchange rates.

30. Nemora and Ng, 2007.

31. Personal conversation with Debbie Matyr, FREELAND, Indonesia. Emails exchanged in January, 2011.

32. Nowell and Ling, 2007.

33. Ibid.

34. Ibid.

35. Ibid.

36. Ibid.

37. Ibid, p. 6.

38. Save the Tiger Fund granted a total of $15.7 million in 313 grants from 1995 through 2007.

39. Save the Tiger Fund, "Who We Are," accessed July 8, 2009, http://www.savethetigerfund.org/Content/NavigationMenu2/Learn/WhoWeAre/default.htm.

40. G. Ananthakrishnan, "Women Walk on the Wild Side," *The Times of India*, accessed January 20, 2010, http://articles.timesofindia.indiatimes.com/2010-01-02/india/28143776_1_vasanta-sena-vasanta-sena-periyar-tiger-reserve.

41. Sanderson et al., 2006.

42. Ibid.

43. Jim Corbett National Park, "Colonel Jim Corbett," accessed August 3, 2009, http://www.jimcorbettnationalpark.com/corbett_coljim.asp.

44. Jim Corbett National Park, "History," accessed August 3, 2009, http://www.jimcorbettnationalpark.com/corbett_history.asp

45. "Project Tiger," accessed August 31, 2009, http://www.lairweb.org.nz/tiger/project5.html.

46. Ibid.

47. Ibid. Also see Buncombe, November 1, 2007.

48. Pallava Bagla, "Poachers Track Poachers in India Wilderness Project," *www.nationalgeographic.com/news*, last modified April 21, 2003, http://news.nationalgeographic.com/news/pf/51115524.html.

49. Ibid.

50. World Conservation Society, "Siberian Tiger Project," accessed May 23, 2010, http://www.wcs.org/globalconservation/Asia/russia/siberiantigerproject.

51. Ibid.

52. Ibid.

53. J. M. Goodrich, D.G. Miquelle, L.L. Kerley, and E.N. Smirnov, "Time for Tigers: Paving the Way for Tiger Conservation in Russia," *Wildlife Conservation* 105 (2002): 22–29.

54. Males in the study also had similar mortality rates.

55. "Phoenix Fund," accessed June 12, 2010, http://www.phoenix.vl.ru/zoom/Pdf/Interreg2004.pdf.

56. Ibid.

57. World Bank, "Amur Tiger: Russian Far East," accessed March 10, 2010, http://siteresources.worldbank.org/INTECA/Resources/Tigers-Russia-Chestin-080609.pdf.

58. WWF, "Amur Tiger: Russian Far East," accessed April 27, 2009, http://www.worldwildlife.org/species/finder/amurtiger/amurtiger.html.

59. A search of the Red List database did not return information or status on the Bwindi gorilla.

60. Information compiled from a number of sources including WWF, Animal Corner, the Smithsonian, and the International Gorilla Conservation Programme.

61. *The Dian Fossey Gorilla Fund International*, "Dian Fossey," accessed January 8, 2010, http://gorillafund.org/dian_fossey.

62. See D. Steklis and N. Gerald-Steklis, "Status of the Virunga Mountain Gorilla Population." In *Mountain Gorilla: Three Decades of Research at Karisoke*, edited by M.M. Robbins, P. Sicotte, and K.J. Stewart, 391–412 (Cambridge, UK: Cambridge University Press , 2001).

63. P.D. Walsh, C.E.G. Tutin, J.F. Oates, J.E.M. Baillie, F. Maisels, E.J. Stokes, S. Gatti, R.A. Bergl, J. Sunderland-Groves, and A. Dunn, "*Gorilla gorilla*," The IUCN Red List of Threatened Species, accessed December 3, 2009, http://www.iucnredlist.org/apps/redlist/details/9404/0.

64. M. Robbins and L. Williamson, "*Gorilla beringei*," The Red List of Threatened Species, accessed December 3, 2009, http://www.iucnredlist.org/apps/redlist/details/39994/0.

65. Convention on International Trade in Endangered Species of Wild Fauna and Flora, "Appendices I, II, and III," accessed November 23, 2009, http://cites.org/eng/app/appendices.shtml.

66. R. Nasi et al., 2007.

67. The BBC report labeled these hunters as "pygmy." According to Dr. John Arthur, an anthropologist who works primarily in Africa, the term is considered to be very derogatory; therefore, it will not be used here. It is unclear from the original source which society these hunters represent. BBC News, "AIDS Warning Over Bushmeat Trade," accessed January 20, 2009 www.news.bbc.co.uk/1/hi/programmes/file_on_4/3954963.stm.

68. See R. Nasi, D. Brown, D. Wilkie, E. Bennett, C. Tutin, G. Van Tol, and T. Christophersen, "Conservation and Use of Wildlife-Based Resources: The Bushmeat Crisis," *Secretariat of the Convention on Biological Diversity, Montreal, and Center for International Forestry Research (CIFOR)*, Bogor, Technical Series no. 33, 2007, accessed June 2, 2009, http://www.cbd.int/doc/publications/cbd-ts-33-en.pdf.

69. Ibid.

70. Ibid.

71. J. Juste, J. E. Fa, J. Perez Del Val, and J. Castroviejo, "Market Dynamics of Bushmeat Species in Equatorial Guinea," *Journal of Applied Ecology* 32, no. 3 (Aug. 1995): 454–467.

72. Sara Goudarzi, "Ape Meat Sold in U.S., European Black Markets," accessed November 3, 2010, http://news.nationalgeographic.com/news/2006/07/060718-ape-meat.html.

73. D.S. Wilkie, "Bushmeat Trade in the Congo Basin," *Smithsonian Institution Press* III, no. 4 (2001): 86–109.

74. Ibid.

75. Ibid.

76. S. Bahuchet and K. Ioveva, "De la Forêt au Marché: Le Commerce de Gibier au Sud Cameroun." In *L'homme et la forêt tropicale* (1999): 533–558. Quoted in R. Nasi, D. Brown, D. Wilkie, E. Bennett, C. Tutin, G. van Tol, and T. Christophersen, "Conservation and Use of Wildlife-Based Resources: The Bushmeat Crisis," Secretariat of the

Convention on Biological Diversity, Montreal, and Center for International Forestry Research (CIFOR), Bogor, Technical Series no. 33, 2007, accessed June 2, 2009, http://www.cbd.int/doc/publications/cbd-ts-33-en.pdf.

77. G. Davies, "Bushmeat and International Development," *Conservation Biology* 16 (2002): 587–589.

78. Ian Redmond, Tim Aldred, Katrin Jedamizik, and Madelaine Westwood, *Recipes for Survival: Controlling the Bushmeat Trade*, (London: Ape Alliance Report funded by World Society for the Protection of Animals, 2006).

79. Karl Ammann, "Bushmeat Hunting and the Great Apes," *Great Apes and Humans: The Ethics of Coexistence*, 3 (2001): 71–85.

80. C. Nellemann, I. Redmond, and J. Refisch (eds.), *The Last Stand of the Gorilla-Environmental Crime and Conflict in the Congo Basin: A Rapid Response Assessment* (United Nations Environment Programme, GRID-Arendal, 2010). Also available online at http://www.unep.org/pdf/GorillaStand_screen.pdf.

81. Redmond et al., 2006.

82. Ammann, 2001.

83. Humane Society International, "Africa News: Primates as Pets, in Entertainment, and in Research," accessed June 3, 2010, http://www.hsi.org/world/africa/index.jsp?page=5.

84. Ibid.

85. Ibid.

86. Ibid.

87. "Massive Great Ape Die-Off in Africa–Ebola Suspected," *www.nationalgeographic.com/news*, last modified February 6, 2003, http://news.nationalgeographic.com/news/2003/02/0205_030205_ebola.html.

88. This university is a pre-eminent research and medical university known for its work in public health and medicine. " 'Bush meat' disease warning," *BBC news*, last modified July 23, 2002, http://news.bbc.co.uk/2/hi/uk_news/politics/2146158.stm.

89. Afrol News, "Bushmeat Warning After Cameroon Virus," accessed October 22, 2010, http://www.afrol.com/articles/13708.

90. WWF, "Rwandan Mountain Gorillas Killed for Wildlife Trade," accessed July 23, 2010, http://wales.wwf.org.uk/wwf_articles.cfm?unewsid=536.

91. Accounts varied in terms of the numbers of gorillas actually killed; for example, *The Sunday Times* (UK) reported eight gorillas, whereas *CNN News* reported four.

92. CNN World, "Mountain Gorillas: Killings of Mountain Gorillas in Congo Prompt U.N. Probe," July 25, 2007, accessed September 20, 2009, http://articles.cnn.com/2007-07-27/world/congo.gorillas_1_mountain-gorillas-virunga-national-park-silverback?_s=PM:WORLD.

93. Jonathan Clayton, "Eight Mountain Gorillas Are Shot Dead in Troubled National Park," *The Sunday Times*, July 28, 2007, accessed September 20, 2009, http://www.timesonline.co.uk/tol/news/world/africa/article2155469.ece.

94. Mark Jenkins., "Who Murdered the Virunga Gorillas?" *National Geographic*, accessed September 20, 2009, http://ngm.nationalgeographic.com/2008/07/virunga/jenkins-text. Also see Lee Poston, "Bodies of Four Critically Endangered Mountain Gorillas Found in Congo's Virunga National Park," accessed June 21, 2009, http://www.worldwildlife.org/who/media/press/2007/WWFPresitem978.html.

95. Ibid.

96. Ibid.

97. Clayton, July 28, 2007.

98. See Jane Goodall Institute, "Controlling Bushmeat Trade," accessed March 11, 2009, www.janegoodall.org/africa-programs/objectives/controlling-bushmeat-trade.asp.

99. See Jane Goodall Institute, "Role of Women in the Community," accessed March 14, 2009, www.janegoodall.org/africa-programs/objectives/role-of-women-in-the -community.asp.

100. Nasi et al., 2007.

101. Ibid.

102. Ibid.

103. Ibid, 37.

104. Redmond et al., 2006.

105. E. Bowen-Jones, "The African Bushmeat Trade–A Recipe for Extinction." *UK Ape Alliance/Fauna and Flora International*, 1998. Also available online at http://www.4apes.com/bushmeat/report/bushmeat.pdf.

106. Anonymous, "Illegal Wildlife Activities in the CAMRAIL Railway and Its Surroundings–Assessment," LAGA, accessed November 21, 2009, http://www.laga -enforcement.org/Portals/0/Documents/CAMRAIL%20assesment%20report%20 -%20October06.pdf. Also see Wildlife Conservation Society, "Keeping Bushmeat Off the Rails in Cameroon," accessed November 28, 2009, http://www.wcs.org/conservation -challenges/natural-resource-use/hunting-and-wildlife-trade/keeping-bushmeat-off-the -rails-in-cameroon.aspx.

107. International Gorilla Conservation Programme, "A Brief History of IGCP," accessed May 20, 2010, http://www.igcp.org/about/history/.

108. WWF, "Protecting Africa's Great Apes," accessed March 20, 2010, http://wwf .panda.org/what_we_do/where_we_work/project/projects/index.cfm?uProjectID=9F0742.

109. P.J. Stephenson and A. Wilson, *African Great Apes Update: Recent News from the WWF African Great Apes Programme* (Gland, Switzerland: WWF, 2005). Also available online at http://www.worldwildlife.org/species/finder/mountaingorilla/WWF Binaryitem12894.pdf.

110. Ibid.

111. The Dian Fossey Gorilla Fund International, "Saving Endangered Gorillas Through Anti-Poaching," accessed January 8, 2010, http://gorillafund.org/page.aspx ?pid=234.

112. WWF, "Key Achievements: Highlights from WWF African Great Apes Projects," accessed September 21, 2009, http://wwf.panda.org/what_we_do/endangered _species/great_apes/apes_programme/achievements/.

113. Ibid.

114. Jane Goodall Institute, "Conservation & Communities," accessed March 11, 2009, http://web.janegoodall.org/cc-education.

115. See A. Choudhury, D.K. Lahiri Choudhury, A. Desai, J.W. Duckworth, P.S. Easa, A.J.T. Johnsingh, P. Fernando, S. Hedges, M. Gunawardena, F. Kurt, U. Karanth, A. Kister, V. Menon, H. Riddle, A. Rübel, and E. Wilkramanayake, "*Elephas maximus*," The IUCN Red List of Threatened Species, accessed December 23, 2009, http://www .iucnredlist.org/apps/redlist/details/7140/0. Also see J. Blanc, "*Loxodonta africana*," The IUCN Red List of Threatened Species, accessed December 23, 2009, http://www .iucnredlist.org/apps/redlist/details/12392/0.

116. Choudhury et al., *"Elephas maximus,"* The IUCN Red List of Threatened Species, accessed December 23, 2009, http://www.iucnredlist.org/apps/redlist/details/7140/0.

117. Ibid.

118. Ibid.

119. Ibid.

120. Peter J. Stephenson, *WWF Species Action Plan: African Elephant 2007–2011,* (Gland, Switzerland: WWF, 2007).

121. The information in this section is a compilation of material from a variety of sources including http://www.arkive.org/asian-elephant/elephas-maximus/, http://www.arkive.org/african-elephant/loxodonta-africana/, http://www.awf.org/content/wildlife/detail/elephant, http://animals.nationalgeographic.com/animals/mammals/asian-elephant/?source=A-to-Z, http://www.ifaw.org/ifaw_international/save_animals/elephants/asian_elephant.php, and http://www.ifaw.org/ifaw_international/save_animals/elephants/african_elephant.php.

122. Ibid.

123. R. Sukumar, U. Ramakrishnan, and J.A. Santosh, "Impact of Poaching on an Asian Elephant Population in Periyar, Southern India: A Model of Demography and Tusk Harvest," *Animal Conservation* 1 (1997): 281–291. Quoted in Chris R. Shepherd and *TRAFFIC* (2008), 2, 12.

124. WWF, "Asian Elephants," accessed July 12, 2010, www.panda.org/about_wwwf/what_we_d0/species_species_factsheets/elephants/asain_elephants/.

125. Animal Planet, "Thai Elephants," accessed November 4, 2009, http://animal.discovery.com/convergence/safari/elephant/thaielephants/thaielephants1.html. Also see The Government Pubic Relations Department, "Inside Thailand: Elephants as Part of Thai Culture and National Symbols," accessed December 4, 2010, http://thailand.prd.go.th/view_inside.php?id=4838.

126. Ibid.

127. UN Special, "The Elephant and His Mahout: A Bond for Life," accessed November 2, 2009, http://www.unspecial.org/UNS635/UNS_635_T01.html.

128. WWF, "African Elephants–Threats," accessed October 3, 2010, http://wwf.panda.org/what_we_do/endangered_species/elephants/african_elephants/afelephants_threats/. Also see WWF, "Asian Elephants-Threats," accessed July 12, 2010, http://wwf.panda.org/what_we_do/endangered_species/elephants/asian_elephants/asianeleph_threats/.

129. WWF, "Gone in an Instant: How the Trade in Illegally Grown Coffee is Driving the Destruction of Rhino, Tiger, and Elephant Habitat," accessed September 23, 2010, http://wwf.panda.org/what_we_do/endangered_species/elephants/asian_elephants/areas/news/trade_coffee/.

130. WWF, "Issues: Human–Elephant Conflict," accessed May 9, 2010, http://wwf.panda.org/what_we_do/endangered_species/elephants/asian_elephants/areas/issues/elephant_human_conflict/. Also see WWF, "African Elephants- Threats," accessed October 3, 2010, http://wwf.panda.org/what_we_do/endangered_species/elephants/african_elephants/afelephants_threats/.

131. WWF, "African Elephants–Threats," accessed October 3, 2010, http://wwf.panda.org/what_we_do/endangered_species/elephants/african_elephants/afelephants_threats/.

132. WWF, "Asian Elephants-Threats," accessed July 12, 2010, http://wwf.panda.org/what_we_do/endangered_species/elephants/asian_elephants/asianeleph_threats/.

133. WWF, "The Tesso Nilo Conservation Landscape, Sumatra, Indonesia," accessed December 15, 2009, http://www.worldwildlife.org/tigers/pubs/riau_profile2.pdf.

134. R.C. Lair, "Gone Astray–The Care and Management of the Asian Elephant in Domesticity," accessed August 4, 2010, www.fao.org/DOCREP/005/AC774E/ac774e00.htm.

135. Mongabay.com, "Tropical Rainforests: Imperiled Riches," accessed November 23, 2009, http://www.mongabay.com/08amphetamine.htm. Also see Animal Planet, "Thai Elephants: The Sordid Underbelly of the Elephant World," accessed November 4, 2009. http://animal.discovery.com/convergence/safari/elephant/thaielephants/thaielephants2.html.

136. Nick Watt, "Elephants Patrol Border Between Man and Beast," accessed December 11, 2007, http://abcnews.go.com/WN/story?id=3985313&page=1.

137. Ibid.

138. See M. Aung, "On the Distribution, Status and Conservation of Wild Elephants in Myanmar," *Gajah* 18 (1997): 47–55. Quoted in C.R. Shepherd and V. Nijam, *Elephant and Ivory in Myanmar* (Petaling Jaya, Selangor, Malaysia: *TRAFFIC*, 2008), 25.

139. Ibid.

140. Ibid.

141. R.C. Lair, "Gone Astray–The Care and Management of the Asian Elephant in Domesticity," accessed August 4, 2010, www.fao.org/DOCREP/005/AC774E/ac774e00.htm.

142. This is based on the value of the U.S. dollar in 1997.

143. See Chris R. Shepherd, "On the Distribution, Status, and Conservation of Wild Elephants in Myanmar," *Gajah* 18 (1997): 47–55. Quoted in C.R. Shepherd and V. Nijam, *Elephant and Ivory in Myanmar* (Petaling Jaya, Selangor, Malaysia: *TRAFFIC*, 2008).

144. See E.B. Martin, "Wildlife Products for Sale in Myanmar," *TRAFFIC Bulletin* 17, no. 1 (1978).

145. Ibid.

146. Ibid.

147. WWF, "The Heart of Borneo Under Siege," accessed September 19, 2009, http://wwf.panda.org/what_we_do/where_we_work/borneo_forests/borneo_deforestation/.

148. WWF–UK, "Fighting Forest Crime and the Illegal Timber Trade," accessed November 21, 2009, http://d2rby7spo76flf.cloudfront.net/downloads/fightingforestcrime.pdf. A hectare is equivalent to 2.47 acres. In the United States, there are 107,593 square feet per hectare, while in the United Kingdom, a hectare is comprised of nearly 10,000 square meters.

149. WWF, "Asian Elephants: Threats," accessed July 12, 2009, http://www.worldwildlife.org/species/finder/asianelephants/threats.html.

150. Ibid.

151. Rob Glastra, *Elephant Forests on Sale: Rain Forest Loss in the Sumatran Tesso Nilo Region and the Role of European Banks and Markets* (WWF Deutschland, 2003). Also see Moch N. Kurnianwan, "NGOs Fight Against Illegal Logging," accessed September 10, 2009, http://www.ecologyasia.com/news-archives/2003/mar-03/thejakartapost.com_20030320_1.htm.

152. B. Schulte-Herbrüggen and H. Rossiter, "Project Las Piedras: A Social-Ecological Investigation into the Impact of Illegal Logging Activity in Las Piedras, Madre de Dios Peru," accessed November 4, 2010, http://www.peruforests.org/documents/Studies/LCLasPiedrasFinalReport.pdf.

153. Asian News, "Borneo, Pygmy Elephant at Risk of Extinction," accessed December 3, 2009, http://www.asianews.it/index.php?l=en&art=14596&size=A.

154. WWF, "Gone in an Instant: How the Trade in Illegally Grown Coffee is Driving the Destruction of Rhino, Tiger, and Elephant Habitat," accessed September 23, 2010, http://wwf.panda.org/what_we_do/endangered_species/elephants/asian_elephants/areas/news/trade_coffee/.

155. Ibid.

156. Ibid.

157. Smithsonian National Museum of African Art, "Ivory: Identification and Regulation of a Precious Material," accessed January 3, 2010, http://africa.si.edu/research/ivory.pdf.

158. WWF-AU, "Myanmar Emerges as Ivory Trade and Elephant Smuggling Hot Spot," last modified December 11, 2008, http://www.wwf.org.au/news/myanmar-emerges-as-ivory-trade- and-elephant-smuggling-hot-spot/.

159. Ibid.

160. WWF, "Asian Elephants," accessed July 12, 2010, www.panda.org/about_wwwf/what_we_d0/species_species_factsheets/elephants/asain_elephants/.

161. Ibid.

162. Shepherd, 2002.

163. Ibid.

164. Ibid.

165. Chris R. Shepherd and Vincent Nijam, *Elephant and Ivory in Myanmar* (Petaling Jaya, Selangor, Malaysia: TRAFFIC, 2008).

166. Daniel Stiles, *An Assessment of the Illegal Ivory Trade in Viet Nam* (Petaling Jaya, Selangor, Malaysia, 2008). Also available online at www.traffic.org/species-reports/traffic_species_mammals42.pdf.

167. Ibid.

168. Flora and Fauna International, 1998, *Conservation of the Asian Elephant in Indochina.* Quoted in The Viet Nam Ecological Association, TRAFFIC Southeast Asia, Indochina Office and the Forest Protection Department of the Ministry of Agriculture and Rural Development, "An Assessment of the Illegal Trade in Elephants and Elephant Products in Viet Nam," *TRAFFIC International* 2 (July 2002): 5. Also available on line at www.traffic.org/species-reports/traffic_species_mammals21.pdf.

169. For detailed discussion see Caitlin O'Connell-Rodwell and Rob Parry-Jones, *An Assessment of China's Management of Trade in Elephants and Elephant Products,* (Cambridge, UK: TRAFFIC International, 2002).

170. Ibid.

171. Ibid.

172. Ibid.

173. Ibid.

174. Ibid.

175. Ibid.

176. Ibid.

177. Ibid.

178. Ibid.

179. Ibid.

180. United Nations Development Programme, *Human Development Report, 2005* (New York: United Nations Development Programme, 2005).

181. TRAFFIC Network Report, *Still in Business: The Ivory Trade in Asia Seven Years After the CITES Ban* (*TRAFFIC*, 1997).

182. International Centre for Trade and Sustainable Development, "CITES Sanctioned Ivory Auctions Underway in Southern Africa," accessed November 2, 2009, http://ictsd.org/i/news/biores/32508/.

183. Andrew M. Lemieux and Ronald V. Clarke, "The International Ban on Ivory Sales and Its Effects on Elephant Poaching in Africa,"*British Journal of Criminology* 49 (2009): 451–471.

184. Ibid.

185. WWF, "WWF's African Elephant Programme," accessed November 3, 2009, http://wwf.panda.org/what_we_do/endangered_species/elephants/african_elephants/elephant_programme/.

186. Ibid.

187. Ibid.

188. Forest Policy Research, "Indonesia: Tesso National Park to Increase in Size," accessed November 4, 2009, http://forestpolicyresearch.com/2009/02/18/indonesia-tesso-national-park-to-increase-in-size/.

189. See WWF, "Legislation Enacted to Curb Illegal Logging,"accessed November 21, 2010, http://wwf.worldwildlife.org/site/PageServer?pagename=can_results_illegal_logging_imports.

190. Ibid.

191. Chris R. Shepherd and Vincent Nijam, *Elephant and Ivory in Myanmar* (Petaling Jaya, Selangor, Malaysia: *TRAFFIC*, 2008).

192. Ibid.

193. Tom Milliken, African Elephants and the Eleventh Meeting of the Conference of the Parties to CITES, 2000. Quoted in Caitlin O'Connell-Rodwell, and Rob Parry-Jones, *An Assessment of China's Management of Trade in Elephants and Elephant Products* (Cambridge, UK: *TRAFFIC International*, 2002), 18.

194. Ibid.

195. Convention on International Trade in Endangered Species of Wild Fauna and Flora, "Monitoring the Illegal Killing of Elephants (MIKE)," accessed May 3, 2010, www.CITES.org/eng/prog/MIKE.

196. Ibid.

197. T. Milliken, R.W. Burn, and L. Sangalakula, "The Elephant Trade Information System (ETIS) and the Illicit Trade in Ivory: A Report to the 14th Meeting of the Conference of the Parties to CITES," CoP15 Doc. 44.1, Annex 1, 2007, accessed December 9, 2010, www.cites.org/eng/cop/14/doc/E14-53-2.pdf.

198. Ibid.

199. O'Connell-Rodwell and Parry-Jones, 2002.

200. Ibid.

Chapter 6

1. WildAid, *"End of the Line?" Global Threats to Sharks* (WildAid, 2007).

2. Ibid.

3. Ibid.

4. Hawaii Sharks, "On 'Aumakua,' Hawaiian Ancestral Spirits," accessed August 26, 2010, http://www.hawaiisharks.com/aumakua.html.

5. WildAid, 2007.

6. Ibid.

7. Ibid.

8. Sarah Fowler and John A. Musick, "Shark Specialist Group Finning Statement," accessed August 26, 2010, http://www.flmnh.ufl.edu/fish/organizations/ssg/ssgfin statementfinal2june.pdf.

9. IUCN and SSC, "Shark Specialist Group," accessed June 4, 2010, http://www.iucnssg.org/index.php/about-the-ssg.

10. Ibid.

11. The term "pelagic" refers to open ocean waters with little contact with the ocean floor.

12. This statement excludes deep-sea species. Data for this category is simply far too flawed.

13. Memorandum of Understanding on the Conservation of Migratory Sharks, Article IV, Convention of Migratory Species, February 12, 2010.

14. See IUCN Red List of Threatened Species, "Taxonomy," accessed December 3, 2009, http://www.iucnredlist.org/technical-documents/data-organization#doc_taxonomy.

15. Shark Research Group, "Great Hammerhead," accessed February 14, 2010, http://www.sharkresearch.com/species/hh-great.html.

16. Ibid.

17. Ibid.

18. See the IUCN Red List of Threatened Species, "*Sphyrna mokarran*, Geographic Range," accessed December 3, 2009, http://www.iucnredlist.org/apps/redlist/details/39386/0.

19. Ibid.

20. IUCN Red List of Threatened Species, "*Carcharodon carcharias*," accessed February 21, 2010, http://www.iucnredlist.org/apps/redlist/details/3855/0.

21. Marine Bio, "*Carcharodon carcharias*, Great White Shark," accessed February 21, 2010, http://marinebio.org/species.asp?id=38.

22. Ibid.

23. Ibid.

24. WildAid, 2007.

25. IUCN Red List of Threatened Species, "*Carcharodon carcharias*," accessed February 21, 2010, http://www.iucnredlist.org/apps/redlist/details/3855/0.

26. Brad Norman, "Whale Shark," *Environment Australia Marine Species Section*, accessed January 3, 2010, http://www.environment.gov.au/coasts/species/sharks/whaleshark/index.html.

27. Ibid.

28. Ibid.

29. No research substantiates claims that shark cartilage actually alleviates pain from arthritis.

30. See WildAid, 2007.

31. BBC News, "Mercury Poison found in Shark Fins," accessed February 21, 2010, http://news.bbc.co.uk/2/hi/asia-pacific/1420029.stm.

32. Joel Arak, "Shark Fin Soup: A Dangerous Delicacy?" accessed February 21, 2010, http://www.cbsnews.com/stories/2002/07/31/world/main517011.shtml.

33. Susie Watts, *Shark Finning: Unrecorded Wastage on a Global Scale* (San Francisco: WildAid), 2003. Also available online at www.protect-The_Sharks.org/pdf/ Wildaid/shark_finning.pdf.

34. David Barboza, "Waiter, There's a Celebrity in My Shark Fin Soup," *The New York Times*, August 13, 2006, www.nytimes.com/2006/08/13/weekinreview/13barboza .html.

35. M. Lack and G. Sant, *Illegal, Unreported and Unregulated Shark Catch: A Review of Current Knowledge and Action* (Canberra: Department of the Environment, Water, Heritage, and the Arts and *TRAFFIC*, 2008).

36. Ibid.

37. Ibid.

38. Animal Welfare Institute, "Sharks At Risk," accessed February 3, 2010, http:// www.awionline.org/ht/a/GetDocumentAction/i/10560.

39. Lack and Sant, 2008.

40. See Julia K. Baum and Ransom A. Myers, "Shifting Baselines and the Decline of Pelagic Sharks in the Gulf of Mexico," accessed May 4, 2010, http://onlinelibrary.wiley.com.

41. Lack and Sant, 2008.

42. Ibid.

43. For more details, see Sea Shepherd Conservation Society, "What is a Long-line?," accessed February 10, 2010, http://www.seashepherd.org/shark/longlining.html.

44. Oceana, "Gillnets: Walls of Death," accessed October 3, 2010, http://na.oceana .org/en/our-work/promote-responsible-fishing/bycatch/learn-act/gillnets-walls-of-death.

45. Lack and Sant, 2008.

46. Ibid., 16.

47. Watts, 2003.

48. FAO produces Fishstat Capture Production reports based on 100 shark species and for an additional 30 groups.

49. M. Lack and Glenn Sant. *Confronting Shark Conservation Head On!* (Cambridge, UK: *TRAFFIC*, 2006), 4–5.

50. Ibid.

51. United Nations Food and Agriculture Organization, "FAO Fisheries Commodities Production and Trade," accessed January 15, 2010, http://www.fao.org/fishery/ statistics/software/fishstat/en.

52. United Nations Food and Agriculture Organization, "International Plan of Action for the Conservation and Management of Sharks," accessed January 15, 2010, http://www.fao.org/fishery/ipoa-sharks/npoa/en.

53. Ibid.

54. United Nations Food and Agriculture Organization, "Fishing Vessel Monitoring Systems (VMS)," accessed January 17, 2010, http://www.fao.org/fishery/vms/en.

55. Commission for the Conservation of Antarctic Marine Living Resources, "Why Does CCAMLR Exist?, Patagonian Toothfish," accessed January 17, 2010, http://www .ccamlr.org/edu/eng/e-why3.htm.

56. Greenpeace International, "Greenpeace International Blacklist," accessed January 15, 2010, http://www.greenpeace.org/international/en/campaigns/oceans/pirate -fishing/Blacklist1/.

57. United Nations Food and Agriculture Organization, "Species Fact Sheets: *Huso huso*," accessed May 4, 2010, http://www.fao.org/fishery/species/2072/en.

58. Arkive, "Beluga (*Huso huso*)," accessed October 13, 2010 http://www.arkive.org/beluga/huso-huso/info.html.

59. University of Michigan Museum of Zoology, Animal Diversity Web, "*Huso huso*," accessed February 10, 2010, http://animaldiversity.ummz.umich.edu/site/accounts/information/Huso_huso.html.

60. Ibid and Arkive, "Beluga (*Huso huso*)," accessed October 13, 2010, http://www.arkive.org/beluga/huso-huso/info.html.

61. Ibid.

62. R.P. Khodorevskaya, G.I. Ruban, and D.S. Pavlov, *Behaviour, Migrations, Distribution, and Stocks of Sturgeons in the Volga-Caspian Basin* (Norderstedt, Germany: Books on Demand GmbH, 2009).

63. M. Kottelat, J. Gesner, M. Chebanov, and J. Freyhof, The IUCN Red List of Threatened Species, "*Huso huso*," accessed May 1, 2010, http://www.iucnredlist.org/apps/redlist/details/10269/0.

64. In non-spawning times, the fish do not congregate in large numbers.

65. See Kottelat et al., 2009.

66. Ibid.

67. Ibid.

68. Khodorevskaya et al., 2009 in Kottelat et. al., 2009.

69. Ibid.

70. Kottelat et al., 2009.

71. Ibid.

72. These data include species of sharks, rays, skates, and chimaeras, class Chondrichthyes.

73. Lack and Sant, 2006.

74. Ibid.

75. Straddling fish stocks are those that migrate across or between the economic exclusive zone of one or more States and on the high seas. See UN Atlas of the Oceans.

76. United Nations, "Convention on the Laws of the Sea," accessed July 23, 2010, http://www.un.org/Depts/los/convention_agreements/texts/unclos/unclos_e.pdf.

77. Lack and Sant, 2006, 2–3.

78. Ibid.

79. U.S. Department of State, "Regional Fisheries Management Organizations," accessed March 12, 2010, http://www.state.gov/g/oes/ocns/fish/regionalorganizations/index.htm.

80. United Nations, "Convention on the Laws of the Sea," accessed July 23, 2010, http://www.un.org/Depts/los/convention_agreements/texts/unclos/unclos_e.pdf.

81. Ibid.

82. Lack and Sant, 2006, 2–3.

83. Ibid.

84. WildAid, 2007.

85. The Maldives is comprised of 1,191 islands, with only 200 islands being inhabited.

86. WildAid, 2007.

87. Ibid.

88. Ibid.

89. See Kottelat et al., 2009.

90. Ibid.

Chapter 7

1. Also known as Brazilian mahogany or large leaved mahogany.
2. According to the U.S. Fish and Wildlife Management Authority, neotropics is a biogeographic region that stretches southward from the Tropic of Cancer and includes southern Mexico, Central and South America, and the West Indies. The area of southern Florida and the Caribbean is also included. See U.S. Fish and Wildlife Service, "Mahogany General Overview," accessed November 23, 2010, www.fws.gov/international/DMA_DSA/CITES/timber/maogany_overview.html.
3. Roberto F. Kometter, Martha Martinez, Arthur G. Bundell, Raymond E. Guillison, Marc K. Steininger, and Richard E. Rice, "Impacts of Unsustainable Mahogany Logging in Bolivia and Peru," *Ecology and Society* 9, no. 1 (2004), 12, accessed June 16, 2009.
4. Ibid.
5. Ann Azbill, "The Majestic Big Leaf Mahogany—Is it on the Verge of Extinction?," *Associate Content*, September 30, 2009, accessed May 2, 2010, www.associatedcontent.com/article/2212109/the_majestic_big_leaf_mahogany_is_it.html?cat=47.
6. Arkive, "Big Leaf Mahogany (*Swietenia macrophylla*)," accessed April 3, 2010, www.ARKive.org/big-leaf-mahogany/swientenia-macrophylla.
7. WWF, "Wildlife Trade: Mahogany Trade FAQs," accessed January 3, 2010, http://worldwildlife.org/what/globalmarkets/wildlifetrade/faqs=mahogany.html.
8. Global Trees Campaign, "*Swietenia macrophylla*," accessed April 3, 2010, http://www.globaltrees.org/tp_swieteniamacrophylla.htm.
9. World Conservation Monitoring Centre, The IUCN Red List of Threatened Species, "*Swietenia macrophylla*," accessed April 3, 2010, http://www.iucnredlist.org/apps/redlist/details/32293/0.
10. In terms of discharge, not length.
11. See WWF Global, "Amazon Keystone Initiative," accessed April 3, 2010, http://wwf.panda.org/what_we_do/where_we_work/amazon/vision_amazon/wwf_projects_amazon_basin_rainforests/index.cfm?uProjectID=BR0940.
12. Ibid.
13. Plants become commercially extinct when, because of logging (legal or illegal), the tree inventory is so low that it is no longer economically viable to harvest the trees.
14. WWF Global, "Amazon Keystone Initiative," accessed April 3, 2010, http://wwf.panda.org/what_we_do/where_we_work/amazon/vision_amazon/wwf_projects_amazon_basin_rainforests/index.cfm?uProjectID=BR0940.
15. Global Trees Campaign, "*Swietenia macrophylla*," accessed April 3, 2010, http://www.globaltrees.org/tp_swieteniamacrophylla.htm.
16. See WWF Global, "Amazon Basin," accessed April 4, 2010, http://wwf.panda/what_we_do/where_we_are/amazon/vision_amazon/wwf-projects_amazon_basin_rainforests/index.cfm?uProjectID=BR0925.
17. Rob Rhykerd (professor and chairperson) in discussion with author, June 24, 2010.
18. Ibid.
19. Transparency International, *Corruption in Logging Licenses & Concessions*, accessed December 20, 2010, http://www.illegal-logging.info/uploads/WPTimberLicensing3November2010.pdf.

20. Tracy Staedter, "Selective Logging Fails to Sustain Rainforest," *Scientific American*, October 21, 2005, accessed December 20, 2009, http://www.scientificamerican.com/article.cfm?id=selective-logging-fails-t. Also see: Mark Schwartz, "Selective Logging Causes Widespread Destruction, Study Finds," *Stanford Report*, October 21, 2005, accessed December 20, 2009, http://news.stanford.edu/news/2005/october26/select-102605.html.

21. Sierra Club, "Responsible Trade: Trade and Illegal Logging," accessed April 20, 2010, www.sierraclub.org/trade/globalization/logging.aspx.

22. Ibid.

23. CEPI. *The European Pulp and Paper Industry's Position Against Illegal Logging and the Trade of Illegally Harvested Wood*. Press Release, August 26, 2002, quoted in *Illegal Logging and Illegal Activities in the Forest Sector: Overview and Possible Issues for the UNECE Timber Committee and FAO European Forestry Commission*, A Paper Presented as Basis of an Expert Presentation at the UNECE Timber Committee Market Discussions on 7–8 October 2003 (Geneva, Switzerland, September 2003): 3.

24. A. Contreas-Hermosilla, R. Doornbosch, and M. Lodge, *Economics of Illegal Logging and Associated Trade*, (Organisation for Economic Co-operation and Development, SG/SD/RT, 1/REV), 2007: 1–46, accessed April 9, 2010, www.illegal-logging.info/uploads/OECD_background_paper_on_illegal_logging.pdf.

25. Environment and Agriculture and Rural Development Departments/Sustainable Development Network, *Strengthening Forest Law Enforcement and Governance: Addressing a Systematic Constraint to Sustainable Development*, (Washington, D.C.: World Bank, 2006).

26. WWF, *Failing the Forests: Europe's Illegal Timber Trade Report* (Surrey, UK: WWF–UK, 2006): 2.

27. Ibid.

28. Ibid.

29. See William F. Laurence, Mark A. Cochrane, Scott Berger, Philip M. Fearnside, Patricia Delamônica, Christopher Barber, Sammya D'Angelo, and Tito Fernandes, "The Future of the Brazilian Amazon," *Science* (January 19, 2001): 438–439.

30. WWF, "Issues: Timber Trade and Illegal Logging," accessed July 20, 2010, http://wwf.panda.org/what_we_do/endangered_species/elephants/asian_elephants/areas/issues/habitat_loss_fragmentation/timber_trade_illegal_logging/.

31. G. Xiang, *Report of the External Commission of the Chamber of Deputies Destined to Investigate the Acquisition of Wood, Lumber Mills and Extensive Portions of Land in the Amazons by Asian Loggers* (Brasilia, Brazil, 1998).

32. Ibid.

33. Nelly Luna Amancio, "Corruption in INRENA is Worse than 'Petro-tapes,'" trans. Canessa Castro Chesterton, accessed April 6, 2010, www.livinginperu.com/features-617-environment-corruption-inrena-is-worse-tha-a?petro-tapes.

34. AIDESEP, *Illegal Logging and International Trade in Mahogany* (Swientenia macrophylla) *from the Peruvian Amazon* (Lima, Peru: AIDESEP, 2007).

35. Ibid.

36. Ibid.

37. See J.N.M. Silva, J.O.P. de Carvalho, J.C.A. do Lopes, and B.F. de Almelda, D.H.M. Costa, L.C. de Oliveria, J.K. Vanclay, and J.P. Skovsgaard, "Growth and Yield of a Tropical Rainforest in the Brazilian Rainforest 13 Years After Logging," *Forest Ecology and Management* 71 (1995): 267–274.

38. Mongabay.com, "Colombia," accessed January 2, 2010, http://rainforests .mongabay.com/20colombia.htm.

39. Sierra Club, "Responsible Trade: Trade and Illegal Logging," accessed August 23, 2010, www.sierraclub.org/trade/globalization/logging.aspx.

40. WWF, "Wildlife Trade: Mahogany Trade FAQs," accessed January 3, 2010, www.worldwildlife.org/what/globalmarkets/wildlifetrade/faqs=mahogany.html.

41. AIDESEP is an acronym for Associatión Interétnica de Desarrollo de la Selva Peruan.

42. AIDESEP and the Rainforest Foundation of Norway, "Peru's Mahogany Exports Threaten Survival of Indigenous Tribes and Violate International Law," *Illegal Logging*, May 30, 2007, accessed May 2, 2010, http://www.illegal-logging.info-item_single.php ?it_id=2134&it.news.

43. Ibid.

44. World Conservation Monitoring Centre, The IUCN Red List of Threatened Species, "*Swietenia macrophylla*," accessed April 3, 2010, http://www.iucnredlist.org/apps/ redlist/details/32293/0.

45. Global Trees Campaign, "*Swietenia Macrophylla*," accessed April 3, 2010, http://www.globaltrees.org/tp_swieteniamacrophylla.htm.

46. WWF Global, "More Than 40 Years in the Amazon. What WWF Is Doing: An Integrated Approach," accessed January 10, 2010, http://wwf.panda.org/what_we_do/ where_we_work/amazon/vision_amazon/.

47. See WWF Global, "Global Forest Trade Network," accessed April 22, 2010, http://gftn.panda.org/.

48. Ibid.

49. Ibid.

50. Lacey Act, 18 USC 42-43, 16 USC 3371-3378.

51. Ibid.

52. WWF, "Activists Help Curb Illegal Logging that Threatens Endangered Species," accessed November 17, 2010, http://wwf.worlwildlife.org/site/pageserver ?pagename=can_results_illegal_logging_CITES&AddInterest=1120.

53. The Peninsula Online, Qatar, "CITES Gives Peru Six Months to Curb Illegal," accessed November 1, 2010, http://www.illegal-logging.info/item_single.php?it _id=4279&it=news.

54. Ibid.

55. WWF Global, "Establishment of the Alto Purús National Park: Protecting an Area Almost the Size of Belgium," accessed April 27, 2010, http://wwf.panda.org/what _we_do/where_we_work/amazon/vision_amazon/models/amazon_protected_areas/ establishment/alto_purus/.

56. See WWF–Peru, "Active Conservation Projects in Peru," accessed April 23, 2010, http://wwf.panda.org/who_we_are/wwf_offices/peru/projects/index.cfm ?ProjectID=PE0867.

57. Ibid.

58. Ibid.

59. Ibid.

60. See WWF, "Amazon: Projects—Amazon Region Protected Areas," accessed April 27, 2010, http://www.worldwildlife.org/what/wherewework/amazon/arpa.html.

61. Ibid.

62. WWF Global, "WWF in the Deep Amazon: Malaria, Infections and One Incredible Park," accessed January 10, 2010, http://wwf.panda.org/what_we_do/where_we_work/amazon/vision_amazon/models/amazon_protected_areas/management/wwf_expedition/.

63. See WWF Global, "Amazon Keystone Initiative," accessed April 3, 2010, http://wwf.panda.org/what_we_do/where_we_work/amazon/vision_amazon/wwf_projects_amazon_basin_rainforests/index.cfm?uProjectID=BR0940.

64. Ibid.

65. WWF–UK, "Fighting Forest Crime and the Illegal Timber Trade," accessed November 21, 2009, http://d2rby7spo76flf.cloudfront.net/downloads/fightingforestcrime.pdf.

66. WWF Global, "Conservation of Guiana's Forests," accessed on April 27, 2010, http://wwf.panda.org/who_we_are/wwf_offices/suriname/index.cfm?uProjectID=9L0807.

67. Ibid.

68. Ruth Nussbaum, Ian Gray, and Sophie Higman, *Modular Implementation and Verification (MIV): A Toolkit for the Phased Application of Forest Management Standards and Certification* (Oxford: ProForest, 2003).

69. Ibid.

70. Ibid.

71. Yarding is the moving of logs to an assembly point once the tree is cut.

72. F.E. Putz, P. Sist, T. Frederickson, and D. Dykstra, "Reduced-impact Logging: Challenge and Opportunities," *Forest Ecology and Management* 256 (2008): 1428.

73. Ibid.

74. Liliana Lozano, *USAID Progress Report: Project #: 527-A-00-02-00134-00*, accessed November 20, 2009, http://pdf.usaid.gov/pdf_docs/PDACF792.pdf

75. See WWF Global, "Responsible Forestry in the Amazon," accessed April 22, 2010, http://wwf.panda.org/what_we_do/where_we_work/amazon/vision_amazon/models/responsible_forestry_amazon/.

76. Jürgen Blaser, *Forest Law Compliance and Governance in Tropical Countries: A Region-by-Region Assessment of the States of Forest Law Compliance and Governance: Recommendations for Improvement* (FAO and ITTO, 2010).

Chapter 8

1. See Stephen F. Pires and Ronald V. Clarke, "Are Parrots CRAVED?: An Analysis of Parrot Poaching in Mexico," *Journal of Research in Crime and Delinquency*, published online March 15, 2011, doi: 10.1177/0022427810397950. Also, Stephen F. Pires and Ronald V. Clarke, "Sequential Foraging, Itinerant Fences, and Parrot Poaching in Bolivia," *British Journal of Criminology* 51, no. 2 (2011): 314.

2. Birdlife International, *"Anodorhynchus leari,"* accessed December 28, 2010, http://www.iucnredlist.org/apps/redlist/details/142575/0.

3. IUCN Red List of Threatened Species, *"Cyanopsitta spixii,"* accessed May 3, 2011, http://www.iucnredlist.org/apps/redlist/details/142578/0.

4. IUCN Red List of Threatened Species, *"Anodorhynchus glaucus,"* accessed May 3, 2011, http://www.iucnredlist.org/apps/redlist/details/142577/0.

5. Ibid.

6. BirdLife International, The IUCN Red List of Threatened Species, "*Anodorhynchus hyacinthinus*," accessed December, 28, 2010, http://www.birdlife.org/datazone/speciesfactsheet.php?id=1543.

7. Meindert Brouwer, "The Hyacinth Macaw Makes a Comeback," accessed June 6, 2010, http://www.worldwildlife.org/science/projects/item8605.html.

8. Arkive, "Hyacinth Macaw" accessed on November 1, 2010, http://www.arkive.org/hyacinth-macaw/anodorhynchus-hyacinthinus/.

9. Ibid.

10. Charles A. Minn, Jorgen B. Thomsen, and Carlos Yamashita, *Report on the Hyacinth Macaw in the Audubon Wildlife Report*, pp. 405–419, accessed November 23, 2010, www.bluemacaws.org/hywild15.htm.

11. WWF, "The Hyacinth Macaw Makes a Comeback," accessed December 10, 2010, http://www.worldwildlife.org/science/projects/item8605.html.

12. Ibid.

13. Ibid.

14. The WWF scientifically ranks the most outstanding bio and habitat regions in which it operates.

15. BirdLife International, "Species Fact Sheet: *Anodorhynchus hyacinthinus*," accessed December 28, 2010, http://www.birdlife.org/datazone/speciesfactsheet.php?id=1543.

16. Ibid.

17. Mauricio Herrera and Bennett Hennessey, "Monitoring Results of the Illegal Parrot Trade in the Los Pozos Market, Santa Cruz de la Sierra, Bolivia," in *Proceedings of the Fourth International Partners in Flight Conference: Tundra to Tropics* (McAllen, TX: Partners in Flight, 2008): 232–234.

18. Ibid.

19. *The New York Times*, February 3, 1996, "A Defender of Rare Birds is Guilty of Smuggling Them," accessed November 1, 2010, www.nytimes/com/1996/02/03/US/a-defender-of-rare-birds-is-guilty-of-smuggling-them.html.

20. Ibid.

21. United States Court of Appeals, Seventh Circuit, "United States v. Silva," accessed November 1, 2010, http://caselaw.findlaw.com/us-7th-circuit/1004794.html.

22. Igor I. Solar, "Brazil: Massive Illegal Traffic of Endangered Fauna Disrupted," *Digital Journal*, accessed September 2, 2010, http://www.digitaljournal.com/article/294263.

23. Ibid.

24. Ibid.

25. University for the Development of the State and Region of the Pantanal, Refrígrò Caiman, Toyota Brasil, Brasil Telecom, and various Brazilian NGOs. Last accessed September 2, 2009.

26. Bill Hinchberger, "Hyacinth Macaw Project: Saving Endangered Birds in the Pantanal," accessed June 14, 2010, http://www.brazilmax.com/news.cfm/tborigem/pl_pantanal/id/7.

27. Meindert Brouwer, WWF, "Science: The Hyacinth Macaw Makes a Comeback," accessed November 1, 2010, http://www.worldwildlife.org/science/projects/item8605.html.

28. Ibid.

29. Patrícia Faria, Neiva M. R. Guedes, Carlos Yamashita, Paulo Martuscelli, and Cristina Y. Miyaki, "Genetic Variation and Population Structure of the Endangered

Hyacinth Macaw (*Anodorhynchus hyacinthinus*): Implications for Conservation," *Biodiversity Conservation* 17 (2008): 765–779.

30. Ibid.

31. S.M. Haig, "Molecular Contributions to Conservation," *Ecology* 79, (1998): 413–435.

32. BirdLife International, The IUCN Redlist of Threatened Species, "*Milvus milvus*," accessed December 28, 2010, http://www.iucnredlist.org/apps/redlist/details/144330/0.

33. Ibid.

34. Arkive, "Red kite (*Milvus milvus*)," accessed December 28, 2010, http://www.arkive.org/red-kite/milvus-milvus/.

35. Ibid.

36. Ibid.

37. Ibid.

38. BirdLife International, "Red Kite (*Milvus milvus*)," accessed December 28, 2010, http://www.birdlife.org/datazone/speciesfactsheet.php?id=3353.

39. Ibid.

40. Ibid.

41. Royal Society for the Protection of Birds, "Red Kite," accessed December 28, 2010, www.rspb.org.uk/wildlife/birdguide/name/r/redkite/index.aspx.

42. Ibid.

43. Ibid.

44. Ibid and BirdLife International, "Red Kite (*Milvus milvus*)," accessed December 28, 2010, http://www.birdlife.org/datazone/speciesfactsheet.php?id=3353.

45. Royal Society for the Protection of Birds, "Red Kite," accessed December 28, 2010, www.rspb.org.uk/wildlife/birdguide/name/r/redkite/index.aspx.

46. Efforts were made to discover what actions Germany was taking to protect the species, but unfortunately, materials were unavailable.

47. The deadly myxoma virus is highly contagious and fatal in the vast majority of rabbits and hares that are infected.

48. Royal Society for the Protection of Birds, "Red Kite: Legal Status," accessed December 28, 2010, http://www.rspb.org.uk/wildlife/birdguide/name/r/redkite/legal.aspx

49. Royal Society for the Protection of Birds, "Red Kite," accessed December 28, 2010, www.rspb.org.uk/wildlife/birdguide/name/r/redkite/index.aspx.

50. Ibid.

51. Ibid.

52. Ibid.

53. BBC News Cumbria, "Red Kites Returned to Cumbria Forest After 160 Years," accessed November 21, 2010, last updated August 3, 2010, www.bbc.co.uk/news/uk-england-cumbria-10849991.

54. Royal Society for the Protection of Birds, "Red Kite: Conservation," accessed December 28, 2010, http://www.rspb.org.uk/wildlife/birdguide/name/r/redkite/conservation.aspx

55. Ibid.

56. BBC News, "Police Probe Red Kite Poisoning: Rare Birds of Prey from an Award Winning Reintroduction Project Have Been Found Poisoned," last updated

November 29, 2007, accessed December 1, 2010, http://news.bbc.co.uk/2/hi/uk_news/tayside_and_central/7118782.stm.

57. Ibid.

58. BBC News, "Red Kite Found Dead Was Poisoned," accessed November 21, 2010, last updated August 26, 2010, accessed December 4, 2010, http://www.bbc.co.uk/news/uk-scotland-tayside-central-11098865.

59. BBC News, "Red Kite Introduced to Cumbrian Forest Shot Dead," last updated September 10, 2010, accessed November 21, 2010, http://www.bbc.co.uk/news/uk-england-cumbria-11264438.

Chapter 9

1. See Jacqueline L. Schneider "Stolen-Goods Markets: Methods of Disposal," *British Journal of Criminology* 45 (2005): 129–140.

2. Ibid.

3. See Stephen F. Pires and Ronald V. Clarke, "Are Parrots CRAVED?: An Analysis of Parrot Poaching in Mexico," *Journal of Research in Crime and Delinquency*, published online March 15, 2011, doi: 10.1177/0022427810397950. Also, Stephen F. Pires and Ronald V. Clarke, "Sequential Foraging, Itinerant Fences, and Parrot Poaching in Bolivia," *British Journal of Criminology* 51, no. 2 (2011): 314.

4. The IUCN Red List of Threatened Species, "Spatial Data Download," accessed November 4, 2010, http://www.iucnredlist.org/technical-documents/spatial-data.

5. Visit the Center for Problem-Oriented Policing Web site for the original 25 techniques of situational crime prevention, http://www.popcenter.org/25techniques/.

6. See Amar Toor, "NutriSmart Prototype Embeds RFID Tags Directly within Food, Traces Your Lunch from Start to Finish (video)," accessed August 8, 2011, http://www.engadget.com/2011/05/30/nutrismart-prototype-embeds-rfid-tags-directly-within-food-trac/.

7. IDTechEx, "Food and Livestock RFID–Where, Why, What Next?," accessed August 8, 2011, http://www.idtechex.com/research/articles/food_and_livestock_rfid_where_why_what_next_00000434.asp.

8. J. Lowther, D. Cook, and M. Roberts, *Crime and Punishment in the Wildlife Trade* (Wolverhampton, UK: WWF–UK, 2002) and D. Cook, M. Roberts, and J. Lowther, *The International Wildlife Trade and Organised Crime: A Review of the Evidence and the Role of the UK* (Wolverhampton, UK: WWF–UK, 2002).

9. Pires and Clarke, 2011.

10. J. Schneider, "Reducing the Illicit Trade in Endangered Species," *Journal of Contemporary Criminal Justice* 24, no. 3 (2008): 274–295. And Schneider, 2005.

Bibliography

Abreu-Grobois, A., and P. Plotkin. *"Lepidochelys olivacea."* The IUCN Red List of Threatened Species. Accessed May 9, 2010. http://www.iucnredlist.org/apps/redlist/details/11534/0.

Achieng, Judith. "Environment: Kenya and India Challenge CITES on Ivory Trade." *Environment Bulletin* March 10 (2000).

African Wildlife Foundation. "Elephant." Accessed November 2, 3009. http://www.awf.org/content/wildlife/detail/elephant.

AIDESEP. *Illegal Logging and International Trade in Mahogany (Swietenia macrophylla) from the Peruvian Amazon.* National Association of Amazon Indians in Peru (Lima, Peru: AIDESEP), 2007. Also available online at http://www.illegal-logging.info/uploads/Mahogany_reportEng.pdf.

AIDESEP, and The Rainforest Foundation of Norway. "Peru's Mahogany Exports Threaten Survival of Indigenous Tribes and Violate International Law." Accessed May 2, 2010. http://www.illegal-logging.info-item_single.php?it_id=2134&it.news.

Alacón, Randi. "The Convention on the International Trade of Endangered Species: The Difficulty in Enforcing CITES and the United States Solution to Hindering the Trade in Endangered Species." *New York International Law Review* 14, no. 2 (2001): 105–108.

Albanese, Jay. "OC: A Perspective from South Africa." In *OC World Perspectives*, edited by Jay S. Albanese, Dilip Das, and Arvina Verma, 438–459. New York: Prentice Hall, 2002.

Amancio, Nelly Luna. "Corruption in INRENA is Worse than 'Petro-Tapes.' " *El Comercio* (December 2008). Translated by Canessa Castro Chesterton. Accessed April 6, 2010. http://www.livinginPeru.com/features-617-environment-corruption-inrena-is-worse-tha-a?petro-tapes.

Ammann, K. "Bushmeat Hunting and the Great Apes." In *Great Apes & Humans: The Ethics of Coexistence*, edited by B.B. Beck, T.S. Stoinski, M. Hutchins, T.L. Maple, B. Norton, A. Rowan, E.F. Stevens, and A. Arluke, 71–85. Washington, D.C.: Smithsonian Institute, 2001.

Amur Tigers. "Preserving Leopards and Tigers in the Wild." Accessed May 2, 3010. http://amur.org.uk/tigers.shtml.

Ananthakrishnan, G. "Women Walk on the Wild Side." *The Times of India*. Accessed January 20, 2010. http://articles.timesofindia.indiatimes.com/2010-01-02/india/28143776_1_vasanta-sena-vasanta-sena-periyar-tiger-reserve.

Anderson, R.S. "Investigation, Prosecution and Sentencing of International Wildlife Trafficking Offenses in the U.S. Federal System." *National Environmental Enforcement Journal* 12: 14 June (1997).

Animal Planet. "Thai Elephants: The Sordid Underbelly of the Elephant World." Accessed November 4, 2009. http://animal.discovery.com/convergence/safari/elephant/thaielephants/thaielephants2.html.

Animal Welfare Institute. "Sharks At Risk." Accessed February 3, 2010. http://www.awionline.org/ht/a/GetDocumentAction/i/10560.

Anonymous. "Black Market Caviar a $748 Million Trade That Puts Fish Stock at Risk." *NZ Herald*, September 27, 2006. Accessed November 9, 2009. http://www.nzherald.co.nz/aquaculture/news/article.cfm?c_id=121&objectid=10403052.

Anonymous.. "Illegal Wildlife Activities in the CAMRAIL Railway and Its Suroundings–Assessment." *LAGA*. Accessed November 21, 2009. http://www.laga-enforcement.org/Portals/0/Documents/CAMRAIL%20assesment%20report%20-%20October06.pdf.

Afrol News. "Bushmeat Warning After Cameroon Virus." Accessed October 22, 2010. http://www.afrol.com/articles/13708.

Arak, Joel. "Shark Fin Soup A Dangerous Delicacy?" Accessed February 21, 2010. http://www.cbsnews.com/stories/2002/07/31/world/main517011.shtml.

Arkive. "African Elephant (*Loxodonta africana*)." Accessed November 2, 2009. http://www.arkive.org/african-elephant/loxodonta-africana/.

Arkive. "Asian Elephant (*Elephas maximus*)." Accessed November 2, 2009. http://www.arkive.org/asian-elephant/elephas-maximus/.

Arkive. "Beluga (*Huso huso*)." Accessed October 13, 2010. http://www.arkive.org/beluga/huso-huso/.

Arkive. "Big-leaf mahogany (*Swietenia macrophylla*)." Accessed October 13, 2010. http://www.arkive.org/big-leaf-mahogany/swietenia-macrophylla/.

Arkive. "Hyacinth Macaw." Accessed November 1, 2010. http://www.arkive.org/hyacinth-macaw/anodorhynchus-hyacinthinus/.

Arkive. "Red Kite." Accessed December 28, 2010. http://www.arkive.org/red-kite/milvus-milvus/.

Arthur, John. University of South Florida, St. Petersburg, Anthropology. Personal Interview, April 12, 2009.

Asian News. "Borneo, Pygmy Elephant at Risk of Extinction." Last modified February 27, 2009. http://www.asianews.it/index.php?1=en&art=14596&size=A.

Associated Press. "Airport Inspection Reveals Smuggled Songbirds." Last modified May 6, 2009. http://www.msnbc.msn.com/id/30598542/ns/travel-news/t/airport-inspection-reveals-smuggled-songbirds/.

Associated Press. "The Ol' Naked Wife Diversion," *San Francisco Chronicle*. Accessed December 10, 2010. http://www.sfgate.com/cgi-bin/article.cgr?f=n/a/2001/12/12/mnwood.

Aung, M., "On the Distribution, Status and Conservation of Wild Elephants in Myanmar," *Gajah* 18 (1997): 47–55. Quoted in C.R. Shepherd and V. Nijam, *Elephant and Ivory in Myanmar* (Petaling Jaya, Selangor, Malaysia: TRAFFIC, 2008), 4, 25, 26.

Azbill, Ann. "The Majestic Big Leaf Mahogany–Is it on the Verge of Extinction?" *Associate Content*. Accessed May 2, 2010. http://www.associatedcontent.com/article/2212109/the_majestic_big_leaf_mahogany_is_it.html?cat=47.

Bahuchet, S., and Ioveva K. "De la Forêt au Marché : Le Commerce de Gibier au Sud Cameroun." In *L'homme et la forêt tropicale* (1999): 533–558. Quoted in R. Nasi, D. Brown, D. Wilkie, E. Bennett, C. Tutin, G. van Tol, and T. Christophersen, "Conservation and Use of Wildlife-Based Resources: The Bushmeat Crisis," Secretariat of the Convention on Biological Diversity, Montreal, and Center for International Forestry Research (CIFOR), Bogor. Technical Series no. 33, 2007, accessed June 2, 2009, http://www.cbd.int/doc/publications/cbd-ts-33-en.pdf.

Bagla, Pallava. "Poachers Track Poachers in India Wilderness Project." *NATIONALGEOGRAPHIC.COM/NEWS*. Last modified April 21, 2003. http://news.nationalgeographic.com/news/pf/51115524.html.

Barboza, David. "Waiter, There's a Celebrity in My Shark Fin Soup." *The New York Times*, August 13, 2006. www.nytimes.com/2006/08/13/weekinreview/13barboza.html.

Barnett, Anthony. "London Raids Expose Mafia Caviar Racket." Accessed November 2, 2009. http://www.guardian.co.uk/uk/2003/Nov/09/ukcrime.london.

Baum, Julia K., and Ransom A. Myers. "Shifting Baselines and the Decline of Pelagic Sharks in the Gulf of Mexico." Accessed May 4, 2010. http://www.fmap.ca/ramweb/papers-total/Baum_Myers_2004.pdf.

BBC News. "AIDS Warning Over Bushmeat Trade." Accessed January 20, 2009. www.news.bbc.co.uk/1/hi/programmes/file_on_4/3954963.stm.

BBC News. "Mercury Poison found in Shark Fins." Accessed February 21, 2010. http://news.bbc.co.uk/2/hi/asia-pacific/1420029.stm.

BBC News. "Police Probe Red Kite Poisonings: Rare Birds of Prey from an Award-Winning Reintroduction Projects Have Been Found Poisoned." Last updated November 29, 2007. Accessed December 1, 2009. http://news.bbc.co.uk/2/hi/uk_news/scotland/tayside_and_central/7118782.stm.

BBC News. "Red Kite Found Dead was Poisoned." Accessed December 4, 2010. http://www.bbc.co.uk/news/uk-scotland-tayside-central-11098865.

BBC News. "Red Kite Reintroduced to Cumbrian Forest Shot Dead." Accessed December 4, 2010. http://www.bbc.co.uk/news/uk-england-cumbria-11264438.

BBC News. "Red Kites Threatened in Scotland." Accessed December 4, 2010. http://news.bbc.co.uk/2/hi/uk_news/scotland/6214969.stm.

BBC News Cumbria. "Red Kites Returned to Cumbria Forest After 160 Years." Accessed November 21, 2010. Last updated August 3, 2010. www.bbc.co.uk/news/uk-england-cumbria-10849991.

Beardsley, Elizabeth R. "Poachers with PCs: The United States' Potential Obligations and Ability to Enforce Endangered Wildlife Trading Prohibitions against Foreign Traders Who Advertise on eBay." *UCLA Journal of Environmental Law & Policy* (2006/2007): 110–124.

Beccaria, Cesare. *On Crimes and Punishment.* Translated by Stephen Gould. New York: Gould & Van Winkle, 1809.

Bemis, W.E., and E.K. Findeis. "The Sturgeon's Plight." *Nature* 370 (1994): 602.

Bird, Maryann. "Black Gold Comeback." *Time* 159, March 18, 2002. Accessed November 2, 2009. www.time.com/time/magazine/europe/0,9263,901020318,00.html.

Birdlife International. "*Anodorhynchus hyacinthinus.*" Accessed December 28, 2010. http://www.iucnredlist.org/apps/redlist/details/142575/0.

Birdlife International. "*Anodorhynchus leari.*" Accessed December 28, 2010. http://www .iucnredlist.org/apps/redlist/details/142575/0.

Birdlife International. "*Milvus milvus.*" Accessed December 28, 2010. http://www .iucnredlist.org/apps/redlist/details/144330/0.

Birdlife International. "Red Kite (*Milvus milvus*)." Accessed December 28, 2010. http:// www.birdlife.org/datazone/speciesfactsheet.php?id=3353.

Birdlife International. "Species Factsheet: *Androhynchrus hyacinthinus.*" Accessed December 28, 2010. http://www.birdlife.org/datazone/speciesfactsheet.php?id=1543.

Blanc, J. "*Loxodonta africana.*" The IUCN Red List of Threatened Species. Accessed December 23, 2009. http://www.iucnredlist.org/apps/redlist/details/12392/0.

Blaser, J. "Forest Law Compliance and Governance in Tropical Countries." FAO and ITTO, 2010. Also available online at www.fao.org/forestry/20060-0ea89047982 ec036d5833bdf42a00663.pdf.

Blaser, Jürgen, Arnoldo Contreras, Tapani Oksanen, Esa Puustjärvi, and Franz Schmithü-sen. *Forest Law Enforcement and Governance (FLEG) in Eastern Europe and Northern Asia (ENA).* Washington, D.C.: World Bank, 2005.

Bowen-Jones, E. "The African Bushmeat Trade–A Recipe for Extinction." *UK Ape Alliance/Fauna and Flora International,* 1998. Also available online at http://www .4apes.com/bushmeat/report/bushmeat.pdf.

Brouwer, Meindert. "The Hyacinth Macaw Makes a Comeback." Accessed June 6, 2010. http://www.worldwildlife.org/science/projects/item8605.html.

Brown, D., Fa, J. E., and L. Gordon. "Assessment of Recent Bushmeat Research and Recommendations to Her Majesty's Government." Accessed September 23, 2009. https://static.zsl.org/files/defra-assessment-of-recent-bushmeat-research-and -recommendations-to-her-majestys-government-298.pdf.

Brown, Nancy C. "Lower Rio Grande Valley National Wildlife Refuge." *Endangered Species Bulletin* 23, no. 4 (July 1998): 36.

Buncombe, Andrew. "Hunter Who Turned to Conservation: The Remarkable Legacy of Tiger Jim." *The Independent on Sunday.* November 1, 2007. Accessed September 8, 2010. http://www.independent.co.uk/environment/nature/hunter-who-turned-to -conservation-the-remarkable-legacy-of-tiger-jim-398493.html.

Buncombe, Andrew. "The Face of a Doomed Species: Tigers Driven to Edge of Extinction by Poachers and Loss of Habitat." *The Independent,* Wednesday, October 31, 2007. Accessed September 8, 2010. http://www.independent.co.uk/environment/ nature/the-face-of-a-doomed-species-398373.html.

Canada Border Service Agency. Accessed November 21, 2010. http://cbsaasfc.gc.ca/ menu-eng.html.

Cantú-Guzmán, Juan-Carlos, María Elena Sánchez-Saldaña, Manuel Grosselet, and Jesús Silva Gamez. "The Illegal Parrot Trade in Mexico." *Defenders of Wildlife,* (January 2007): 7–121.

Center for Problem-Oriented Policing. "Twenty Five Techniques of Situational Prevention." Accessed November 2, 2009. http://www.popcenter.org/25techniques/.

CEPI. *The European Pulp and Paper Industry's Position Against Illegal Logging and the Trade of Illegally Harvested Wood.* Press Release, August 26, 2002. Quoted in *Illegal Logging and Illegal Activities in the Forest Sector: Overview and Possible Issues for the UNECE Timber Committee and FAO European Forestry Commission.* A Paper Presented as Basis of an Expert Presentation at the UNECE Timber Committee Market Discussions on 7-8 October 2003, Geneva, Switzerland (September 2003): 3.

China's Biodiversity: A Country Study. Beijing: China Environmental Science Press, 1998. Also available online at http://bpsp-neca.brim.ac.cn/books/cntrysdy_cn/index.html.

Choudhury, A., D.K. Lahiri Choudhury, A. Desai, J.W. Duckworth, P.S. Easa, A.J.T. Johnsingh, P. Fernando, S. Hedges, M. Gunawardena, F. Kurt, U. Karanth, A. Kister, V. Menon, H. Riddle, A. Rübel, and E. Wilkramanayake. *"Elephas maximus."* The IUCN Red List of Threatened Species. Accessed December 23, 2009. http://www.iucnredlist.org/apps/redlist/details/7140/0.

Christy, Bryant. "The Serpent King." *Foreign Policy* (Dec. 28, 2010.) Accessed January 4, 2011. http://www.foreignpolicy.com/articles/2010/12/28/the_serpent_king.

Chundawat, R.S., B. Habib, U. Karanth, K. Kawanishi, J. Ahmad Khan, T. Lynam, D. Miquelle, P. Nyhus, S. Sunarto, R. Tilson, and S. Wang. *"Panthera tigris."* The IUCN Red List of Threatened Species. Accessed August 30, 2008). http://www.iucnredlist.org/apps/redlist/details/15955/0.

Circle of Asia. Accessed January 25, 2009. http://www.circleofasia.com/.

CITES BWG/IUCN, P. Ibrahima, and Y. Bello. "Study on Wildlife Legislation and Policies in Central African Countries." Accessed November 20, 2010. http://www.cites.org/common/prog/bushmeat/rep_legislation.pdf.

Clarke, Roger S. *The United Nations Crime Prevention and Criminal Justice Program: Formulation of Standards and Efforts at Their Implementation.* Philadelphia: University of Pennsylvania Press, 1994.

Clarke, Ronald V. "Hot Products: Understanding, Anticipating, and Reducing Demand for Stolen Goods." *Police Research Series Paper 112* (1999). Also available online at http://www.popcenter.org/problems/shoplifting/PDFs/fprs112.pdf.

Clayton, Jonathan. "Eight Mountain Gorillas Are Shot Dead in Troubled National Park," *The Sunday Times,* July 28, 2007. Accessed September 20, 2009. http://www.timesonline.co.uk/tol/news/world/africa/article2155469.ece.

CNN. *Planet in Peril.* Accessed December 23, 2009. http://www.cnn.com/SPECIALS/2009/planet.in.peril/.

CNN Wire Staff. "Live Tiger Cub Found in Suitcase at Thai Airport." *CNN World,* August 27, 2010. Accessed September 3, 2010. http://articles.cnn.com/2010-08-27/justice/thailand.tiger_1_tiger-cub-thai-airport-suitcase?_s=PM:CRIME.

CNN Wire Staff. "Major Mexican Wildlife Trafficker Arrested, Officials Say." *CNN World,* July 6, 2010. Accessed August 1, 2010. http://articles.cnn.com/2010-07-06/world/mexico.animal.traffic.arrest_1_wild-animals-trafficker-wildlife?_s=PM:WORLD.

CNN World. "Mountain Gorillas: Killings of Mountain Gorillas in Congo Prompt U.N. Probe." July 25, 2007. Accessed September 20, 2009. http://articles.cnn.com/

2007-07-27/world/congo.gorillas_1_mountain-gorillas-virunga-national-park
-silverback?_s=PM:WORLD.

Cockburn, Patrick. "Black Gold, Black Death." *The Independent*, May 25, 2000. Accessed February 3, 2009. http://www.independent.co.uk/news/world/europe/black-gold
-black-death-716387.html.

Commission for the Conservation of Antarctic Marine Living Resources. "Why Does CCAMLR Exist?, Patagonian Toothfish." Accessed January 17, 2010. http://www
.ccamlr.org/edu/eng/e-why3.htm.

Contreas-Hermosilla, A., R. Doornbosch, and M. Lodge. "Economics of Illegal Logging and Associated Trade." Organisation for Economic Co-operation and Development. SG/SD/RT1/RV2007, 2007. Accessed April 9, 2010. www.illegal
-logging.info/uploads/OECD_background_paper_on_illegal_logging.pdf.

Convention on International Trade in Endangered Species of Wild Fauna and Flora. "A Brief History of Sturgeons and CITES." Accessed May 31, 2010. http://www
.cites.org/eng/prog/Sturgeon/history.shtml.

Convention on International Trade in Endangered Species of Wild Fauna and Flora. "Appendices I, II, and III." Accessed November 23, 2009. http://cites.org/eng/
app/appendices.shtml.

Convention on International Trade in Endangered Species of Wild Fauna and Flora. *CITES Trade Data Dashboards*. Accessed December 20, 2010. http://www.cites
-dashboard.unep-wcmc.org/about.

Convention on International Trade in Endangered Species of Wild Fauna and Flora. "CITES Trade Database." Accessed December 22, 2010. http://www.unep
-wcmc.org/citestrade/docs/CITESTradeDatabaseGuide_v7.pdf.

Convention on International Trade in Endangered Species of Wild Fauna and Flora. "Monitoring the Illegal Killing of Elephants (MIKE)." Accessed May 3, 2010. www.CITES.org/eng/prog/MIKE.

Convention on International Trade in Endangered Species of Wild Fauna and Flora. "National Reports, Reporting Under the Convention." Accessed August 3, 2009. http://www.cites.org/eng/resources/reports.shtml.

Convention on International Trade in Endangered Species of Wild Fauna and Flora. "Sixteenth Meeting of the CITES Animals Committee Shepherdstown." Accessed October 2, 2010. http://www.cites.org/eng/com/ac/16/index.shtml/.

Convention on International Trade in Endangered Species of Wild Fauna and Flora. "Text on the Convention." Accessed August 3, 2009. http://cites.org/eng/disc/text.shtml.

Convention on International Trade in Endangered Species of Wild Fauna and Flora. "The Elephant Trade Information System (ETIS): What is ETIS?." Accessed November 5, 2009. http://www.cites.org/eng/prog/etis/index.shtml.

Convention on Migratory Species. "Convention on Conservation of Migratory Species." Accessed May 9, 2010. http://www.cms.int/about/index.htm.

Cook, Dee, M. Roberts, and J. Lowther. *The International Wildlife Trade and Organized Crime: A Review of the Evidence and the Role of the UK. WWFUK*. Wolverhampton, UK: University of Wolverhampton, 2002.

Coonan, Clifford. "Chinese Bid to Lift Ban on Tiger Trade Will Result in Extinction, Say Conservationists." *The Independent on Sunday*, Friday May 29, 2007. Accessed September 19, 2009. http://www.independent.co.uk/news/world/asia/chinese-bid-to
-lift-ban-on-tiger-trade-will-result-in-extinction-say-conservationists-449346.html.

Cowdrey, David. "Switching Channels: Wildlife Trade Routes into Europe and the UK." *WWF/TRAFFIC Report*. Wolverhampton: University of Wolverhampton, 2002.

David Suzuki Foundation. "Canada's Species At Risk Act." Accessed December 29, 2010. http://www.davidsuzuki.org/issues/wildlife-habitat/science/endangered-species -legislation/canadas-species-at-risk-act.

Davies, G. "Bushmeat and International Development." *Conservation Biology* 16 (2002): 587–589.

Davis, Ben. *Black Market: Inside the Endangered Species Trade in Asia*. San Rafael, CA: Earth Awareness Editions, 2005.

Defra. *Wildlife Crime: A Guide to the Use of Forensic and Specialist Techniques in the Investigation of Wildlife Crime*. London: HMSO, 2009.

Denham, J., J. Stevens, C.A. Simpfendorfer, M.R. Heupel, G. Cliff, A. Morgan, R. Graham, M. Ducrocq, N.D. Dulvy, M. Seisay, M. Asber, S.V. Valenti, F. Litvinov, P. Martins, M. Lemine Ould Sidi, P. Tous, and D. Bucal. "*Sphyrna mokarran*." The IUCN Red List of Threatened Species. Accessed March 20, 2010. http://www.iucnredlist.org/ apps/redlist/details/39386/0.

Department of the Interior. "Endangered and Threatened Wildlife and Plants." *Federal Register* 41, no. 115 (1976): 24062–24067.

DeSombre, Elizabeth R. *Global Environmental Institutions*. London: Routledge, 2006.

Dickinson, M.B., J.C. Dickinson, and F.E. Putz. "Natural Forest Management as a Conservation Tool in the Tropics: Divergent Views on Possibilities and Alternatives." *Commonwealth Forestry Review* 75 (1996): 309–315.

Dinerstein, E., C. Loucks, A. Heydlauff, E. Wikramanayake, G. Bryja, J. Forrest, J. Ginsberg, S. Klenzendorf, P. Leimgruber, T. O'Brien, E. Sanderson, J. Seidensticker, and M. Songer. *Setting Priorities for the Conservation and Recovery of Wild Tigers: 2005–2015*. Also available online at http://www.savethetigerfund.org/AM/Template .cfm?Section=Full_Reports&Template=/CM/ContentDisplay.cfm&ContentID=2714.

Doward, Jamie. "Health Fears Row as Mountains of Meat are Smuggled into the UK." *The Observer*, Sunday June 10, 2007. http://www.guardian.co.uk/environment/2007/ jun/10/food.medicineandhealth.

E! Science News. "Weddings Boost Shark's Fin Consumption in Singapore: Report." *Biology and Nature*, May 10, 2008. Accessed March 6, 2009. http://esciencenews .com/sources/physorg/2008/05/10/weddings.boost.sharks.fin.consumption.singapore .report.

Edwards, Holly. "When Predators Become Prey: The Need for International Shark Conservation." *Ocean and Coastal Law Journal* 12 (2006–2007): 305.

"Endangered Species Act of 1973: As Amended by the 108th Congress." Department of the Interior, U.S. Fish & Wildlife Service. Accessed June 24, 2010, http://www .fws.gov/endangered/esa-library/pdf/ESAall.pdf.

Environment and Agriculture and Rural Development Departments/Sustainable Development Network. *Strengthening Forest Law Enforcement and Governance: Addressing a Systematic Constraint to Sustainable Development*. Washington, D.C.: World Bank, 2006.

Environment Florida. "Why We Need a Strong Endangered Species Act." Accessed May 24, 2011. http://www.environmentflorida.org/preservation/endangered -species/why-we-need-a-strong-endangered-species-act.

Environmental Crimes. "Profiting at the Environmental." *Environmental Health Perspective* 112, no. 2 (2004): A97–A103.

Environmental Investigative Agency (EIA). *How China's Illegal Ivory Trade is Causing a 21st Century African Elephant Disaster.* Washington, D.C.: EIA, 2007.

Esmond, Martin and Daniel Stiles. "Ivory Markets of Europe." Save the Elephants, 2005. Accessed February 10, 2010. www.savetheelephants.org/files/pdf/publications/2005%20MARTIN%20&20STYLES%20IVORY%20Markets%20of%20Europe.pdf.

European Commission Environment. "Wildlife Trade Legislation." Accessed August 20, 2010. http://ec.europa.eu/environment/cites/legis_wildlife_en.htm

Evolutionary Distinct & Globally Endangered (EDGE). "68. Western Gorilla (*Gorilla gorilla*)." Accessed December 10, 2009. http://www.edgeofexistence.org/mammals/species_info.php?id=161.

Fa, John E., Carlos A. Peres, and Jessica Meeuwig. "Bushmeat Exploitation in Tropical Forests: An Intercontinental Comparison." *Conservation Biology* 16, no. 1. (2002): 232–237.

Fagan, C., and D. Shoobridge. "An Investigation of Illegal Mahogany Logging in Peru's Auto Purús National Park and its Surroundings." Accessed October 8, 2010. http://www.illegal-logging.info/uploads/2007AltoPurusReport.pdf.

Faria, Patrícia J., Neiva Guedes, Carlos Yamashita, Paulo Martuscelli, and Cristina Miyaki. "Genetic Variation and Population Structure of the Endangered Hyacinth Macaw: Implications for Conservation." *Biological Conservation* 17 (January 2008): 765–796.

Fasulo, Linda. *An Insider's Guide to the UN.* New Haven, CT: Yale University Press, 2004.

Favre, D. "Elephants, Ivory and International Law." *Review of European Community & International Environmental Law* 10 (2001): 277–286.

Fiadjoe, Yvonne. "CITES in Africa: An Examination of Domestic Implementation and Compliance." *American University/Sustainable Development Law & Policy* (Spring 2004): 152–169.

Fischer, Carolyn. "The Complex Interactions of Markets for Endangered Species Products." *Journal of Environmental Economics and Management* 48 (2004): 926–953.

Fishermen's Protective Act (Pelly Amendment) 22 U.S.C. §§ 1971–1979. August 27, 1954, as amended 1968, 1972, 1976–1981, 1984, 1986–1988, 1990, 1992, and 1995.

Flora and Fauna International. 1998. *Conservation of the Asian Elephant in Indochina.* Quoted in The Viet Nam Ecological Association, TRAFFIC Southeast Asia, Indochina Office and the Forest Protection Department of the Ministry of Agriculture and Rural Development. "An Assessment of the Illegal Trade in Elephants and Elephant Products in Viet Nam." *TRAFFIC International* 2 (July 2002): 1.

Food and Agriculture Organization of the United Nations. "*Workshop on Tropical Secondary Forest Management in Africa: Reality and Perspectives.* Rome, Italy: FAO, 2003. Also available online at http://www.fao.org/DOCREP/006/J0628E/J0628E00.HTM.

Forest Policy Research. "Indonesia: Tesso National Park to Increase in Size." Accessed November 4, 2009. http://forestpolicyresearch.com/2009/02/18/indonesia-tesso-national-park-to-increase-in-size/.

Foundation WILDLIFE RIGHTS. "Welcome To the In Situ Wildlife Conservation Organization: The Wildlife Rights Foundation." Accessed June 4, 2009. http://www.insituwildlifeconservation.org.

Fowler, Sarah, and John A. Musick. "Shark Specialist Group Finning Statement." Accessed December 28, 2010. http://www.flmnh.ufl.edu/fish/organizations/ssg/ssgfinstatementfinal2june.pdf.

Funk, P. "On Effective Use of Stigma as a Crime-Deterrent." *European Economic Review* 48 (2004): 715–728.

Galster, Steven R. "Big-Game Smugglers: The Trail Leads to South Africa." *The Nation* (February 1993): 195–198.

Gibson, Claudine, Sarah V. Valenti, Sarah L. Fowler, and Sonja V. Fordham. *The Conservation Status of Northeast Atlantic Chondrichthyans: Report of the IUCN Shark Specialist Group*. Newbury, UK: IUCN Species Survival Commission. Also available online at http://www.iucnssg.org/tl_files/Assets/pdf/Reports/SSG_NEA_Shark_Report.pdf.

Gigrin Farm. "Threats to Red Kites." Accessed December 28, 2010. http://www.gigrin.co.uk/threats_to_red_kites.html.

Gilling, Daniel. *Crime Prevention: Theory, Policy and Politics*. London: Routledge, 1997.

Glastra, Rob. *Elephant Forests on Sale: Rain Forest Loss in the Sumatran Tesso Nilo Region and the Role of European Banks and Markets*. WWF–Deutschland, 2003.

Global Trees Campaign. "Global Trees Campaign." Accessed October 12, 2010. http://globaltrees.org.

Global Trees Campaign. "*Swietenia macrophylla*." Accessed April 3, 2010. www.globaltrees.org.

Gnam, Rosemarie. "Protecting the Source of Caviar." Accessed October 29, 2010. http://findarticles.com/p/articles/mi_m0ASV/is_1_23/ai_54023069/.

Goodrich, J.M., D.G. Miquelle, L.L. Kerley, and E.N. Smirnov. "Time for Tigers: Paving the Way for Tiger Conservation in Russia." *Wildlife Conservation* 105 (2002): 22–29.

Gorilla Journal. "The Gorilla Population of Bwindi Continues to Increase." Accessed June 21, 2009. http://www.berggorilla.org/english/gjournal/texte/34bwindi-census.html.

Goudarzi, Sara. "Ape Meat Sold in U.S., European Black Markets." *National geographic.com/news*, July 18, 2006. Accessed November 3, 2009. http://news.nationalgeographic.com/news/2006/07/060718-ape-meat.html.

Greenpeace. "Oceans, Whales, & Seafood." Accessed March 22, 2011. www.greenpeace.org/usa/campaigns/oceans.

Greenpeace. "Protect Forests" Accessed March 22, 2011. www.greenpeace.org/usa/campaigns/forests.

Greenpeace International. "Greenpeace International Blacklist." Accessed January 15, 2020. http://www.greenpeace.org/international/en/campaigns/oceans/pirate-fishing/Blacklist1/.

Gudmia-Mfonfu, Vincent. "High Level Fight Against Corruption in the Wildlife Section in Cameroon." *Wildlife Justice* 6 (June 2009): 3.

Gudmia-Mfonfu, Vincent. " 'Those Who Want to Deplete our Wildlife Species Cannot Succeed,' His Excellency, Elvis Ngolle Ngolle, Minister of Forestry and Wildlife." *Wildlife Justice* 5 (November 2007): 3.

Haig, S.M. "Molecular Contributions to Conservation." *Ecology* 79 (1998): 413–435.

Hawaii Sharks. "On 'Aumakua,' Hawaiian Ancestral Spirits." Accessed August 26, 2010. http://www.hawaiisharks.com/aumakua.html.

Hemley, Ginette, ed. *International Wildlife Trade: A CITES Sourcebook*. World Wildlife Fund, 1994.

Herrera, Mauricio, and Bennett Hennessey. "Monitoring Results of the Illegal Parrot Trade in the Los Pozos Market, Santa Cruz de la Sierra, Bolivia." In *Proceedings of the Fourth International Partners in Flight Conference*. McAllen, TX: Partners in Flight, 2008.

Hinchberger, Bill. "Hyacinth Macaw Project: Saving Endangered Birds in the Pantanal." Accessed June 14, 2010. http://www.brazilmax.com/news.cfm/tborigem/pl_pantanal/id/7.

Home Office, Research Development Statistics. "Organised Crime." Accessed March 9, 2009. http://webarchive.nationalarchives.gov.uk/20110220105210/http://rds.homeoffice.gov.uk/rds/orgcrime1.html.

Humane Society International. "Africa News: Primates as Pets, in Entertainment and in Research." Accessed June 3, 2010. http://www.hsi.org/world/africa/index.jsp?page=5.

IDTechEx. "Food and Livestock RFID–Where, Why, What Next?." Accessed August 8, 2011. http://www.idtechex.com/research/articles/food_and_livestock_rfid_where_why_what_next_00000434.asp.

International Centre for Trade and Sustainable Development. "CITES Sanctioned Ivory Auctions Underway in Southern Africa." Accessed November 2, 2009. http://ictsd.org/i/news/biores/32508/.

International Fund for Animal Welfare (IFAW). "African Elephant." Accessed November 3, 2009. http://www.ifaw.org/ifaw_international/save_animals/elephants/african_elephant.php.

International Fund for Animal Welfare (IFAW). "Asian Elephant." Accessed November 3, 2009. http://www.ifaw.org/ifaw_international/save_animals/elephants/asian_elephant.php.

International Gorilla Conservation Programme. "A Brief History of IGCP." Accessed May 20, 2010. http://www.igcp.org/about/history/.

International Tropical Timber Organization. *Making the Mahogany Trade Work: Report of the Workshop on Capacity-building for the Implementation of the CITES Appendix-II Listing of Mahogany*. INRENA, 2004. Also available on line at http://www.cites.org/common/prog/mwg/E-report.pdf.

INTERPOL. "About INTERPOL." Accessed June 20, 2010. http://www.interpol.int/public/icpo/default.asp.

INTERPOL. "Wildlife Crime." Accessed April 30, 2010. http://www.interpol.int/Public/EnvironmentalCrime/Wildlife/Default.asp.

IRNA. "German Authorities Clamp Down on Caspian Sea Caviar Smuggling." Accessed December 21, 2010. http://www.mathaba.net/news/?x=613665?flattr.

IUCN. *"Gorilla beringei."* Accessed December 3, 2009. http://www.iucnredlist.org/apps/redlist/details/39994/0.

IUCN. *"Gorilla gorilla."* Accessed December 3, 2009. http://www.iucnredlist.org/apps/redlist/details/9404/0.

IUCN. *Illegal Logging: A Commitment to Change Through Tripartite Action*. Accessed June 30, 2010. http://cmsdata.iucn.org/downloads/iucn_fleg_brochure_may2006.pdf.

IUCN. *Shark Specialist Group*. Accessed June 4, 2010. http://www.iucnssg.org/index.php/about-the-ssg.

IUCN. "Sturgeon More Critically Endangered Than any Other Group of Species." Accessed June 2, 2010. http://www.iucn.org/?4928/Sturgeon-more-critically -endangered-than-any-other-group-of-species.

IUCN. "What We Do." Accessed November 1, 2009. http://www.iucn.org/what/.

IUCN and SSC. "Shark Specialist Group." Accessed June 4, 2010. http://www.iucnssg .org/index.php/about-the-ssg.

IUCN Red List of Threatened Species. "*Anodorhynchus glaucus*." Accessed May 3, 2011. http://www.iucnredlist.org/apps/redlist/details/142577/0.

IUCN Red List of Threatened Species. "*Carcharodon carcharias*." Accessed February 21, 2010. http://www.iucnredlist.org/apps/redlist/details/3855/0.

IUCN Red List of Threatened Species. "*Cyanopsitta spixii*." Accessed May 3, 2011. http://www.iucnredlist.org/apps/redlist/details/142578/0.

IUCN Red List of Threatened Species. "Data Organization." Accessed May 24, 2009. http://www.iucnredlist.org/technical-documents/data-organization#documentation.

IUCN Red List of Threatened Species. "Geographic Patters." Accessed May 9, 2010. http://www.iucnredlist.org/initiatives/mammals/analysis/geographic-patterns.

IUCN Red List of Threatened Species. *IUCN Red List Categories and Criteria: Version 3.1*. Gland, Switzerland and Cambridge, UK: IUCN Species Survival Commission, 2001.

IUCN Red List of Threatened Species. "Mammal Key Findings." Accessed May 9, 2010. www.iucnredlist.org/mammals/key_findings.

IUCN Red List of Threatened Species. "Red List Overview." Accessed November 22, 2010. http://www.iucnredlist.org/technical-documents/data-organization# documentation.

IUCN Red List of Threatened Species. "Spatial Data Download." Accessed February 15, 2011. http://www.iucnredlist.org/technical-documents/spatial-data.

IUCN Red List of Threatened Species. "*Sphyrna mokarran*, Geographic Range." Accessed December 3, 2009. http://www.iucnredlist.org/apps/redlist/details/ 39386/0.

IUCN Red List of Threatened Species. "Summary Statistics." Accessed December 12–15, 2010. http://www.iucnredlist.org/about/summary-statistics.

IUCN Red List of Threatened Species. "Taxonomy." Accessed December 3, 2009. http:// www.iucnredlist.org/technical-documents/data-organization#doc_taxonomy.

Jackson, R., and R. Norton. "Improving Ethical Behavior in Hunters." *Transactions of the North American Wildlife and Natural Resources Conference* 44 (1979): 306–318.

Jane Goodall Institute. "Conservation & Communities." Accessed March 11, 2009. http:// web.janegoodall.org/cc-education.

Jane Goodall Institute. "Controlling Bushmeat Trade." Accessed March 11, 2009. www .janegoodall.org/africa-programs/objectives/controlling-bushmeat-trade.asp.

Jane Goodall Institute. "Role of Women in the Community." Accessed March 14, 2009. www.janegoodall.org/africa-programs/objectives/role-of-women-in-the-community .asp.

Japanese Auto Pages. "Ports." Accessed November 23, 2010. http://www.japanautopages .com/useful_resources/ports.php.

Jenkins, Mark. "Who Murdered the Virunga Gorillas?" *National Geographic*. Accessed September 20, 2009. http://ngm.nationalgeographic.com/2008/07/virunga/jenkins -text.

Jim Corbett National Park. "Colonel Jim Corbett." Accessed August 3, 2009. http://www
.jimcorbettnationalpark.com/corbett_coljim.asp.

Jim Corbett National Park. "History." Accessed August 3, 2009. http://www
.jimcorbettnationalpark.com/corbett_history.asp.

Joint Nature Conservation Committee. "The Wildlife and Countryside Act 1981."
Accessed August 23, 2010. http://jncc.defra.gov.uk/page-1377.

Juste, J., J. E. Fa, J. Perez Del Val, and J. Castroviejo. "Market Dynamics of Bushmeat
Species in Equatorial Guinea." *Journal of Applied Ecology* 32, no. 3 (August 1995):
454–467.

Kashka, Babukar. "Illicit Wildlife Trade Third Largest After Arms, Drugs." *In Depth
News*, February 13, 2010.

Kazmar, Jonathon. "The International Illegal Plant and Wildlife Trade: Biological
Suicide." *University of California Davis Journal of International Law and Policy*
6, no. 105 (2009).

Khodorevskaya, R.P., Ruban, G.I., and D.S. Pavlov. 2009. "Behaviour, Migrations,
Distribution and Stocks of Sturgeons in the Volga-Caspian Basin." Quoted in
M. Kottelat, J. Gesner, M. Chebanov, and J. Freyhof, The IUCN Red List of Threatened Species. "*Huso huso*." Accessed May 1, 2010. http://www.iucnredlist.org/
apps/redlist/details/10269/0.

Knapp, A., C. Kitschke, and S. von Meibom. "Proceedings of the International Sturgeon
Enforcement Workshop to Combat Illegal Trade in Caviar." Accessed January 18,
2010. www.traffic.org/species-reports/traffic_species_fish14.pdf.

Kometter, Roberto F., Martha Martinez, Arthur G. Blundell, Raymond E. Gullison, Marc
K. Steininger, and Richard E. Rice. "Impacts of Unsustainable Mahogany Logging
in Bolivia and Peru." *Ecology and Society* 9, no. 1 (2004): 12. Accessed June 16,
2009. http://www.ecologyandsociety.org/vol9/iss1/art12/print.pdf.

Korobeinikov, Dmitry. "Astrakhan Police Destroy 300 kg of Contraband Black Caviar."
Accessed December 1, 2010. http://en.rian.ru/crime/20090803/155714409.html.

Kottelat, M., J. Gesner, M. Chebanov, and J. Freyhof. "*Huso huso*." The IUCN Red List of
Threatened Species. Accessed May 1, 2010. http://www.iucnredlist.org/apps/
redlist/details/10269/0.

Kurnianwan, Moch N. "NGOs Fight Against Illegal Logging." Accessed September 10,
2009. http://www.ecologyasia.com/news-archives/2003/mar-03/thejakartapost
.com_20030320_1.htm.

"Lacey Act." 18 USC 42-43, 16 USC 3371-3378.

Lack, M., and G. Sant. *Illegal, Unreported and Unregulated Shark Catch: A Review of
Current Knowledge and Action.* Canberra: Department of the Environment, Water,
Heritage, and the Arts and TRAFFIC, 2008. Also available online at www.traffic
.org/species-reports/traffic_species_fish30.pdf.

Lack, Mary, and Glenn Sant. *Confronting Shark Conservation Head On!* Cambridge, UK:
TRAFFIC, 2006. Also available online at www.traffic.org/species-reports/traffic
_species_fish4.pdf.

Lack, Mary, and Glenn Sant. *Trends in Global Shark Catch and Recent Developments in
Management.* Cambridge, UK: TRAFFIC, 2009. Also available online at www
.traffic.org/species-reports/traffic_species_fish34.pdf.

Lair, R.C. "Gone Astray—The Care and Management of the Asian Elephant in Domesticity." Accessed August 4, 2010. www.fao.org/DOCREP/005/AC774E/ac774e00.htm.

Laurence, William F., Mark A. Cochrane, Scott Berger, Philip M. Fearnside, Patricia Delamónica, Christopher Barber, Sammya D'Angelo, and Tito Fernandes. "The Future of the Brazilian Amazon." *Science* January 19 (2001): 438–439.

LeDuc, J.P. "Trafficking in Animals and Plants: A Lucrative form of Crime." *International Criminal Police Review* (1996): 458–459.

Lemieux, Andrew M., and Ronald V. Clarke. "The International Ban on Ivory Sales and Its Effects on Elephant Poaching in Africa." *British Journal of Criminology* 49 (2009): 451–471.

Levy, Adrian, and Cathy Scott-Clark. "Poaching for Bin Laden." Accessed November 1, 2010. http://www.guardian.co.uk/world/2007/may/05/terrorism.animalwelfare.

Lowther, J., D. Cook, and M. Roberts. *Crime and Punishment in the Wildlife Trade.* Wolverhampton, UK: WWF–UK, 2002.

Lozano, Liliana. *USAID Progress Report: Project #: 527-A-00-02-00134-00.* Accessed November 20, 2009. http://pdf.usaid.gov/pdf_docs/PDACF792.pdf

Lucas, K. "Environment-Eduador: Rising Concern over Trafficking of Animals." *Environment Bulletin* September (2000): 20.

MacDonald, Kenneth Iain. "IUCN: A History of Constraint." Accessed September 2, 2010. http://perso.cpdr.ucl.ac.be/maesschalck/MacDonaldInstitutional_Reflexivity_and_IUCN-17.02.03.pdf.

Maggio, Gregory F. "Recognizing the Vital Role of Local Communities in International Legal Instruments for Conserving Biodiversity." *UCLA Journal of Environmental Law & Policy* (1997/1998): 213–247.

Magrath, William B. "Basic Concepts of Crime Prevention and Asset Security." In *Timber Theft Prevention: Introduction to Security for Forest Managers*, edited by W.B. Magrath, R. Grandalski, G. Stuckey, G.B. Vikanes, and G.R. Wilkinson, 4–12. World Bank Sustainable Development in Asia and Pacific Region, 2007. Also available online at vle.worldbank.org/bnpp/files/TF05369310888WBTimberheftWEB.pdf.

Magrath, William B.. "Conclusions: Policies and Strategies to Promote Timber Theft Prevention." In *Timber Theft Prevention: Introduction to Security for Forest Managers*, edited by W.B. Magrath, R. Grandalski, G. Stuckey, G.B. Vikanes, and G.R. Wilkinson, 87–92. World Bank Sustainable Development in Asia and Pacific Region, 2007. Also available online at vle.worldbank.org/bnpp/files/TF05369310888WBTimberheftWEB.pdf.

Magrath, William B., R. Grandalski, G. Stuckey, G.B. Vikanes, and G.R. Wilkinson. *Timber Theft Prevention: Introduction to Security for Forest Managers.* World Bank Sustainable Development in Asia and Pacific Region, 2007. Also available online at vle.worldbank.org/bnpp/files/TF05369310888WBTimberheftWEB.pdf.

Mameli, Peter. "Stopping the Illegal Trafficking of Human Beings: How Transnational Police Work Can Stem the Flow of Forced Prostitution." *Crime Law and Social Change* 38 (2002): 67–80.

Mank, Bradford C. "Protecting Intrastate Threatened Species: Does the Endangered Species Act Encroach on Traditional State Authority and Exceed the Outer Limits of the Commerce Clause?" *Georgia Law Review* (Spring 2002): 99–151.

Marine Bio. "*Carchrodon carcharias*, Great White Shark." Accessed February 21, 2010. http://marinebio.org/species.asp?id=38.

Marine Bio. "*Delphinapterus leucas*: Beluga Whale." Accessed July 30, 2010. http://marinebio.org/species.asp?id=159.

Marine Bio. "*Sphyrna mokarran*: Great Hammerhead Shark." Accessed July 30, 2010. http://marinebio.org/species.asp?id=87.

Marghescu, Tamás. "Trading Wildlife." *European Newsletter* 14 (2007): 1–16. Accessed June 2, 2009. http://cmsdata.iucn.org/downloads/iucn_no14_eng _internet.pdf.

Marshall, Andrew. "Making a Killing: Driven by Low Risks and High Profits, the Global Black-Market Trade in Wildlife Endangers Animals and Humans Alike." *Bulletin of the Atomic Scientist* 62, no. 2 (2006): 36–43.

Martin, E.B. "Wildlife Products for Sale in Myanmar." *TRAFFIC Bulletin* 17, no. 1 (1978): 33–44.

"Massive Great Ape Die-Off in Africa–Ebola Suspected." *NATIONALGEOGRAPHIC .COM/NEWS*. Last modified February 6, 2003. http://news.nationalgeographic. com/news/2003/02/0205_030205_ebola.html.

Matyr, Debbie. FREELAND, Indonesia, emails exchanged in January, 2011.

McKenzie, David. "Singaporeans Arrested in Kenya for Suspected Ivory Smuggling." *CNN World*, December 11, 2010. Accessed January 15, 2011. http://articles.cnn .com/2010-12-11/world/kenya.ivory.bust_1_elephant-ivory-elephant-populations -african-elephants?_s=PM:WORLD.

McOmber, Elizabeth M. "Problems in Enforcement of the Convention on International Trade in Endangered Species." *Brooklyn Journal of International Law* 27, Part 2 (2002): 673–702.

Metropolitan Police. "Fact Sheet." *Operation Charm*. Accessed November 21, 2009. http://www.operationcharm.org/documents/facsheet_english.pdf.

Metropolitan Police. "Wildlife Crime Unit." Accesed July 8, 2010. http://www.met .police.uk/wildlife/index.htm.

Milliken, Tom. "African Elephants and the 14th Meeting of the Conference of the Parties to CITES." Accessed August 22, 2010. http://www.andrews-elephants.com/docs/ traffic_pub_cop14_13.pdf.

Milliken, T., R.W. Burn, and L. Sangalakula. "The Elephant Trade Information System (ETIS) and the Illicit Trade in Ivory: A Report to the 14th meeting of the Conference of the Parties to CITES." CoP15 Doc. 44.1, Annex 1, 2007. Accessed December 9, 2010. www.cites.org/eng/cop/14/doc/E14-53-2.pdf.

Mills, J.A. "Tiger Bone Trade in South Korea." *Cat News* 19 (1993): 13–16.

Minn, Charles A., Jorgen B. Tomsen, and C. Yamashita. "Report on the Hyacinth Macaw in the Autoban." *Wildlife Report*: 405–419. Accessed November 23, 2010. http:// www.bluemacaws.org/hywild15.htm.

Mongabay.com. "Colombia." Accessed January 2, 2010. http://rainforests.mongabay .com/20colombia.htm.

Mongabay.com. "Tropical Rainforests: Imperiled Riches." Accessed November 23, 2009. http://www.mongabay.com/08amphetamine.htm.

Nahkuna Mfonfu, Olive. "Is Corruption Hampering Conservation Efforts?" *Wildlife Justice*, no. 005 (2007): 3.

Nasi, R., D. Brown, D. Wilkie, E. Bennett, C. Tutin, G. van Tol, and T. Christophersen. "Conservation and Use of Wildlife-Based Resources: The Bushmeat Crisis." Secretariat of the Convention on Biological Diversity, Montreal, and Center for International Forestry Research (CIFOR), Bogor. Technical Series no. 33, 2007. Accessed June 2, 2009. http://www.cbd.int/doc/publications/cbd-ts-33-en.pdf.

National Geographic. "Poachers Track Poachers in India Wilderness Project." Accessed June 3, 2010. http://news.nationalgeographic.com/news/2003/04/0421_030421_indiapoachers.html.

National Oceanic and Atmospheric Administration Fisheries, Office of Protected Resources. "Marine Mammal Protection Act (MMPA) of 1972." Accessed November 2, 2010. http://www.nmfs.noaa.gov/pr/laws/mmpa.

National Wildlife Crime Intelligence Unit. Accessed December 1, 2009. http://www.ncis.co.uk/wildlifecrime.asp.

Nellemann, C., I. Redmond, and J. Refisch (eds). *The Last Stand of the GorillaEnvironmental Crime and Conflict in the Congo Basin: A Rapid Response Assessment.* United Nations Environment Programme, GRID-Arendal, 2010. Also available online at http://www.unep.org/pdf/GorillaStand_screen.pdf.

NEP-WCMC Species Database. Accessed May 25 2010. http://www.unep-wcmc.org/isdb/Taxonomy/tax-species-result.cfm?SpeciesNo=11534&tabname=distribution#

New York Times. "A Defender of Rare Birds is Guilty of Smuggling Them." *The New York Times*, February 3, 1996. Accessed November 1, 2010. http://www.nytimes.com/1996/02/03/us/a-defender-of-rare-birds-is-guilty-of-smuggling-them.html.

Ng, Julia and Nemora. *Tiger Trade Revisited in Sumatra, Indonesia.* Petaling Jaya, Malaysia: TRAFFIC Southeast Asia, 2007. Also available online www.traffic.org/species-reports/traffic_species_mammals37.pdf.

Norman, Brad. "Whale Shark." *Environment Australia Marine Species Section.* Accessed January 3, 2010. http://www.environment.gov.au/coasts/species/sharks/whaleshark/index.html.

Nowell, Kristen, and Xu Ling. *Taming the Tiger Trade: China's Markets for Wild and Captive Tiger Products Since the 1993 Domestic Trade Ban.* East Asia: TRAFFIC, 2007. Also available online at http://www.worldwildlife.org/species/finder/tigers/WWFBinaryitem15400.pdf.

NRDC. "Trade in Bigleaf Mahogany: The Need for Strict Implementation of CITES." *NRDC, The Earth's Best Defense, Forest Facts*, 2006. Accessed October 1, 2010. http://www.nrdc.org/international/files/int_06100201a.pdf.

Nussbaum, Ruth, Ian Gray, and Sophie Higman. *Modular Implementation and Verification (MIV): A Toolkit for the Phased Application of Forest Management Standards and Certification.* London: ProForest, 2003. Also available online at assets.panda.org/downloads/mivtoolkit.pdf.

O'Connell-Rodwell, Caitlin, and Rob Parry-Jones. *An Assessment of China's Management of Trade in Elephants and Elephant Products.* Cambridge, UK: TRAFFIC International, 2002. Also available online at www.traffic.org/species-reports/traffic_species_mammals19.pdf.

Oceana. "Congress Ends Shark Finning in the U.S." Accessed January 4, 2011. http://na.oceana.org/en/news-media/press-center/press-releases/congress-ends-shark-finning-in-us.

Oceana. "Gillnets: Walls of Death." Accessed October 3, 2010. http://na.oceana.org/en/our-work/promote-responsible-fishing/bycatch/learn-act/gillnets-walls-of-death.

Phoenix Fund. "Phoenix Fund." Accessed June 12, 2010. http://www.phoenix.vl.ru/zoom/Pdf/Interreg2004.pdf.

Phoenix Fund. "Support for the Antipoaching Activities." Accessed January 15, 2011. http://www.phoenix.vl.ru/support.htm.

Phuah, Lin Ken. "Smuggling Syndicate Caught with Python Skin, Gold Ore." *New Straits Times*, January 9, 2009. Accessed June 23, 2010. http://www.asiaone.com/News/AsiaOne%2BNews/Crime/Story/A1Story20090109-113422.html.

Pikitch, Ellen K., Phaedra Dookakis, Liz Lauck, Prosanta Chakrabarty, and Daniel L. Erikson. "Status, Trends, and Management of Sturgeon and Paddlefish Fisheries." *Fish and Fisheries* 6 (2005): 233–265.

Pillai, K. Rajasekharan, and B. Suchintha. "Women Empowermen for Biodiversity Conservation Through Self Help Groups: A Case From Periyar Tiger Reserve, Kerala, India." *International Journal of Agricultural Resources Governance and Ecology* 5, no. 4 (2006): 338–355.

Pires, Stephen F., and Ronald V. Clarke. "Are Parrots CRAVED? An Analysis of Parrot Poaching in Mexico." *Journal of Research in Crime and Delinquency*. First published online March 15, 2011. Accessed March 29, 2011. doi: 10.1177/0022427810397950.

Pires, Stephen F., and Ronald V. Clarke. "Sequential Foraging, Itinerant Fences and Parrot Poaching in Bolivia." *British Journal of Criminology* 51, no. 2 (2011): 314–335.

Plowden, Campbell, and David Bowles. "The Illegal Market in Tiger Parts in Northern Sumatra, Indonesia." *Oryx* 31, no. 1 (1997): 51–66.

Poston, Lee. "Bodies of Four Critically Endangered Mountain Gorillas Found in Cong's Virunga National Park." Accessed June 21, 2009. http://www.worldwildlife.org/who/media/press/2007/WWFPresitem978.html.

Project Tiger. "Project Tiger." Accessed August 31, 2009. http://www.lairweb.org.nz/tiger/project5.html.

Putz, F.E., P. Sist, T. Frederickson, and D. Dykstra. "Reduced-impact Logging: Challenge and Opportunities," *Forest Ecology and Management* 256 (2008): 1428.

Redmond, Ian, Tim Aldred, Katrin Jedamizik, and Madelaine Westwood. *Recipes for Survival: Controlling the Bushmeat Trade*. London: Ape Alliance Report funded by World Society for the Protection of Animals, 2006.

Renctas. *1st National Report on the Traffic of Wild Animals*. Brasilia, Brazil: Renctas, 2001.

Reuters. "Thai Customs Seize Hundreds of Smuggled Turtles: Live Turtles and Other Rare Reptiles were Stuffed into Four Suitcases and Smuggled into Bangkok's Suvamabhumi Airport." Accessed July 1, 2011. http://www.guardian.co.uk/environment/2011/jun/02/thai-customs-turtles-suitcase-smuggled

Rhykerd, Rob. Illinois State University Department of Agriculture, Personal Interview. June 24, 2010.

Robbins, M., and L. Williamson. "*Gorilla beringei*." The Red List of Threatened Species. Accessed December 3, 2009. http://www.iucnredlist.org/apps/redlist/details/39994/0.

Round River Conservation Studies. "The Race for Peru's Last Mahogany Trees, Illegal Logging and the Alto Purús Park." Accessed October 8, 2010. http://www.illegal-logging.info/uploads/2007AltoPurusReport.pdf.

Rowcliffe, J. Marcus, Emmanuel de Merode, and Guy Cowlishaw. "Do Wildlife Laws Work? Species Protection and the Application of a Prey Choice Model to Poaching Decisions." *Proceedings: Biological Sciences* 271, no. 1557 (2004): 2631–2636.

Royal Society for the Protection of Birds. "Red Kite." Accessed December 28, 2010. http://www.rspb.org.uk/wildlife/birdguide/name/r/redkite/index.aspx.

Rubin, J., *and S.* Stucky. "Fighting Black Markets and Oily Water: The Department of Justice's National Initiatives to Combat Transnational Environmental Crime." *Sustainable Development Law and Policy*, 21 (2004): 21–26.

Saenz, Dianne. "U.S. Government Issues Shark Finning Ban in Atlantic Ocean and Gulf of Mexico Waters." *Oceana Press Releases*, June 19, 2008. Accessed September 9, 2010. http://na.oceana.org/en/news-media/press-center/press-releases/us -government-issues-shark-finning-ban-in-atlantic-ocean-and-gulf-of-mexico-waters.

Sanderson, E. J. Forrest, C. Loucks, J. Ginsberg, E. Dinerstein, J. Seidensticker, P. Leimgruber, M. Songer, A. Heydlauff, T. O'Brien, G. Bryja, S. Klenzendorf, and E. Wikramanayake. *Setting Priorities for the Conservation and Recovery of Wild Tigers: 2005–2015. The Technical Assessment.* Washington, D.C.: WCS, WWF, Smithsonian, and NFWF-STF, 2006.

Save the Tiger Fund. "The Facts and Fallacies of Tiger Farming." Accessed July 8, 2009. http://www.worldwildlife.org/species/finder/tigers/WWFBinaryitem15401.pdf.

Save the Tiger Fund. "Who We Are." Accessed July 8, 2009. http://www.savethetiger fund.org/Content/NavigationMenu2/Learn/WhoWeAre/default.htm.

Schwartz, Mark. "Selective Logging Causes Widespread Destruction, Study Finds." *Stanford Report*, October 21, 2005. Accessed December 20, 2009. http://news .stanford.edu/news/2005/october26/select-102605.html.

Schneider, Jacqueline L. "The Link Between Shoplifting and Burglary: The Booster Burglar." *British Journal of Criminology* 45, no. 3 (2005): 395–401.

Schneider, Jacqueline L. "Stolen Goods Markets: Methods of Disposal." *British Journal of Criminology* 45, no. 2 (2005): 129–140.

Schneider, Jacqueline L. "Reducing the Illicit Trade in Endangered Wildlife: The Market Reduction Approach." *Journal of Contemporary Criminal Justice* 24 (2008): 274–295.

Schulte-Herbrüggen, B., and H. Rossiter. "Project Las Piedras: A Social-Ecological Inves- tigation into the Impact of Illegal Logging Activity in Las Piedras, Madre de Dios Peru." Edinburgh: University of Edinburgh, 2003. Also available online at http:// www.peruforests.org/documents/Studies/LCLasPiedrasFinalReport.pdf.

Sea Shepherd Conservation Society. "Sea Shepherd Conservation Society." Accessed March 22, 2011. www.seashepherd.org.

Sea Shepherd Conservation Society. "What is a Longline?." Accessed February 10, 2010. http://www.seashepherd.org/shark/longlining.html.

Sellar, John M. "Anti-Smuggling, Fraud, and Organized Crime." Accessed November 14, 2010. http://www.policechiefmagazine.org/magazine/index.cfm?fuseaction= display_arch&article_id=1203&issue_id=62007.

Shark Research Group. "Great Hammerhead." Accessed February 14, 2010. http://www .sharkresearch.com/species/hh-great.html.

Shark Specialist Group. "Review of Migratory Chondrichthyan Fishes." *CMS Technical Series No. 15.* Bonn, Germany: IUCN and UNEP/CMS Secretariat. Also available online at http://www.iucnssg.org/tl_files/Assets/pdf/Reports/CMS_Technical Series15_Migratory_sharks.pdf.

Shepherd, Chris R. "On the Distribution, Status and Conservation of Wild Elephants in Myanmar," *Gajah* 18 (1997): 47–55. Quoted in C.R. Shepherd and V. Nijam, *Elephant and Ivory in Myanmar.* (Petaling Jaya, Selangor, Malaysia: TRAFFIC, 2008).

Shepherd, Chris R. *The Trade of Elephants and Elephant Products in Myanmar.* Cambridge, UK: TRAFFIC International, 2002. Also available online at www .traffic.org/species-reports/traffic_species_mammals29.pdf.

Shepherd, C.R., and V. Nijman, "An Assessment of Wildlife Trade at Mong La Market on the Mynamar-China Border." *TRAFFIC Bulletin* 21, no. 2 (August 2007): 85–88.

Shepherd, Chris R. and Nolan Magnus. *Nowhere to Hide: The Trade in Sumatran Tiger.* Southeast Asia: TRAFFIC International, 2004. Also available online at www .traffic.org/species-reports/traffic_species_mammals15.pdf.

Shepherd, Chris R., and Vincent Nijam. *Elephant and Ivory in Myanmar.* Petaling Jaya, Selangor, Malaysia: TRAFFIC, 2008.

Shwartz, Mark. "Selective Logging Causes Widespread Destruction, Study Finds." *Standford Report*, October 21, 2005. Accessed December 20, 2009. http://news.stanford .edu/news/2005/october26/select-102605.html.

Sierra Club. "Responsible Trade: Trade and Illegal Logging." Accessed August 23, 2010. http://www.sierraclub.org/trade/globalization/logging.aspx.

Silva, J.N.M., J.O.P. De Carvalho, J. do C.A. Lopes, B.F. DeAlmvada, D.H.M. Costa, L.C. DeOliveria, J.K. Vanclay, and J.P. Skovsgaard. "Growth and Yield of a Tropical Rainforest in the Brazilian Rainforest 13 Years After Logging." *Forest Ecology Management* 17 (1995): 267–274.

Smithsonian National Museum of African Art. "Ivory: Identification and Regulation of a Precious Material." Accessed January 3, 2010. http://africa.si.edu/research/ivory .pdf.

Solar, Igor I. "Brazil: Massive Illegal Traffic of Endangered Fauna Disrupted." *Digital Journal*, July 5, 2010. Accessed September 2, 2010. http://www.digitaljournal .com/article/294263.

Species at Risk Public Registry. "Species at Risk Act, Compliance and Enforcement." Accessed November 21, 2010. http://www.sararegistry.gc.ca/virtual_sara/files/ reports/ar_SARA-AnnualReport_0209_e.pdf.

Staedter, Tracy. "Selective Logging Fails to Sustain Rainforest." *Scientific American*, October 21, 2005. Accessed December 20, 2009. http://www.scientificamerican .com/article.cfm?id=selective-logging-fails-t.

Steklis, D., and N. Gerald-Steklis. "Status of the Virunga Mountain Gorilla Population." In *Mountain Gorilla: Three Decades of Research at Karisoke*, edited by M. M. Robbins, P. Sicotte, and K.J. Stewart, 391–412. Cambridge, UK: Cambridge University Press, 2001.

Stephenson, P.J., and A. Wilson. *African Great Apes Update: Recent News from the WWF African Great Apes Programme.* Gland, Switzerland: WWF, 2005. Also available online at http://www.worldwildlife.org/species/finder/mountaingorilla/WWF Binaryitem12894.pdf.

Stephenson, Peter J. *WWF Species Action Plan: African Elephant 2007–2011.* Gland, Switzerland: WWF, 2007.

Stiles, Daniel. *An Assessment of the Illegal Ivory Trade in Viet Nam.* Petaling Jaya, Selangor, Malaysia, 2008. Also available online at www.traffic.org/species-reports/ traffic_species_mammals42.pdf.

Stuckey, Gerald L., and William B. Magrath. "Securing Timber Transactions: Technologies and Systems." In *Timber Theft Prevention: Introduction to Security for Forest Managers*, edited by W.B. Magrath, R. Grandalski, G. Stuckey, G.B. Vikanes,

G.R. Wilkinson, 44–67. World Bank Sustainable Development in Asia and Pacific Region, 2007. Also available online at vle.worldbank.org/bnpp/files/TF05369310888 WBTimberheftWEB.pdf.

Sukumar, R., U. Ramakrishnan, and J.A. Santosh. "Impact of Poaching on an Asian Elephant Population in Periyar, Southern India: A Model of Demography and Tusk Harvest," *Animal Conservation* 1 (1997): 281–291. Quoted in Chris R. Shepherd and TRAFFIC, 2008, 2, 12.

Sullivan, Kathleen. "Body Part by Body Part, Sumatran Tigers Are Being Sold into Extinction." *WWF Press Release*, 12 February 2008. http://www.worldwildlife .org/who/media/press/2008/WWFPresitem6629.html.

Sullivan, Nancy J., Anthony Sanchez, Pierre E. Rollin, Zhi-yong Yang, and Gary J. Nabel, "Development of a Preventative Vaccine for Ebola Virus Infection in Primates," *Nature* 408, no. 6812: 605–610.

Sutton, Mike. "Supply by Theft: Does the Market for Second-hand Goods Play a Role in Keeping Crime Figures High?." *British Journal of Criminology* 35, no. 3 (1995): 400–416.

Sutton, Mike. "Handling Stolen Goods and Theft: A Market Reduction Approach." *Home Office Research Study 178*. London: Research, Development, and Statistics Directorate, Home Office, 1998.

Sutton, Mike, Jacqueline Schneider, and Sarah Hetherington. "Tackling Theft with the Market Reduction Approach." *Crime Reduction Series, Paper 8*. London: Research, Development, and Statistics Directorate, Home Office, 2001.

Swanepoel, G. "The Illegal Trade in Rhino Horn: An Example of an Endangered Species." *International Journal of Risk, Security and Crime Prevention* 3, no. 3 (1998): 207–220.

The Control of Trade in Endangered Species (Enforcement) (Amendment) Regulations 2009. Accessed January 2, 2010. http://www.legislation.gov.uk/uksi/2009/1773/contents/made.

The Dian Fossey Gorilla Fund International. "Dian Fossey." Accessed January 8, 2010. http://gorillafund.org/dian_fossey.

The Dian Fossey Gorilla Fund International. "Saving Endangered Gorillas Through Anti-Poaching." Accessed January 8, 2010. http://gorillafund.org/page.aspx ?pid=234.

The Government Pubic Relations Department. "Inside Thailand: Elephants as Part of Thai Culture and National Symbols." Accessed December 4, 2010. http://thailand.prd .go.th/view_inside.php?id=4838.

The Human Society of the United States. Accessed October 10, 2009. www.humane society.org.

The Peninsula Online, Qatar. "CITES Gives Peru Six Months to Curb Illegal Mahogany Logging." Accessed November 1, 2010. http://www.illegal-logging.info/item _single.php?it_id=4279&it=news.

The Telegraph (New Zealand). "Reptile Collector Who Smuggled Geckos in his Underwear Jailed in New Zealand." Accessed June 19, 2010. http://www.telegraph.co.uk/news/worldnews/australiaandthepacific/newzealand/7080799/Reptile-collector -who-smuggled-geckos-in-his-underwear-jailed-in-New-Zealand.html.

The Viet Nam Ecological Association, TRAFFIC Southeast Asia, Indochina Office and the Forest Protection Department of the Ministry of Agriculture and Rural

Development. "An Assessment of the Illegal Trade in Elephants and Elephant Products in Viet Nam." *TRAFFIC International* 2 (July 2002): 1–29. Also available on line at www.traffic.org/species-reports/traffic_species_mammals21.pdf.

Tigris Foundation. "Anti-Poaching." Accessed October 19, 2010. http://www.tigris foundation.nl.

Tilson, Ronald. "Tiger and Rhino Protection Units are Merged in Way Kambas National Park." *Tiger Field News: Sumatra, Indonesia* (August 13, 2003). Accessed December 2, 2009. http://aazkbfr.org/docs/2003_SumatranAntiPoachingTeamsMerge .html.

Tomaselli, I., and S.R. Hirakuri. "Converting Mahogany–Peru's Efforts to Monitor Trade and Contribute to Sustainability of Endangered Timber Species." *ITTO Tropical Forest Update 18/4*. ITTO.

Toor, Amar. "NutriSmart Prototype Embeds RFID Tags Directly within Food, Traces Your Lunch from Start to Finish (video)." Accessed August 8, 2011. http://www .engadget.com/2011/05/30/nutrismart-prototype-embeds-rfid-tags-directly-within -food-trac/.

TRAFFIC. "Beluga Caviar Seized in Transit." *TRAFFIC News*, December 12, 2010. Accessed January 18, 2011. http://www.traffic.org/home/2010/12/3/beluga-caviar -seized-in-transit.html.

TRAFFIC. "Black Gold: The Caviar Trade in Western Europe." *TRAFFIC Fact Sheet*. Accessed March 13, 2010. www.traffic.org/species-reports/caviar-factsheet -english-2.pdf.

TRAFFIC. "Chinese Citizens Risk Imprisonment for Ivory Smuggling." *TRAFFIC News*, September 13, 2010. Accessed December 2, 2010. http://www.traffic.org/home/ 2010/9/13/chinese-citizens-risk-imprisonment-for-ivory-smuggling.html.

TRAFFIC. "Hotline Tip Leads to Bust by Wildlife Crime Unit." *TRAFFIC News*, April 4, 2008. Accessed September 3, 2009. http://www.traffic.org/home/2008/4/4/hotline -tip-leads-to-bust-by-wildlife-crime-unit.html.

TRAFFIC. "Man Arrested Over Tiger Poisoning Incident." *TRAFFIC News*, June 22, 2010. Accessed January 18, 2011. http://www.traffic.org/home/2010/6/22/man -arrested-over-tiger-poisoning-incident.html.

TRAFFIC. "Monkey Smuggler Arrested in Mexico." *TRAFFIC News*, July 20, 2010. Accessed January 18, 2011. http://www.traffic.org/home/2010/7/20/monkey -smuggler-arrested-in-mexico.html.

TRAFFIC. "Over-Harvesting a Key Threat According to a New IUCN Red List." Accessed June 30, 2010. http://www.traffic.org/home/2008/10/6/over-harvesting -a-key-threat-according-to-new-iucn-red-list.html.

TRAFFIC. "Police in Viet Nam Uncover Wildlife Bone Trade." *TRAFFIC News*, September 20, 2010. Accessed January 18, 2011. http://www.traffic.org/home/2010/9/20/ police-in-viet-nam-uncover-wildlife-bone-trade-network.html.

TRAFFIC. "Seized Notebooks Give Unique Insight Scale of Illicit Pangolin Trade." *TRAFFIC News*, October 28, 2010. Accessed January 18, 2011. http://www .traffic.org/home/2010/10/28/seized-notebooks-give-unique-insight-into-scale-of -illicit-p.html.

TRAFFIC. "Thai Customs Seize Four Suitcases Filled With Ivory." *TRAFFIC News*, September 27, 2010. Accessed December 18, 2010. http://www.traffic.org/home/ 2010/9/27/thai-customs-seize-four-suitcases-filled-with-ivory.html.

TRAFFIC. "Tough Penalties for Organized Smuggling Gang." *TRAFFIC News*, May 30, 2008. Accessed December 21, 2010. http://www.traffic.org/home/2008/5/30/ tough-penalties-for-organized-smuggling-gang.html.

TRAFFIC. *What's Driving the Wildlife Trade? A Review of Expert Opinion on Economic and Social Drivers of the Wildlife Trade and Trade Control efforts in Cambodia, Indonesia, Lao PDR and Vietnam.* East Asia and Pacific Region Sustainable and Development Discussion Papers. Washington, D.C.: East Asia and Pacific Region Sustainable Development Department, World Bank, 2008.

TRAFFIC. "While Supplies Last: The Sale of Tiger and Other Endangered Species Medicines in North America." *TRAFFIC* (January 1998): 1–3. Accessed June 1, 2009. www.traffic.org/species-reports/traffic_species_mammals18.pdf.

TRAFFIC Network Report. *Still in Business: The Ivory Trade in Asia Seven Years After the CITES Ban.* TRAFFIC, 1997.

Transparency International. *Corruption in Logging Licenses & Concessions.* Accessed December 20, 2010. http://www.illegal-logging.info/uploads/WPTimberLicens ing3November2010.pdf.

Transparency International. *The Global Corruption Report, 2009: Corruption and the Private Sector.* Cambridge, UK: Cambridge University Press, 2009. Also available online at http://www.cgu.gov.br/conferenciabrocde/arquivos/English-Global -Corruption-Report-2009.pdf.

Trivedi, Bijal P. "Shark-Soup Boom Spurs Conversationalist DNA Study." *National Geographic News*, September 17, 2002. Accessed November 23, 2009. http://news .nationalgeographic.com/news/2002/09/0917_020917_sharks.html.

UN Special. "The Elephant and His Mahout: A Bond for Life." Accessed November 2, 2009. http://www.unspecial.org/UNS635/UNS_635_T01.html.

U.S. Department of Justice. "Operation Jungle Trade." Accessed January 2, 2010. http:// www.justice.gov/enrd/3339.htm.

U.S. Department of State. "Regional Fisheries Management Organizations." Accessed March 12, 2010, http://www.state.gov/g/oes/ocns/fish/regionalorganizations/index.htm.

U.S. Federal Bureau of Investigation. "Organized Crime." Accessed April 10, 2009. http:// www.fbi.gov/about-us/investigate/organizedcrime/organized_crime.

U.S. Fish and Wildlife Service. "History and Evolution of the Endangered Species Act of 1973, including its Relationship to CITES." Accessed November 30, 2010. http:// www.fws.gov/filedownloads/ftp_DJCase/endangered/ESA/esasum.html.

U.S. Fish and Wildlife Service. "Mahogany General Overview." Accessed November 23, 2010. http://www.fws.gov/international/DMA_DSA/CITES/timber/mahogany _overview.html.

U.S. Government Accountability Office. *International Environment: U.S. Actions to Fulfill Commitments Under Five Key Agreements.* Washington, D.C.: GAO, 2003. Also available online at http://www.environmental-auditing.org/Portals/0/Audit Files/us272eng03ar_ft_fivekeyagreements.pdf.

U.S. Government Accountability Office. "Protected Species: International Convention and U.S. Laws Protect Wildlife Differently. Report to the Chairman, Committee on Resources, House of Representative." Accessed August 8, 2010. http://www .gao.gov/new.items/d04964.pdf.

U.S. Government. *International Crime Threat Assessment*, n.d. Accessed May 29, 2010. http://www.fas.org/irp/threat/pub45270index.html.

United Nations. "Basic Information on Secretariats of Multilateral Environmental Agree-
    ments: Mission, Structure, Financing and Governance." Accessed March 9, 2010.
    http://www.un.org/ga/president/60/summitfollowup/060612d.pdf.
United Nations. "Convention on the Laws of the Sea." Accessed July 23, 2010. http://
    www.un.org/Depts/los/convention_agreements/texts/unclos/unclos_e.pdf.
United Nations. "International Environmental Governance: Multilateral Environmental
    Agreements (MEAs)." Accessed April 3, 2010. http://www.unep.org/environment
    algovernance/Home/tabid/180/Default.aspx.
United Nations. "United Nations Convention Against Transnational Organized Crime and
    its Protocols." Accessed November 3, 2009. http://www.unodc.org/unodc/en/
    treaties/CTOC/index.html or http://www.un-documents.net/uncatoc.htm.
United Nations. "United Nations Fish Stocks Agreement." Accessed April 5, 2010. http://
    www.daff.gov.au/fisheries/legal-arrangements/un-fishstocks.
United Nations Development Programme. *Human Development Report, 2005*, New York:
    United Nations Development Programme, 2005.
United Nations Food and Agriculture Organization. *Best Practices for Improving Law
    Compliance in the Forestry Sector*. Rome: Food and Agriculture Organization of
    the United Nations International Tropical Timber Organization, 2005
United Nations Food and Agriculture Organization. "Capture Production 1950–2004."
    Accessed January 15, 2010. http://www.fao.org/fishery/statistics/software/fishstat/en.
United Nations Food and Agriculture Organization. "FAO Fisheries Commodities Produc-
    tion and Trade." Accessed January 15, 2010. http://www.fao.org/fishery/statistics/
    software/fishstat/en.
United Nations Food and Agriculture Organization. "Fishing Vessel Monitoring Systems
    (VMS)." Accessed January 17, 2010. http://www.fao.org/fishery/vms/en.
United Nations Food and Agriculture Organization. "Global Trade in Forest Products
    Worth USD 159 Billion Annually." *Forest Products Yearbook*, 2005.
United Nations Food and Agriculture Organization. "International Plan of Action for the
    Conservation and Management of Sharks." Accessed January 15, 2010. http://www
    .fao.org/fishery/ipoa-sharks/npoa/en.
United Nations Food and Agriculture Organization. "Species Fact Sheets: *Huso huso*."
    Accessed May 4, 2010. http://www.fao.org/fishery/species/2072/en.
United Kingdom. *Customs and Excise Management Act 1979*. Accessed January 2, 2010.
    http://www.legislation.gov.uk/ukpga/1979/2/contents
University of Canberra Media Centre. "Blackmarket Wildlife Sold Online: UC Research-
    ers." Accessed December 1, 2010. http://www.canberra.edu.au/media-centre/2008/
    december-2008/19_wildlife.
University of Michigan Museum of Zoology, Animal Diversity Web. Accessed February
    10, 2010. http://animaldiversity.ummz.umich.edu/site/accounts/information/Huso
    _huso.html.
U.S. Court of Appeals, 7th Circuit. (U.S. v. Silva). Accessed November 1, 2010. http://
    caselaw.findlaw.com/us-7th-circuit-1004794.html.
U.S. Department of Homeland Security, Customs and Border Protection. "Locate a Port of
    Entry–Air, Land, or Sea. Accessed November 21, 2010. http://www.cbp.gov/xp/
    cgov/toolbox/ports/.
Van Heijnsbergen, P. *International Legal Protection of Wild Fauna and Flora*. Amsterdam,
    Netherlands: IOS Press, 1997.

Vikanes, Garry B. "Securing Forest Land and Resources: Technologies and Systems." In *Timber Theft Prevention: Introduction to Security for Forest Managers*, edited by W.B. Magrath, R. Grandalski, G. Stuckey, G.B. Vikanes, and G.R. Wilkinson, 29–43. World Bank Sustainable Development in Asia and Pacific Region, 2007. Also available online at vle.worldbank.org/bnpp/files/TF05369310888WB TimberheftWEB.pdf .

Vorobjiov, S. "Main Problems and Challenges: Combating Illegal Trade in Caviar-Expectations and Needs of Range States." Accessed October 16, 2010 in Knapp et al., 2006, p. 70. http://www.cites.org/common/com/SC/54/E54i-06.pdf.

Walsh, P.D., C.E.G. Tutin, J.F. Oates, J.E.M. Baillie, F. Maisels, E.J Stokes, S. Gatti, R.A. Bergl, J. Sunderland-Groves, and A. Dunn. "*Gorilla gorilla.*" The IUCN Red List of Threatened Species. Accessed December 3, 2009. http://www.iucnredlist.org/apps/redlist/details/9404/0.

Warchol, G.L.; Zupan, L., and W. Clack. "Transnational Criminality: An Analysis of the Illegal Wildlife Market in Southern Africa." *International Criminal Justice Review* 13, no. 1 (2003): 1–27.

Watt, Nick. "Elephants Patrol Border Between Man and Beast." *ABC World News*. Last modified December 11, 2007. http://abcnews.go.com/WN/story?id=3985313&page=1.

Watts, Susie. *Shark Finning: Unrecorded Wastage on a Global Scale*. San Francisco: WildAid, 2003. Also available online at www.protect-The_Sharks.org/pdf/Wildaid/shark_finning.pdf.

Watts, Susie and Victor Wu. *At Rock Bottom: The Declining Sharks of the Eastern Tropical Pacific*. San Francisco, C.A.: WildAid, 2003. Also available online at http://www.wildaid.org/PDF/reports/AtRockBottom.pdf.

Watters, Lawrence, and Wang Xi. "The Protection of Wildlife and Endangered Species in China." *Georgetown International Environmental Law Review* 14, no. 3 (2002): 489–525.

Wikramanayake, M. McKnight, E. Dinerstein, A. Joshi, B. Gurung, and D. Smith. "Designing a Conservation Landscape for Tigers in Human-Dominated Environments." Conservation Biology 18 (2004): 839–844.

WildAid. *End of the Line?: Global Threats to Sharks*. WildAid, 2007. Also available online at http://na.oceana.org/sites/default/files/o/fileadmin/oceana/uploads/Sharks/EndoftheLine_Spread_sm.pdf.

WildAid. *Shark Finning: Unrecorded Wastage on a Global Scale*. WildAid, 2003. Also available online at http://www.protect-the sharks.org/pdf/Wildaid/Shark_Finning.pdf.

Wildlife Conservation Society. "Cameroon." Accessed February 24, 2010. http://www.wcs.org/where-we-work/africa/cameroon.aspx.

Wildlife Conservation Society. "Keeping Bushmeat Off the Rails in Cameroon." Accessed November 28, 2009. http://www.wcs.org/conservation-challenges/natural-resource-use/hunting-and-wildlife-trade/keeping-bushmeat-off-the-rails-in-cameroon.aspx.

Wildlife Conservation Society. "Shark Fin Trade Greater Than Previously Thought, Study Finds." *Science Daily*, February 20, 2003. Accessed March 23, 2010. http://www.sciencedaily.com/releases/2003/02/030220082002.htm.

Wiles, Paul, and Andrew Costello. "The 'Road to Nowhere': The Evidence for Travelling Criminals." *Home Office Research Study No. 207*. Home Office: London, 2000.

Wilkie, D.S. "Bushmeat Trae in the Congo Basin." *Smithsonian Institution Press* III, no. 4 (2001): 86–109.

Wilkie, D.S., and J.F. Carpenter. "Bushmeat Hunting in the Congo Basin: An Assessment of Impacts and Options for Mitigation." *Biodiversity and Conservation* 8, no. 7 (1999): 927–955.

Wilkinson, Graham L. "Forest Management Planning: Basis for Operations and Control." In *Timber Theft Prevention: Introduction to Security for Forest Managers*, edited by W.B. Magrath, R. Grandalski, G. Stuckey, G.B. Vikanes, and G.R. Wilkinson, 13–28. World Bank Sustainable Development in Asia and Pacific Region, 2007. Also available online at vle.worldbank.org/bnpp/files/TF05369310888WB TimberheftWEB.pdf.

Wolfe N.D., Daszak P., Kilpatrick A.M., and D.S. Burke. "Bushmeat Hunting, Deforestation, and Prediction of Zoonotic Disease." *Emerging Infectious Diseases* 11 no. 12 (Dec. 2005): 1822–1827.

World Bank. "Amur Tiger: Russian Far East." Accessed March 10, 2010. http://siteresources.worldbank.org/INTECA/Resources/Tigers-Russia-Chestin-080609.pdf.

World Conservation Monitoring Centre. The IUCN Red List of Threatened Species. "*Swietenia macrophylla*." Accessed April 3, 2010. http://www.iucnredlist.org/apps/redlist/details/32293/0.

World Conservation Society. "Russia." Accessed February 3, 2010. http://www.wcs.org/where-we-work/asia/russia.aspx.

World Conservation Society. "Siberian Tiger Project." Accessed May 23, 2010. http://www.wcs.org/globalconservation/Asia/russia/siberiantigerproject.

WWF. "Activists Help Curb Illegal Logging That Threatens Endangered Species." Accessed November 17, 2010. http://wwf.worldwildlife.org/site/PageServer?pagename=can_results_illegal_logging_CITES&AddInterest=1120.

WWF. "African Elephants–Threats." Accessed October 3, 2010. http://wwf.panda.org/what_we_do/endangered_species/elephants/african_elephants/afelephants_threats/.

WWF. "Amazon, Projects–Amazon Region Protected Areas." Accessed April 27, 2010. http://www.worldwildlife.org/what/wherewework/amazon/arpa.html.

WWF. "Amur Tiger: Russian Far East." Accessed April 27, 2009. http://www.worldwildlife.org/species/finder/amurtiger/amurtiger.html.

WWF. "Amazon, Projects–Amazon Region Protected Areas." Accessed April 27, 2010. http://www.worldwildlife.org/what/wherewework/amazon/arpa.html.

WWF. "Asian Elephants." Accessed July 12, 2010. www.panda.org/about_wwwf/what_we_d0/species_species_factsheets/elephants/asain_elephants/.

WWF. "Asian Elephants: Threats." Accessed July 12, 2009. http://wwf.panda.org/what_we_do/endangered_species/elephants/asian_elephants/asianeleph_threats/.

WWF. "Borneo and Sumatra: Elephant Flying Squad." Accessed November 3, 2009. http://www.worldwildlife.org/what/wherewework/borneo/elephantflyingsquad.html.

WWF. "Program of Combating Illegal Logging: Program of Combating Forest Crime in Tesso Nilo Landscape." Accessed January 2, 2010. http://www.wwf.or.id/en/about_wwf/whatwedo/forest_species/where_we_work/tessonilobukittigapuluh/whoweare/combating_illog/.

WWF. "Conserving Tigers in the Wild: A WWF Framework and Strategy for Action 2002–2010." *Species Programme* (February 2002): 1–32.

WWF. "Elephants." Accessed October 3, 2010. http://wwf.panda.org/what_we_do/
endangered_species/elephants/.

WWF. "Establishment of Alto Puru's National Park." Accessed December 10, 2010.
http://wwf.panda.org/what_we_do/where_we_work/amazon/vision_amazon/
models/amazon_protected_areas/establishment/alto_purus/.

WWF. "Extinct Javan Elephants May Have Been Found Again–in Borneo." Accessed
October 2, 2010. http://singapore.panda.org/news_stories/?131101/Extinct-Javan
-elephants-may-have-been-found-again-in-Borneo.

WWF. *Failing the Forests: Europe's Illegal Timber Trade Report.* Surrey, UK: WWF–
UK (2006): 2.

WWF. "Gone in an Instant: How the Trade in Illegally Grown Coffee is Driving the
Destruction of Rhino, Tiger, and Elephant Habitat." Accessed September 23,
2010. http://wwf.panda.org/what_we_do/endangered_species/elephants/asian
_elephants/areas/news/trade_coffee/.

WWF. "Issues: Habitat Loss and Fragmentation." Accessed July 20, 2010. http://wwf.
panda.org/what_we_do/endangered_species/elephants/asian_elephants/areas/
issues/habitat_loss_fragmentation/.

WWF. "Issues: Human–Elephant Conflict." Accessed May 9, 2010. http://wwf.panda.org/
what_we_do/endangered_species/elephants/asian_elephants/areas/issues/elephant
_human_conflict/.

WWF. "Issues: Rubber Bands for Elephants." Accessed May 22, 2010. http://wwf.panda.
org/what_we_do/endangered_species/elephants/asian_elephants/areas/issues/
elephant_human_conflict/rubber_bands/.

WWF. "Issues: Timber Trade and Illegal Logging." Accessed July 20, 2010. http://wwf.
panda.org/what_we_do/endangered_species/elephants/asian_elephants/areas/
issues/habitat_loss_fragmentation/timber_trade_illegal_logging/.

WWF. "Key Achievements: Highlights from WWF African Great Apes Projects."
Accessed September 21, 2009. http://wwf.panda.org/what_we_do/endangered
_species/great_apes/apes_programme/achievements/.

WWF. "Legislation Enacted to Curb Illegal Logging." Accessed November 21, 2010.
http://wwf.worldwildlife.org/site/PageServer?pagename=can_results_illegal_logging
_imports.

WWF. "Myanmar Emerges as Ivory Trade and Elephant Smuggling Hot Spot." *WWF*.
Last modified December 11, 2008. http://www.wwf.org.au/news/myanmar
-emerges-as-ivory-trade- and-elephant-smuggling-hot-spot/.

WWF. "Projects Across the AREAS Region." Accessed July 23, 2010. http://wwf.panda
.org/what_we_do/endangered_species/elephants/asian_elephants/areas/projects/.

WWF. "Protecting Africa's Great Apes." Accessed March 20, 2010. http://wwf.panda
.org/what_we_do/where_we_work/project/projects/index.cfm?uProjectID
=9F0742.

WWF. "Resumption of Mountain Gorilla Poaching After 17 Years Sends Shockwaves
Through Conservation Circles." *WWF News*, November 27, 2002. Accessed
November 12, 2009. http://wwf.panda.org/who_we_are/wwf_offices/eastern
_southern_africa/news/?10148/Resumption-of-mountain-gorilla-poaching-after
-17-years-sends-shockwaves-through-conservation-circles.

WWF. "Rwandan Mountain Gorillas Killed for Wildlife Trade." Accessed July 23, 2010.
http://wales.wwf.org.uk/wwf_articles.cfm?unewsid=536.

WWF. "The Facts and Fallacies of Tiger Farming." Accessed March 16, 2010. http://
www.worldwildlife.org/species/finder/tigers/WWFBinaryitem15401.pdf.

WWF. "The Heart of Borneo Under Siege." Accessed September 19, 2009. http://wwf
.panda.org/what_we_do/where_we_work/borneo_forests/borneo_deforestation/.

WWF. "The Hyacinth Macaw Makes a Comeback." Accessed December 10, 2010. http://
www.worldwildlife.org/science/projects/item8605.html.

WWF. "The Tesso Nilo Conservation Landscape, Sumatra, Indonesia. Accessed December 15, 2009. http://www.worldwildlife.org/tigers/pubs/riau_profile2.pdf.

WWF. "Wildlife Trade: Mahogany Trade FAQs." Accessed January 3, 2010. http://
worldwildlife.org/what/globalmarkets/wildlifetrade/faqs=mahogany.html.

WWF. "WWF on the Ground in Nepal–The Area." Accessed March 1, 2010. http://www
.wwfnepal.org/our_solutions/conservation_nepal/tal/area/.

WWF. "WWF's African Elephant Programme." Accessed November 3, 2009. http://wwf
.panda.org/what_we_do/endangered_species/elephants/african_elephants/elephant
_programme/.

WWF–AU. "Myanmar Emerges as Ivory Trade and Elephant Smuggling Hot Spot." Last
modified December 11, 2008, http://www.wwf.org.au/news/myanmar-emerges-as
-ivory-trade- and-elephant-smuggling-hot-spot/.

WWF Global. "Amazon Basin." Accessed April 4, 2010. http://wwf.panda/what_we_do/
where_we_are/amazon/vision_amazon/wwf-projects_amazon_basin_rainforests/
index.cfm?uProjectID=BR0925.

WWF Global. "Amazon Keystone Initiative." Accessed December 3, 2009). http://wwf
.panda.org/what_we_do/where_we_work/amazon/vision_amazon/wwf_projects
_amazon_basin_rainforests/index.cfm?uProjectID=BR0940.

WWF Global. "Conservation of Guiana's Forests." Accessed December 3, 2009. http://
wwf.panda.org/who_we_are/wwf_offices/suriname/index.cfm?uProjectID=9L0807.

WWF Global. "Establishment of the Alto Purús National Park: Protecting an Area Almost
the Size of Belgium." Accessed April 27, 2010. http://wwf.panda.org/what_we_do/
where_we_work/amazon/vision_amazon/models/amazon_protected_areas/
establishment/alto_purus/.

WWF Global. "Global Forest Trade Network." Accessed April 27, 2010. http://gftn.
panda.org.

WWF Global. "More Than 40 Years in the Amazon. What WWF is doing: An Integrated
Approach." Accessed January 10, 2010. http://wwf.panda.org/what_we_do/where
_we_work/amazon/vision_amazon/.

WWF Global. "Responsible Forestry in the Amazon." Accessed April 22, 2010. http://
wwf.panda.org/what_we_do/where_we_work/amazon/vision_amazon/models/
responsible_forestry_amazon/.

WWF Global. "WWF in the Deep Amazon: Malaria, Infections and One Incredible Park."
Accessed January 10, 2010. http://wwf.panda.org/what_we_do/where_we_work/
amazon/vision_amazon/models/amazon_protected_areas/management/wwf
_expedition/.

WWF–Peru. "Active Conservation Projects in Peru." Accessed April 23, 2010. http://wwf.
panda.org/who_we_are/wwf_offices/peru/projects/index.cfm?ProjectID=PE0867.

WWF–UK. "Fighting Forest Crime and the Illegal Timber Trade." Accessed November
21, 2009. http://d2rby7spo76flf.cloudfront.net/downloads/fightingforestcrime
.pdf.

Wyler, Liana Sun, and Pervaze A. Sheikh. *CRS Report for Congress: International Illegal Trade in Wildlife: Threats and U.S. Policy*. Washington, D.C.: Congressional Research Service, August 2008.

Xiang, G. *Report of the External Commission of the Chamber of Deputies Destined to Investigate the Acquisition of Wood, Lumbermills, and Extensive Portions of Land in the Amazon by Asian Loggers*. Brasilia, Brazil, 1998.

Zimmerman, Mara E. "The Black Market for Wildlife: Combating Transnational Organized Crime in Illegal Wildlife Trade." *Vanderbilt Journal of Transnational Law* 36, no. 5 (November 2003): 1657–1689.

Index

Page locaters with b., f., or t. preceding the page number indicate the entry found in a Box, Figure, or Table.

Association for the Preservation of Game (India), 82

Beccaria, Cesare, 4
Beluga sturgeon. *See* Great sturgeon
Big leaf mahogany (*Swietenia macrophylla*), 144; characteristics, 145; CITES status, 144, 146, 152; conservation, 152–56, 158; consumers, 151–52; ecosystem and, 147; habitat, 145–46; hardwood, 145; imports, t.151; indigenous tribes and, 152; IUCN Red List status, 144, 152; overharvesting, 145–46; range states, 145–46, 149; sister trees, 144, 145, 146; threats, 146–47
Blacklist method, 135
Brazilian Biodiversity Fund, 155
Brazilian National Network Against the Trafficking of Wild Animals (RENCTAS), 54
Bukit Barisan Selatan National Park (Sumatra Island), 108
Burma Forest Act (1902), 116
Bushmeat, 7; consumption, 89–90; defined, 89–90; impact on communities, 90; trade, 89–93, 94–95

Camino, José Luis, 150
Canada Border Services Agency, 47
Canadian Endangered Species Conservation Council, 42
Carcharodon carcharias. See Great white shark
Caviar, 53, 57–61; beluga, 49, 57–58, 59, 60, 137; black, 60; illegal trade, 59–61; legal trade, 58–59. *See also* Great sturgeon
Certification and Development of the Forest Sector (CEDEFOR), 157
Charcoal trade, 89, 91, 93–94, 96, 108, 183
CITES (Convention on International Trade in Endangered Species), 12; 14–15; Animals Committee, 139; appendices of, 34–35; black market and, 91; Conference of Parties, 13–14,

34–35; creation of, 33; databases. *See* CITES data; description of, 13, 33; documents, 186; ecosystem conservation work, 33–36; effectiveness of, 35–36; enforcement, 43–45, 46–50, 93; Gaborone Amendment, 38; implementation, 36–42; Management and Scientific Authorities, 150; marine species, 119; member compliance, 18; Secretariat, 13, 32, 35, 60, 106, 111, 186; Shark Working Group, 139; Standing Committee, 35
CITES data, 16; comparative reports, 16–19; databases, 17–19; limitations of, 17–18, 19
Clarke, Ronald, V., b.161; CRAVED model, 71, b.73, 160, 164
Code of Conduct for Responsible Fisheries, 139–40
Coffee, illegally grown, 105, 106, 107, 108
Concealable, Removable, Available, Enjoyable, Disposable model. *See* CRAVED
Congolese Wildlife Authority, 93, 97
Conservation (Natural Habitats, &c.) Regulations 1994 (UK), 39
Container Security Initiative, 46, 47
Control of Trade in Endangered Species (Enforcement) Regulations, 1994 (UK), 38–39
Convention for Preservation and Protection of Fur Seals (1893), 31
Convention on Biological Diversity, 90, 95
Convention on the Conservation of Antarctic Marine Living Resources (CCAMLR), 135
Convention on International Trade in Endangered Species. *See* CITES
Convention on Migratory Species (CMS) of Wild Animals, 32, 43; Conference of Parties, 43; enforcement, 43–45; marine species and, 119, 122; membership, 43; Secretariat of, 43

About the Author

Dr. JACQUELINE L. SCHNEIDER is the chair of and an associate professor in the Department of Criminal Justice Sciences at Illinois State University. Her doctorate is from the University of Cincinnati and her Master's in Public Administration is from The Ohio State University. She spent more than six years teaching and conducting research in England where her work on reducing stolen goods markets has been put forward as best practice and has attracted interest by policy makers in other countries. In addition to her many grants, she was the first recipient of the UK Home Office's Innovative Research Challenge Grant. Since 1990, Dr. Schneider has been teaching at various universities in England and the United States. She received an outstanding teaching award from the University of Cincinnati while completing her Ph.D. She has authored several academic papers and chapters in books. Her main research areas include gangs, stolen goods markets, and the illegal trade in endangered flora and fauna.